Charles V

Charles V

The World Emperor

Harald Kleinschmidt

SUTTON PUBLISHING

First published in the United Kingdom in 2004 by
Sutton Publishing Limited · Phoenix Mill
Thrupp · Stroud · Gloucestershire · GL5 2BU

British Library Cataloguing in Publication Data
A catalogue record for this book is available from the British Library.

ISBN 0-7509-2404-7

Typeset in 11/14.5pt Sabon.
Typesetting and origination by
Sutton Publishing Limited.
Printed and bound in England by
J.H. Haynes & Co. Ltd, Sparkford.

Contents

Contents

List of Illustrations

Maps

List of Abbreviations

Cal. Venice	*Calendar of State Papers and Manuscripts, Relating to English Affairs, Existing in the Archives and Collections of Venice and in Other Libraries of Northern Italy*, ed. Rawdon Brown *et al.* (London, 1864–).
Kohler, ed., *Quellen*	*Quellen zur Geschichte Karls V.*, ed. Alfred Kohler (Darmstadt, 1990) (Ausgewählte Quellen zur deutschen Geschichte der Neuzeit, 15).
Lanz, ed., *Correspondenz*	*Correspondenz des Kaisers Karl V. Aus dem Königlichen Archiv und der Bibliothèque de Bourgogne zu Brüssel*, 3 vols, ed. Karl Friedrich Wilhelm Lanz (Leipzig, 1844–46) [repr. (Frankfurt, 1966)].
Lanz, ed., *Staatspapiere*	*Staatspapiere zur Geschichte Kaiser Karls V. Aus dem Königlichen Archiv und der Bibliothèque de Bourgogne zu Brüssel*, ed. Karl Friedrich Wilhelm Lanz (Stuttgart, 1845) (Bibliothek des Litterarischen Vereins, 11).
LP	*Letters and Papers, Foreign and Domestic, Relating to the Reign of Henry VIII*, ed. John Sherren Brewer *et al.*, 22 vols (London, 1862–1930).
MGH, *SS*	Monumenta Germaniae Historica, *Scriptores*

MGH, *SS rer. Merov.*	Monumenta Germanie Historica, *Scriptores rerum Merovingicarum*
RTA 1	*Deutsche Reichstagsakten.* Jüngere Reihe, vol. 1, ed. August Kluckhohn (Gotha, 1893).
RTA 2	*Deutsche Reichstagsakten.* Jüngere Reihe, vol. 2, ed. Adolf Wrede (Gotha, 1896).
RTA 7	*Deutsche Reichstagsakten.* Jüngere Reihe, vol. 7, ed. Johannes Kühn (Göttingen, 1962).
RTA 8	*Deutsche Reichstagsakten.* Jüngere Reihe, vol. 8, ed. Wolfgang Steglich (Göttingen, 1970).
SP Spain	*Calendar of Letters, Despatches, and State Papers Relating to the Negotiations between England and Spain, preserved in the Archives at Simancas, Vienna, Brussels, and Elsewhere*, ed. G.A. Bergenroth *et al.*, 14 vols (London, 1862–1940).
Weiss, ed., *Papiers*	*Papiers d'état du cardinal de Granvelle d'après les manuscrits de la bibliothèque de Besançon*, 9 vols, ed. Charles Weiss (Paris, 1841–43).

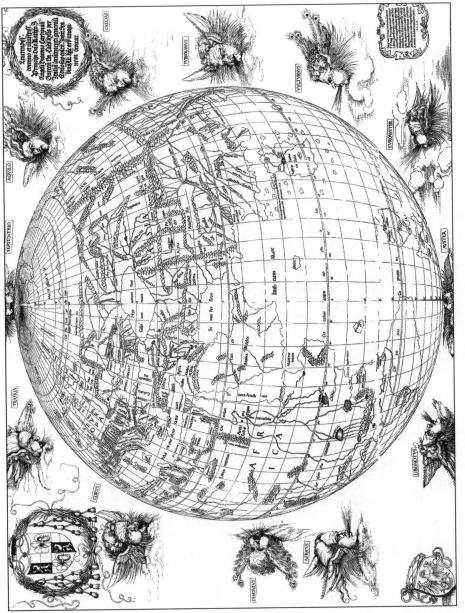

Stabius-Dürer, map of the world, 1515. (*London, British Library*)

Peter Apian, map of the world, 1530. (*London, British Library*)

Introduction

Peter Paul Rubens's portrait of 1635 eternalises Emperor Charles V as a warrior and as a world emperor. Wearing a laurel wreath and dressed in full armour underneath a tunic, Charles holds a globe (*sphaira*) in his left hand and a sword in his right. He extends his right hand and presents the sword with its blade upwards but pushes the globe towards his chest. He appears to be ready to strike with his right hand while seeking to protect the globe against an attack (Plate 1).

Rubens drew on the medieval occidental iconography of emperors. From the tenth century occidental rulers bearing the imperial title were often shown holding the *sphaira* as the symbol of universal rule in their extended left hand and the sceptre as the symbol of virtue and equity in their extended right hand. Rubens modified the medieval model in two important respects: he replaced the symbol of virtue and equity by the symbol of war-proneness and did not allow Charles to extend his left hand. Rubens's portrait thus visualises a tension between Charles as a daring warrior and Charles as the peace-bringing emperor. Readiness to use military force and willingness to protect the world do not seem to go together.

Rubens's portrait is part of a tradition of scepticism that constitutes a conflict between the tasks of a warrior and the tasks of a ruler; that juxtaposes the values of heroism against the values of stoicism; that recognises the obligation of warriors to risk their lives while it imposes upon rulers the obligation to preserve their lives as long as they can. Again, the tradition is old. It can be traced back to the tenth century. But did Charles himself accept the view that there was a conflict between warriors' and rulers' norms, values and rules? Certainly, some of his advisers urged him not to risk his life, and Charles died peacefully, though not as a ruler. Yet he consciously risked his life on several occasions, was trained in combat, acted as a military commander and reflected on aspects of the theory of war. Contrary to the legacy of the medieval tradition of rulers' ethics Charles combined rather than juxtaposed warriors' and rulers' norms, values and rules. This book will show that Charles saw the fulfilment of his warrior tasks as the precondition for the accomplishment of his obligations as a ruler. War was an element of life, peace a dream about the future at best. Although he lived with medieval traditions, Charles was not a man of the Middle Ages.

Charles was born as a Burgundian nobleman at Ghent in the Netherlands on 24 February 1500. He took the office of the duke of Burgundy at the age of six. He succeeded as ruler of the Spanish kingdoms in 1516 and was elected emperor in 1519. As a young man Charles raised the most exalted hopes: that he could unify Christendom and that he could pacify the world. Indeed, he journeyed back and forth between the Iberian peninsula and central Europe attempting to 'bring peace and good government' to his many subjects. But, after forty years in office, his many foes denounced him as 'the butcher of Flanders' and nicknamed him 'Charles of Ghent who claims to be emperor'. At the age of fifty-five he felt ill and so tired that he abdicated and spent his remaining years in the vicinity of a monastery, where he died in 1558.

Charles's experience was the most extravagant among the unusual lives that many holders of high office have led. As a ruler he bore different numbers. As duke of Burgundy and ruler over the Netherlands he has been known as Charles II, as Spanish ruler he has been Charles I, and as emperor he has received the number V. At times he was also archduke of Austria and duke of Milan. He was in control of the island worlds to which Columbus had journeyed, the Native American empires that Hernán Cortés and Francisco Pizarro had conquered and, at times, the Spice Islands in the South Pacific that the Magellan expedition had visited. His nearest relatives were his brother Ferdinand, to whom he granted his title of archduke of Austria and who was also king of Bohemia and Hungary and king of the Romans; his sister, who was regent for the Netherlands; the king of Denmark, Sweden (with Finland) and Norway, who was his brother-in-law; the king of France, who was another brother-in-law; the kings of Portugal, one of whom was his brother-in-law, another his son-in-law; the queen of England, who was his daughter-in-law; the duke of Florence, who was his son-in-law; and the duke of Parma, who was also his son-in-law. His rivals and enemies regarded Charles and his closest kin as a threat to peace in Christendom, criticised them for their accumulation of offices and accused them of excessive ambition. In response to these charges Charles insisted that, in all his wars, he never wanted anything for himself but was only trying to do his best to promote peace in the world. But he envisioned peace as an order that he and only he was going to establish.

Charles was an elusive figure, his world paradoxical. Historians must search for him by tracing his footprints. But footprints can only show where he was, not who he was. While political scientists may be able to stand on tiptoe observing politicians in action in front of them, historians cannot look over Charles's shoulder. For historians, he remains behind a veil of texts recording his movements. There is an abundance of texts bearing Charles's name. But he never saw most of these and among the minority of letters that he did write with his own hand are some which do not reflect his own thoughts but those of his advisers. Charles was an elusive figure not merely because he was an itinerant ruler but because, despite his remarkable rhetorical skills, he did not communicate with many people. Dr Martin Luther, who liked to talk, and confronted him on two occasions, called him 'our silent emperor'. I have tried to penetrate behind the veil of texts by letting Charles respond to the paradoxical world in which he was moving as a warrior and ruler. I do not attempt to explain the paradoxes of his world; for I have neither the intention of undoing them nor the ability to instil meaning into them retrospectively. Instead, I allow the paradoxes to remain in Charles's world and record Charles's responses primarily through his actions and less often through his words. Keeping silent is also a way of responding and, needless to say, a type of manifest action.

In a biography the hero determines the framework of chronology, not the historian. Nevertheless, it is the historian's task to mark time. I have used the years 1515, 1519, 1521, 1530 and 1548 as major epochal breaks. In Chapter One, I introduce Charles's family and describe his youth to 1515. In Chapter Two, I examine his ascendance to the Spanish kingdoms to 1519. In Chapter Three, I relate the story of his early years as emperor to 1521. In Chapter Four, I trace his movements to 1530. The period from 1530 to 1548 poses difficulties for Charles's biographer because he was simultaneously engaged in activities concerning many different peoples and places. Rather than jumping back and forth from one scene to another, I have forced Charles to pass through these crucial years twice. Thus, in Chapter Five, I display him engaged in European military and diplomatic strife and Spanish overseas affairs, and in Chapter Six, I observe him in his struggles against Turkish armies and adherents to what Charles persistently referred to as the 'Lutheran heresy'. Chapter Seven covers the final years.

Each chapter consists of three sections. The first section always gives the narration of events, following the chronological framework. The second section establishes the background of the world in which these events took place. The third section reviews carefully selected sources relevant to the main contents of the chapter.

Charles's world was the remote world of courts. Unlike his grandfather, Emperor Maximilian I, he was not a popular figure and did not become a hero of literature. Nevertheless, there remains something artificial about Charles and his world, as if it were the world of the stage.

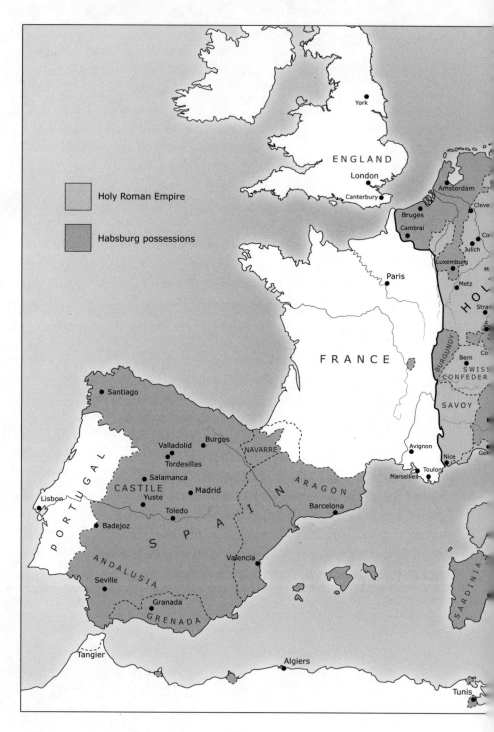

Holy Roman Empire

Habsburg possessions

York

ENGLAND

London

Canterbury

Amsterdam

Cleve

Bruges

Co

Cambrai

Julich

Luxemburg

M

Metz

H O L

Stras

Paris

F R A N C E

BURGUNDY

Bern

SWISS

Co

CONFEDER

SAVOY

Santiago

Avignon

Nice

Ge

Valladolid

Burgos

Marseilles

Toulon

Tordesillas

NAVARRE

A R A G O N

Salamanca

CASTILE

Madrid

Barcelona

Yuste

Lisbon

Toledo

P
O
R
T
U
G
A
L

S
P
A
I
N

Badejoz

Valencia

A N D A L U S I A

SARDINIA

Seville

Granada

G R E N A D A

Tangier

Algiers

Tunis

Europe and the Habsburg possessions at the time of Charles V.

ONE

Dramatis Personae: *The Dynasties*

CREATING A FAMILY OF RULERS

A duke meets the emperor

Appearances matter. Charles the Bold, Duke of Burgundy and ruler over a plethora of territories within the Holy Roman Empire and beyond its western fringes, spared no pomp when he met Emperor Frederick III in the city of Trier in 1473. Trier was gleaming with symbols of empire. Once a residential imperial capital in the bygone days of antiquity, it still featured ruins of once-lavish Roman baths, of imperial palaces and a well-preserved gate that remained in use as a church. In the Middle Ages, the city became the seat of an archbishopric, and as an archiepiscopal metropolis it wielded considerable influence over the empire, the Netherlands as well as France. When meeting the emperor in the monastery of St Maximin, Charles the Bold brought along stupendous manifestations of his wealth, decorating the meeting-place with tapestries and precious pieces of art and dressing himself up in the most elegant of garments that his manufacturers could produce.[1] Frederick III was unable to equal Charles's splendour. The emperor was poor as an office-holder, as he depended on the revenues that the lesser rulers in the empire were willing to award to him. But Frederick had immaterial treasures to offer, namely an impressive genealogy of ancestors and the right to designate his successor. In 1473, Frederick had been at the helm of the empire for thirty-three years while using the time to advance the fame of his dynasty, the Habsburgs. He tried to keep his own branch of the dynasty in the imperial office, and thus boosted the expectation that his son Maximilian, born in 1459, would be

1

the heir to all Habsburg dominions. The Habsburgs were in control of areas scattered in what is today Austria, Switzerland, southern Germany, northern Italy and Slovenia, outnumbering the holdings of Charles the Bold. Frederick's marriage to Eleonore of Portugal secured him good connections to one of the most dynamic economies in fifteenth-century Europe next to the realms under the control of Charles the Bold. Imperial genealogists were compiling preposterous family trees that connected Frederick with the Frankish kings of the early Middle Ages; the ancient Roman aristocratic family of the Colonna; Hector and Aeneas, the heroes of the Trojan War; the ancient Roman emperors; Osiris, the ancient Egyptian hero; and Noah, the biblical father. Frederick did not forget to bring a booklet with his genealogies to Trier, which he put on display before his counterpart.[2]

By Frederick's standards, Charles was nobody. As a descendant of the French royal dynasty of the Valois he could reiterate their claim to descent from the Trojans. Moreover, if Frederick's wife was a Portuguese princess, so was Charles's mother Isabella. But his own branch had split off from the French royal dynasty merely four generations ago when establishing itself as the dukes of Burgundy. True, Charles cared little about legal niceties and used his wealth to demonstrate his power. He even created a propagandistic fancy that portrayed the duke of Burgundy at a rank similar to that of the Roman emperor. But King Louis XI of France, Charles's archrival, contended these claims and insisted that the dukes of Burgundy were his disloyal vassals. Charles could only hope to be able to continue to live up to his image of a wealthy and powerful ruler equal to the emperor and kings of France, England and Portugal if he succeeded in demonstrating his ability to resist Louis's claims for suzerainty. Charles's dilemma was thus that he could use his wealth and power only as long as he was able to keep his position of autonomy, but could hope to succeed in the long run merely if he found an alliance partner. Frederick, of course, knew Charles's dilemma well. Yet at Trier, Charles had his trump cards. His third wife, whom he had married in 1468, was Margaret of York, sister of King Edward IV. Through this marriage he was thus allied with the English kings. By his second wife Isabella of Bourbon he had a daughter, Mary, born in 1457 and thus matching Maximilian in age. And this was why the two rulers met at Trier: if it was possible to mate their children, a power house would come into existence that could bring together the ruling dynasties of the Roman Empire, Burgundy, England and Portugal. The combination could not only secure Charles's position against Louis XI of France, but offered golden opportunities in the dreams of ambitious fathers.

As Frederick wanted Charles's money together with his daughter and Charles wanted Frederick's status together with his son, the deal seemed to be straightforward. But Charles knew his value. He demanded nothing less than the imperial crown in exchange for his daughter. In Charles's view, the deal was this: Mary would marry Maximilian, Charles would succeed Frederick as emperor, and Maximilian would succeed Charles. Nicknamed 'the rash' by his junior contemporaries, Charles would neither take into account that the ageing Frederick might continue to occupy the imperial throne for another twenty years nor imagine that Louis XI would be able to mobilise a formidable enemy against his disloyal vassal. Nevertheless, Charles's conditions were tough for Frederick. The empire was not a hereditary monarchy, as the emperors were elected by a college of seven rulers bearing the appropriate title 'electors'. What if these electors refused to consent to Charles's demands? Frederick hesitated, and the meeting ended in a draw. Mary was betrothed to Maximilian and further decisions were postponed to the future.

The future that forced Frederick to make decisions came sooner than he may have anticipated. Louis XI concluded an agreement with the Swiss canton of Bern that allowed him to rally Swiss warriors against Charles. By 1476, the Swiss were ready for battle, and Charles decided to face the enemy. Drawing on his revenues, he assembled the most modern of armies, equipped with high-technology weapons, such as mortars, cannon and portable firearms, and staffed with numerous well-trained warriors. He loaded the big cannon on wheels, so that they could be hauled quickly and with ease wherever they were needed. He added a large cavalry and requested enforcements with longbowmen from his English relatives. He carefully planned tactical arrangements for battle that allowed him a maximum of flexible responses. The Swiss appeared to be no match for this fighting force. They relied mainly on a long variant of the lance, called the pike, a weapon that farmers could use with ease, together with a small cavalry and a few firearms. They ordered the pikemen into one large battalion called 'the heap', which could march straight forwards to strike at the enemy but could hardly manoeuvre. Hence, all odds pointed against the Swiss, and yet they won the first battle against Charles at Grandson early in 1476 because Charles simply could not break into the carefully maintained Swiss rank and file. Charles was again defeated at Murten later in the same year, when he lost much of his valuable equipment. In the third battle, at Nancy in January 1477, Charles's army was completely destroyed and the duke's body was discovered in the mud only days after the battle had ended. Louis XI's proxy warriors had done their job well.

The emperor's son and the duke's daughter get married

Maximilian, then approaching the age of eighteen, was eager to have his marriage concluded. Under the given conditions Mary, the new reigning duchess of Burgundy, had no choice but to accept the deal. Maximilian thus entered the stage as a juvenile warrior willing to take up the defence of the Burgundian realms against Louis XI, the old man in Paris. The campaigns proved protracted and difficult. The loyalty of the estates, namely the urban governments and seigneurial lords in Charles's vast realms, was shaken by the defeats at Grandson, Murten and Nancy. Revenue came in less easily and, above all, there were thorny legal issues. With Charles the Bold gone, Maximilian was the unquestioned heir apparent in the empire. As the husband of the reigning duchess of Burgundy, he was theoretically a vassal to the French king. As the future emperor could hardly accept being dependent on the French king, Burgundy would have to be constituted as a polity of its own, so to speak, between France and the empire. But this strategy would lead to a

Habsburg–Valois rift and deepen the antagonism between the empire and the kingdom of France. Through his campaigns for the Habsburg succession over Burgundy, Maximilian tried to prevent Louis XI from calling back his fief. Maximilian thus faced the awkward task of restoring the loyalty of the Burgundian estates without breaking with the French king. Luckily, Maximilian's fighting force of German lansquenets gained a victory at Guinegate in 1479, rescuing Artois, Tournai and Picardy for Maximilian. Through her so-called 'Great Privilege' of 1477, Mary succeeded in soliciting support from the Burgundian estates by confirming their liberties, some of which the previous dukes had alienated. The privilege restored the right of self-government and became the equivalent of a constitution for Burgundy and the Netherlands. However, Maximilian failed to retain the core part of the duchy of Burgundy around the city of Dijon, once the residential capital of the dukes. The Franche-Comté of Burgundy around Besançon remained contested, although the dukes continued to hold extensive stretches of land there. Yet the ducal power base moved northwards near the urban landscapes of Brabant and Flanders, with Brussels strengthening its position as the administrative centre.

Meanwhile, the Burgundian ducal family grew. Two children, Philip and Margaret, were born in 1478 and 1480. They were named after Mary's grandfather and her stepmother and thus, through their names, displayed their parents' willingness to continue the Burgundian heritage. Maximilian was deeply impressed by the splendour of Burgundian court life, the rigour of administrative techniques and the aesthetic refinement of production and reproduction in the arts and crafts. Burgundy appeared to have a future not only as an intermediary between France and the empire but also as a type of polity later to be referred to as the state. However, that bright future was seriously jeopardised when Mary fell from her horse in 1482 while enjoying a hunting excursion and died. Mary's sudden and premature death was a shock for Maximilian, as his emotional ties to his wife were strong. Even as an old man he remembered her with love and devotion in a lavish piece of literature that described his Burgundian campaign in the style of a medieval wooing epic.[3] Yet the grief over the sudden loss of his beloved wife was surmounted by political worries. King Louis XI of France died in 1483, leaving the French throne to his son, a young man who succeeded as Charles VIII. Fortunately for Maximilian, Charles VIII displayed less concern for Burgundian affairs than his father but developed a keener interest in Italian matters. But the question was whether the Burgundian estates accepted Maximilian as their ruler. Maximilian decided to take the risk and had himself quickly invested as duke of Burgundy. At least he had two children, was himself ready for another marriage and intended to use the opportunity strategically to promote a Habsburg–Valois *rapprochement*. By 1483, he had sent his daughter Margaret to the court of Louis XI to prepare her for the marriage with the future Charles VIII. In 1489, he agreed to marry Anne, the reigning duchess of Brittany, at Rennes where she was under siege by French troops seeking to incorporate the duchy into the French kingdom. Because Maximilian could not reach Rennes in person, Anne had her marriage concluded by proxy. Anne appealed for help to a coalition consisting of Maximilian, King Henry VII of England and King Ferdinand of Aragon. But French military pressure continued until, eventually, Anne agreed to cancel her marriage with Maximilian and, instead, to wed Charles VIII. After Charles's death in 1498, she married his successor Louis XII and her daughter Claude married Francis of Angoulême in 1514, who followed Louis XII as Francis I in 1515. Maximilian shelved his plans for a dynastic union between Habsburg and Valois in 1490 and Margaret returned to her father.

To make things worse, Maximilian's Yorkist relatives were defeated at the battle of Bosworth in 1485. Maximilian hastily supported an abortive rebellion by Yorkist loyalists against the new king, Henry VII. The rebellion collapsed in 1487 but Henry remained a difficult partner for Maximilian. Moreover, Maximilian's position in the Netherlands remained shaky. Some of the Flemish cities insisted that Maximilian should confirm Mary's 'Great Privilege'. But he was reluctant to do so. While his lansquenets were campaigning in Flanders he was engaged in negotiations with urban governments to restore their loyalty by means of diplomacy. Soon his lansquenets' arrogance sent some cities into revolt. At Bruges angry citizens arrested Maximilian early in 1488 and detained him for about two months until he promised to confirm their liberties. A year later, when his position had been strengthened by his lansquenets' victory at Thérouanne, Maximilian returned to Bruges, levelled the house where he had been detained to the ground and punished the citizens for their insurgency.[4] Meanwhile, trouble was mounting in the empire, and Maximilian was summoned to his duties there. In 1486, Frederick III arranged for the coronation of his son as 'king of the Romans', an office that was understood to make apparent the heir to the imperial throne. The ceremony was necessary because in 1485, Matthew Corvinus, king of Hungary, had conquered Vienna, driving Frederick out of his residential capital. Maximilian received the task of restoring Vienna to Habsburg control. At the same time, Frederick placed a further burden upon his son's shoulders, and that was the crusade against the Ottoman Turkish Empire. In the proclamation announcing Maximilian's installation as 'king of the Romans', Frederick announced that the new king would march against the Turkish sultan in the foreseeable future and requested support from everyone in the empire.[5] The crusade, the defence of the Roman Empire and the maintenance of Habsburg rule over the Netherlands remained the three issues that dominated Maximilian's world and European and local politics to the end of his life.

The old emperor dies and his son succeeds

Pursuing policies at these three levels and with equal rigour proved to be a formidable task. Control over the Netherlands involved fewer difficulties than expected although the relationship with France remained strained. Maximilian succeeded in ending Matthew Corvinus's control over Vienna in 1490, and Frederick could return home. When Frederick finally died in 1493, Maximilian succeeded to the helm of the empire without any problems, although he never received his imperial coronation from the pope. Yet Charles VIII opened a new front in 1494 by intervening in Italian affairs and leading an army that penetrated into the peninsula as far south as Naples. Although Charles's efforts to impose himself as a major actor in Italian affairs were soon thwarted by shortages of supply and a want of devoted partners in 1495, the intervention sent shock waves through the establishments of territorial rulers and urban governments as well as into the mindsets of private intellectuals.[6] Members of all three groups became beset with the impression that the Italian peninsula was politically divided and militarily weak. They traded on the fear that Italian liberties were at stake and demanded strong measures of defence against possible future invasions. This momentous quest for autonomy raised Maximilian's concerns because the emperor was legally the overlord of a variety of Italian polities, the most important being the duchy of Milan. Hence, any Habsburg strategy in pursuit of expanding the imperial influence over these polities against France would inevitably trigger anti-Habsburg responses from territorial rulers, urban governments and the intellectual public opinion-makers.

Moreover, even after Charles VIII's withdrawal the French party continued to have many supporters, specifically in the republic of Venice, at whose formal request Charles had intervened, and in the duchy of Milan, where French troops took control and remained until 1521. Maximilian tried to solve the problem in his own way by using his marriage with Bianca Maria Sforza, niece of Lodovico il Moro, Milan's ruler from 1476 to 1499. The marriage had been concluded in 1493 in an attempt to secure Milan for the Habsburgs. But Lodovico il Moro had his own strategy for keeping Milan under Sforza sway and used Bianca as a spy. Maximilian kept a distanced relationship with his wife, and the marriage produced no offspring. Yet of all of Maximilian's burdens, the crusades weighed most heavily because they were costly. More than his father, Maximilian could rely on the Habsburg hereditary lands over which he wielded full control. He could also draw on revenue from the Netherlands as long as he succeeded in persuading the estates that his expenses were necessary and good for the Netherlands. He could also try to make profitable marriage deals, expecting that the dowries would be paid to him. But the crusades demanded more. The ruler of the empire yielded an aura of respect and fame but commanded little control over revenue. At the end of the fifteenth century, the Ottoman Turkish Empire covered large portions of western Asia and the Balkans. The Turkish sultan could draw on support from Muslim rulers in North Africa. In order to have a chance of success, a crusade against this empire needed thorough preparation, long-term financial support and a measure of consensus and stability within the Occident that allowed the pursuit of a protracted campaign without the danger of resurfacing internal rivalries. Even if Maximilian's position was not entirely hopeless, the prospects for meeting these demands were grim.

Up until the middle of the 1490s, we see Maximilian engaged in diplomatic negotiations to the end of creating this consensus and stability. His efforts reached their first peak during the imperial diet held at Worms in 1495. Towards the end of the fifteenth century the imperial diet was emerging as the highest decision-making institution. It was usually convened and chaired by the emperor. It was attended by those territorial rulers and urban governments in the empire who were regarded as imperial estates (or states). Imperial estates were rulers over land and people within the empire who exercised their control in accordance with traditional privileges that they often called liberties. Territorial rulers as imperial estates were normally not in need of imperial legitimisation. Urban governments as imperial estates could claim rights of self-government and were usually free from control by neighbouring territorial lords and stood merely under imperial suzerainty. All estates could thus take the view that they were free from direct control by the emperor and could make their own decisions with regard to their own and imperial affairs. The diet launched a programme for the reform of the empire into a territorial polity under the control of the emperor, against the resistance by some estates. It also established a special tax to support the preparations for the crusade and laid the foundations for a framework of the peaceful adjudication of conflicts among imperial estates.[7] However, after the end of the diet, little happened that could implement this strategic design. For Maximilian, the most pressing need was to achieve his coronation as emperor, and in order to allow the coronation to happen, Maximilian had to establish favourable political conditions in the Italian peninsula. Thus Maximilian became absorbed in Italian affairs, while Charles VIII's campaign was going on, and postponed the more far-reaching plan. Yet despite all the woes confronting him in his own present, when imperial estates were reluctant to endorse his designs for reforms, and when rulers outside the empire challenged the imperial claim for leadership at least over the Occident, Maximilian had his children as foundations of hope. In 1495, Philip was seventeen and Margaret was fifteen. Thus both were ready for use as trump cards in future marriage deals. At Worms, therefore, Maximilian began negotiations with the Spanish courts.

The new emperor expands his kin network

That Maximilian would cast an eye on the Spanish courts in his search for marriage partners for his children was all but self-evident. True, he was familiar with the Portuguese court through his mother and one of his wife's grandmothers. But he was ill informed about current affairs in the Iberian peninsula. This can be gleaned from a letter that the Nuremberg physician Hieronymus Müntzer addressed to King John II of Portugal on 14 July 1493. On Maximilian's behalf Müntzer recommended a westward voyage across the ocean as the nearest and cheapest way to Asia.[8] Müntzer used arguments that the Portuguese Junta de Matematicos had previously rejected when Columbus had presented them in the 1480s.[9] Hence, Maximilian had no idea that his suggestions were well known at the Portuguese court, and was equally unfamiliar with the fact that, meanwhile, Columbus had returned from his first transoceanic voyage, and was now in Spanish service. Maximilian was also ignorant of the fact that Columbus had landed at Lisbon, where he had been interrogated at the request of the Portuguese king. Finally, he knew nothing of the negotiations between the Spanish and Portuguese rulers going on in the town of Tordesillas in 1494 about the regulation of access to the seaways west of Europe and Africa. The involuntary demonstration of imperial provincialism stands against the suggestion that Maximilian approached the Spanish courts as partners in a marriage alliance with an eye on the expeditions. Moreover, Maximilian had little knowledge of Spanish domestic affairs. At the turn of the sixteenth century, the Spanish peninsula was a promising but difficult terrain. There was no united Spanish kingdom but an agglomeration of the two polities of Castile and Aragon, the latter of which consisted of several units (Aragon proper, Catalonia, Leon, and Navarre, as well as overseas dependencies in Naples and Sicily), each with their own histories and institutions. Aragon was under the rule of King Ferdinand, who had ascended the throne in 1479, whereas Castile stood under the government of Queen Isabel, whose actual reign began in the same year. Isabel took over from her half-brother Henry IV, who had occupied the throne in 1454. Henry IV had a daughter Juana, born from his second wife in 1462. As Henry's first marriage had remained without offspring, the Castilian court immediately suspected that Juana was actually not the king's offspring but the daughter of a courtier, namely the Duke of Albuquerque, Don Beltran de la Cueva, and nicknamed her Juana la Beltraneja. Henry IV betrothed Juana to King Alfonso of Portugal and designated Isabel as his successor in 1468 but revoked this designation when Isabel decided to marry Ferdinand of Aragon in 1469. When Henry died in 1474, a war of succession broke out between Isabel and King Alfonso V of Portugal. Although supported by Alfonso, Juana eventually renounced her claims in 1479 and retreated to a monastery where she lived on until 1530. Being recognised as reigning queen of Castile, Isabel could jointly rule the two separate kingdoms with her husband so as to lay the foundations for a future unification under their successors. Their surviving children were four daughters, namely Isabel, Juana, Mary and Catherine, and one son, Juan.

Religious controversy added to dynastic rivalries. Throughout the later Middle Ages, a series of military campaigns in the Iberian peninsula aimed at expelling Muslim rulers whose power base was in the southern region of Andalusia. In the course of the 1480s and early 1490s, Ferdinand and Isabel made joint efforts to conclude these campaigns, which were conducted in the form of a crusade under the name *reconquista*. Early in January 1492 the emir of Granada, the last of the Muslim rulers in the peninsula, voluntarily withdrew from the city to North Africa without giving up his rights to rule. Spanish armed forces that had been assembled in a camp outside Granada moved into the city. The event marked the end of the military phase of the *reconquista* and was followed by the forced conversion of Muslims and Jews who chose to stay in the territories now coming under the control of the Spanish rulers. The two rulers manifested their control by establishing an inquisition to investigate whether the converts had in fact become Christians or had merely, by lip service, renounced their previous faiths.

At the Worms Diet, the recent fiasco of the Habsburg–Valois union seems to have induced Maximilian to gather information about other suitable marriage partners for his children. But the Spanish kingdoms were a more complicated case. Maximilian made no explicit statement justifying the expectation that he was acting in pursuit of some grand political strategy although he may have considered long-term prospects.[10] In 1495, Juan and Juana were seventeen and sixteen years old; that is, they were excellent matches for his two children, Margaret and Philip. To prevent another dynastic disaster, Maximilian tried to arrange a double marriage of two couples. This arrangement would make the Habsburg–Spanish alliance so tight that it was reasonable to expect that neither political disturbances nor the ravages of death could overthrow the long-term prospects of the incorporation of the Spanish kingdoms into the Habsburg-led system of polities with the empire at its core. From the Spanish side, the deal was equally attractive. Ferdinand and Isabel had married their eldest daughter Isabel to heir Alfonso of Portugal and, upon his death, to his son Manuel I. They had done so to maintain peaceful relations among the polities in the Iberian peninsula and to exclude future rival claims from Juana la Beltraneja. The decision revealed their willingness to join Maximilian in using dynastic relations as instruments of diplomacy. The establishment of kin ties with the imperial dynasty offered the strategic advantages of establishing equality with the Portuguese

12

court. It also helped elevate the ruling dynasties in the Spanish kingdoms to a position of supremacy over the many local Castilian, Aragonese, Navarrese, Leonese and southern Italian aristocratic families with their own seigneurial rights and traditions. Moreover, kin ties with prominent dynasties elsewhere in Europe could position the royal government above the representative bodies (Cortes) where deputies of cities had political participation rights. For the Spanish rulers, Maximilian was as helpful as a provider of glory, honour and fame to the end of promoting the interests of the Spanish rulers as the Spanish rulers were for Maximilian in his quest to demonstrate his capacity for leadership at the helm of the empire. Thus the deal was struck. Juana married Philip in 1496, and Margaret married Juan in 1497. Treaties were carefully drawn up specifying legal details, such as the dowries to be paid and the succession rights to be observed. In accordance with these treaties, Philip became the heir apparent to the throne of the future united kingdom of Spain.

Philip and Juana settled in Ghent, where he was acknowledged as duke of Burgundy and lord of the polities in the Netherlands in succession to his father. They enjoyed the festival culture with its court feasts and tournaments. Philip earned a reputation as a knightly aristocrat, well trained in decorum and pageantry. Unlike his father, he was hardly noteworthy for his interest in government and military affairs, although he developed a certain pride, claiming to be the foremost vassal of the French king, due to his position as the duke of Burgundy. Thus, contrary to Maximilian's expectation, Habsburg relations with France appeared to improve through the attractive young couple. Juana was a productive woman. Within a period of about ten years, she gave birth to seven children, of whom six survived to adulthood. In 1498, she bore a daughter who received the name of her paternal Portuguese great-grandmother Eleanor. The next child was a son, born on 25 February 1500. He was given the name of his paternal Burgundian great-grandfather Charles. The other children were a daughter, born in 1501 and named after her maternal grandmother Isabel; a boy, born in 1503 and baptised with the name of his maternal grandfather Ferdinand;

a daughter, born in 1505 and christened after her paternal grandmother Mary; and a daughter, born in 1507 and given the name Catherine.

When Queen Isabel died in 1504, Philip and Juana were due to move to Spain to take up rule in Castile. The preparations for the journey took some time. Eventually, in 1506, most of the family left the Netherlands en route for Juana's home through the realms of Philip's royal lord. Eleanor and Charles were left behind to grow up and receive their education in the Netherlands.

COMING OF AGE IN THE NETHERLANDS

The lives of the Habsburg–Spanish family from 1496 to 1506 resembled a drama wherein a cruel fate removes some of the actors from the scene. Juan was the first to depart. His marriage with Margaret appears to have been happy, too happy perhaps, as the couple devoted most of their time and energy to each other. Only six months after the wedding, Juan died suddenly, apparently of exhaustion. Juan's early departure buried all hopes for a Spanish succession in the empire.[11] Margaret decided to marry again, this time to Philibert of Savoy. As her second husband died prematurely in 1504, he left Margaret widowed and once again at her father's disposal, but she refused to remarry. The next to go was Isabel, wife of King Manuel I of Portugal. She died without issue in 1498. In order not to jeopardise their reconciliation policy, Ferdinand and Isabel gave their unmarried daughter Mary into wedlock with Manuel. Yet the biggest blow was still to come. While travelling in France in 1506, Philip caught a cold but ignored it. He continued the journey until he arrived at Burgos, where he passed away on 25 September (Plate 2).

Despite Ferdinand's reluctance, Philip had been accepted as joint ruler of Castile together with his wife Juana, but his position was not formally recognised at the time of his death. Juana, pregnant with Catherine, refused to accept the fact of Philip's death. She attended the official funeral in a bright colourful garment, decorated with flowers, while all the other mourners appeared in black. For months, she continued to travel in the peninsula, demanding that Philip's coffin should follow her. Courtiers in her entourage were unable to accept her behaviour. During her mother's lifetime, she had already acquired the reputation of being eccentric. On occasions she reproached Philip, who seems to have cultivated his womanising capability. Philip himself was annoyed at what he considered to be unwarranted outbursts of jealousy and reportedly kept a diary. In the diary he apparently noted down what he categorised as fits of madness. No traces of the alleged diary are extant, but Philip's assertions gained currency after his death. Although Juana wanted to succeed her mother as legitimate ruler of Castile, she was declared unfit to rule even though her title as queen of Castile remained uncontested.[12] In retrospect, Juana's behaviour appears to have been less outrageous than Philip and the courtiers claimed. Womanising was indeed a favourite pastime of Burgundian aristocrats, as Maximilian himself demonstrated on many occasions, but women's toleration of marital infidelity grew stronger at the turn of the sixteenth century. Thus Juana may merely have been more self-reliant and assertive than most females of her time.[13] Moreover, like Juana, Maximilian developed the habit of pulling a coffin with him while he was on the move. The scene was equally macabre even though Maximilian had books placed into the coffin rather than a corpse.[14] Finally, Maximilian did not go so far as completely refusing to accept Philip's death; but he did reject the interpretation that it had occurred as a sudden blow of some evil fate. Instead, he speculated publicly that King Louis XII of France had had Philip poisoned while the heir to the Spanish realms was travelling in France.[15]

Be that as it may, Juana was not allowed to act as reigning queen of Castile. Instead she was kept in confinement without access to most of her children and unable to interfere in government affairs. Hence the succession problem was again on the agenda. Soon after Isabel's death Ferdinand married again, in 1505, hoping to generate new offspring. His choice fell on Germaine de Foix. She was great-granddaughter of King Charles VII of France through her grandmother Madeleine de France. Madeleine had married Gaston de Foix, Prince of Viana in Navarre. The area was of strategic interest to the king of Aragon because it was then a French stronghold south of the Pyrenees. Ferdinand may have chosen his third wife with the intention of laying the dynastic basis for the future expansion of Aragonese rule on to Navarre. In 1512, however, he changed his strategy and conquered the area by military force. As Ferdinand had no children from Germaine, he was forced to accept one of his grandsons as his successor. The choice was between Charles and Ferdinand. The ageing king's initial preference was for his namesake grandson.

To make things worse, Philip's death also raised concerns over the governance of the Netherlands. Maximilian, who had long been worried about increasing French anti-Habsburg initiatives, foresaw a French attack on the western fringes of the empire. He was also fearful of outbursts of disgruntlement among the seigneurial lords and urban people in the Netherlands that the French king might use to end Habsburg rule there. He thus responded quickly to the emergency that Philip's death had created and established his widowed daughter Margaret as his regent in the Netherlands. Young Charles succeeded his father as archduke of Austria and duke of Burgundy, while Margaret acted as the imperial and Habsburg lieutenant and, simultaneously, as the provider of funds for the imperial coffers. She retained her position until she died in 1530. Margaret proved to be Maximilian's best choice. Not only was she fit to execute her many duties; she was also a respectable educator for Eleanor and Charles.

What did it mean to grow up in a family of rulers? The first observation to be made in response to this question is that the Habsburg–Spanish dynasty was different from what might be called a standard 'bourgeois' family, then as now. The very idea that the education of children should fall into the parents' competence was absent, not merely because Philip, the father, had died prematurely. Whether Juana would have educated her children well can no longer be determined as she was removed from that task. But this condition was far from unusual in ruling dynasties, where parents would rarely develop intimate relationships with their offspring and left their education to professional nannies, teachers and senior relatives at the courts. It was also common for members of ruling dynasties to search for marriage partners in distant places. Thus it had been customary from the early Middle Ages for elders of these kin groups to dispatch young princesses as consorts to remote places. As a consequence, European rulers were connected through continent-wide kin networks that linked people of widely diverse back-grounds. Hence parents and their advisers often held widely divergent views about educational principles.[16]

Moreover, the Habsburg–Spanish family displayed some further distinctive features. In this kin group, there does not seem to have been any strong prejudice against daughters. Although women were excluded from imperial succession by Roman law, they were not so in the Iberian peninsula and the Netherlands. Neither Ferdinand of Aragon nor Maximilian, the surviving grandfathers, regarded daughters as less important than sons, although both gave preference to male successors where they were available. Thus, much as it was a perfectly normal experience for children in ruling dynasties to be educated by close relatives and professionals rather than their parents, it was not common in ruling dynasties to elevate women to positions of rulers or regents. Second, Philip and Juana, and Juan and Margaret, showed no hesitation in asserting themselves as individuals, living out their extravagances at least as long as they could avoid the burdens of official duties. In their worldview, education had the task of shaping individual characters rather than uniform kin members, males and females alike.[17] Isabel, Queen of Castile, had insisted that all of her children should have a broad education, and Margaret in the Netherlands thought likewise. Thus she invited prominent scholars to her court. Foremost among them was Archbishop Adrian of Utrecht, whom she asked to instruct her niece and nephew in religion, ethics and law. Adrian of Utrecht seems to have been a conscientious teacher. He instilled into the minds of his pupils a strong faith in Catholicism and trust in divine justice. Throughout his life, Charles gave ample evidence of his strong conviction that the divinity would be his ultimate judge and that he intended to perform well on Judgement Day. Margaret also commissioned one of her principal counsellors, William of Croy, sieur de Chièvres, to reveal to them the secrets of government work. The two children thus grew up learning to become familiar with the specific norms and rules, the exceptional etiquette and pastimes of court life. In a word, the courts were the world for them.

It is difficult to overestimate the exceptional features of court life at the turn of the sixteenth century. Courts offered access to possibilities that were far from the dreams of ordinary people. At the same time, court life was lonely and took place in a well-ordered and minutely controlled environment. At court the display of emotions could be treated as a sign of madness; personal ties could become subject to the stern logic of dynastic ambition, and plots and intrigues could have fatal consequences. It is remarkable that against this background Margaret succeeded in generating an atmosphere of mutual trust among all of her nieces and nephews, not merely those who grew up under her immediate control. Against the often-ruthless conventions of court life, trust helped establish bonds of loyalty between Eleanor, Charles, their brother and their sisters that were to last throughout their lives.

Although life in the courts followed similar standards throughout much of Europe, language was a dividing factor. Eleanor and Charles spent much of their youth at Malines in the vicinity of Brussels, where Margaret had her favourite court. French was the language of communication there. The children absorbed French traditions, and French remained the principal means of communication throughout their lives. By contrast, their brother and sisters who had followed Juana to the Spanish kingdoms or were born there received their education in Spanish. Ferdinand, for one, was under the wing of his maternal grandfather who saw to it that his grandson became familiar with Spanish traditions. Whereas Charles grew up as a nobleman who looked for his future in Burgundy and the Netherlands, the Spanish kingdoms appeared to be the lands of Ferdinand's future.

The Habsburg–Spanish family of rulers was also different from other dynasties with regard to the relations between old and young.

Age was defined by a variety of different systems. The most popular schematic division of age during the Middle Ages was informed by the work of the elder Seneca and consisted of five grades. In the late fourth century St Augustine amplified Seneca's original scheme of 'infancy, boyhood, adolescence, young age and old age' by distinguishing two old-age grades, namely the age of advanced years and senility. Presumably, Augustine opted for six age grades in lieu of Seneca's five because he wanted to equate the six age grades with the six world ages and the six creation days of biblical tradition. In any case, Isidore of Seville canonised St Augustine's age grade scheme in the seventh century.[18] These schematic age grades were conspicuous for the absence of a distinct concept of adult age as the intermediary between young and old age. Among the many later references to the Augustinian–Isidorian scheme was the fourteenth-century exegesis of the Bible by the Paris theologian Jean Hesdin, who continued to portray the sequence of age grades as the process of a power transition from the young to the old without any intermediate age.[19]

Yet at the turn of the sixteenth century, a new perception evolved according to which the generation change no longer occurred directly from the old to the young but indirectly from the old to some intermediate group of kin members who were no longer young but not yet old. The extension of the Augustinian–Isidorian age-grade scheme became possible after it had lost its connection with the world ages and thus allowed further ages to be added. Among others, Shakespeare used the resulting scheme of seven age grades,[20] and it featured frequently in other verbal and pictorial sources during the sixteenth and seventeenth centuries. The conceptualisation of adulthood as a distinct age grade or set of age grades had the important consequences that adults acted as intermediaries between the old and the young, and that the young and the old no longer depended on each other, but both depended on the adults. The new schemes also informed the perception that the power transition occurred from the ageing to the adults and was of no concern to the young. Instead, adult age could be described and depicted as the peak of a person's life.[21]

In the case of the Habsburg–Spanish dynasty, the father was dead and the mother lived in seclusion. The young thus grew up in a world of grandfathers and aunts. With the intermediate generation of parent adults thus eliminated, any power transition was to take place directly from the grandparents or their lieutenants to the grandchildren. This was so not because the family followed the medieval conventions but because parent adults were simply not available. Nevertheless, there were tricky legal issues to be observed in power transitions. Maximilian was busy with imperial affairs. Margaret was obliged to help her father. Ferdinand continued as king of Aragon and showed little willingness to accept the consequences of the marriage arrangements of 1496/97. Juana retained her title of queen of Castile throughout her life in seclusion. Ferdinand did not dare to touch upon her rights but acted as a regent for Castile until the maturity of her children. Among her children, Charles continued to preserve her rights until Juana died in 1555. As an adult, Charles thus shared the view that it was his task to take care of the old, and he repeatedly saw to it that his mother continued to live in acceptable conditions.

In summary, Eleanor, Charles, their brother and sisters thus grew up in a family that, despite a broad platform of common standards of court life, displayed several important, distinctive features. Some of its senior members were notorious for their outbursts of emotions, the pursuit of their own happiness during their days of youth and, as far as they could decide by themselves, they were willing to grant some freedoms to the younger generation. This family of rulers was atypical in that there was no active intermediate group of parent adults and that the mother Juana demanded special care for almost fifty years of her life. Her children were capable of developing a basis for mutual trust despite exposure to different cultural traditions and were thus able to keep together as a group of friends and reliable partners in a world of political intrigue and personal animosity.

This platform of trust was crucial in the family's struggle against its many adversaries. The grandfathers insisted that marriage alliances were of critical importance to the continuity of the dynasty. But marriage alliances could only be accomplished if the young abided by the dictates of the old. There were thus conflicts between the dynastic concerns that the old pursued and the individual desires that the young wished to follow. These conflicts were particularly dramatic for women. Margaret, whom her father had sent to the French court at the age of three to become the wife of the future French king, knew the conflict from her own experience. Yet she joined her father in requesting subservience from her nieces.

Ferdinand of Aragon did not display more mercy. While Isabel was alive, the Spanish rulers and King Henry VII of England had reached an agreement according to which Catherine, the youngest daughter of the Spanish rulers, was to marry Henry's eldest son Arthur, the English heir apparent. Accompanied by some Spanish courtiers and a lavish dowry, Catherine travelled to England, where she was received with tournaments and pageants in November 1501.[22] But Arthur died less than six months later. As Henry VII did not want to lose the dowry, he proposed that Catherine should marry his younger and apparently more robust son with the same name. But the younger Henry protested.[23] While Catherine stayed in England, the king shelved the issue and offered the marriage of his daughter Mary to Charles in return. But, as both were still children, definitive arrangements in the form of a marriage treaty had to wait. Meanwhile, Henry VII was widowed, became preoccupied with his remarriage and regarded the political aspects of the relationship with the Spanish kingdoms as less urgent. In 1505, he sent his emissaries to the kingdom of Naples to suggest to the recently widowed queen of Naples, Isabella de Baux, that he should marry her daughter Charlotte. While these delicate negotiations were going on, young Henry changed his mind and agreed to marry Catherine, who was still in England. But negotiations were protracted, as Henry VII was not willing to go ahead with his son's marriage until his daughter Mary was married to Charles. Instead the ageing king considered marrying Juana, being flattered by the remark that he was the best husband for Juana, whether or not she was insane.[24] Eventually, the younger Henry had to wait until his father died in

1509. Upon his recognition as King Henry VIII, the marriage ceremonies took place and concluded with Catherine's investiture as queen of England. Meanwhile Mary continued to wait until Charles came of age. Diplomats in charge of the relations between England and the Spanish kingdoms kept an eye on the future marriage alliance and praised Princess Mary's decorum, her comportment and education, and deplored the fact that she had no more than an unfavourable portrait of her potential future husband. Presumably, this was one of the many portraits of young Charles with his mouth open and his chin sticking out.[25]

Maximilian was no less ruthless. He planned to repeat the double marriage arrangement of 1496/97 with his grandchildren. As Charles was already reserved for Mary, the only other available grandson was Ferdinand, while several granddaughters remained ready for choosing. In 1515, Maximilian pressured Juana's daughter Isabel to marry Christian II, King of Denmark, in order to establish the prospect of a dynastic union with the Scandinavian kingdoms. At this time, the king of Denmark had control of Sweden (with Finland) and Norway, and Maximilian hoped to be able to impose Habsburg rule in the Baltic. Looking out elsewhere for a suitable pair of marriage partners, Maximilian detected the children of Ladislaus, King of Hungary and Bohemia, successor to Matthew Corvinus. They seemed to be ideal candidates. The idea was to settle ancient rivalries between the imperial dynasty and these kingdoms by marrying Ferdinand to Ladislaus's daughter Anne and to give Ferdinand's sister Mary to Ladislaus's son Louis. The negotiations were tough, as Ferdinand of Aragon, his third marriage being without issue, was inclined to designate his grandson Ferdinand as successor for Aragon and Castile. But Maximilian supported Charles's succession. According to Maximilian's design, Eleanor was to marry a reigning king, and Charles was to succeed the elder Ferdinand in Aragon and Juana in Castile. According to this plan Charles would move to Spain, while the younger Ferdinand would be transferred from Aragon to Vienna, to succeed his brother as archduke of Austria, take control of the Habsburg hereditary lands and have the option of succeeding as king of Hungary and Bohemia in the future. Maximilian thus envisaged the Habsburg–Spanish dynasty in control of the empire, Burgundy with the Netherlands, England, the Spanish kingdoms with their Italian dependencies, Portugal and its dependencies, the Scandinavian kingdoms as well as Hungary and Bohemia. The Bohemian crown was particularly valuable as a prey because its bearer was one of the seven imperial electors. Through their control of Bohemia the Habsburgs would thus be able to neutralise one electoral vote.

Grand as Maximilian's strategy was, it roused anxieties not only in France but also in the Iberian peninsula and the empire itself. It is small wonder that the Habsburgs were accused of striving for universal monarchy. The accusation was another way of protesting by way of public propaganda against what appeared to critics of Habsburg policy as excessive dynastic ambition. Thus the two grandfathers played a high-level, risky and protracted political game with, as it were, Maximilian pulling the strings and Ferdinand pulling the legs. In his desperate and notorious need for revenue, Maximilian even went so far in 1516 as to offer the imperial crown to Henry VIII in exchange for a large sum of money. The proposal was a repetition of Charles the Bold's plan of 1473: Henry was to succeed Maximilian as the emperor's adopted son and then pass the imperial crown on to Charles, who was then designated to become Henry's brother-in-law. Although Henry responded with keen interest,[26] Maximilian did not pursue the idea, as he was more focused on concluding the double marriage treaty with Ladislaus of Hungary and Bohemia. In 1515, the Habsburg–Hungarian deal was settled. Ferdinand eventually married Anne in 1521, and Louis and Mary married in 1522. Anticipating Maximilian's success, Ferdinand of Aragon seems to have arrived at the conclusion that his cause was lost. Early in 1516, he designated Charles as his successor.[27] Maximilian won the game, and Henry VIII's candidacy for the imperial succession vanished from the emperor's memory (Plate 3).

Personal relations in families of rulers were thus political matters. Boys and girls born into these families had to accept the reality that arrangements about their lives were made for them, not by them. The decision of who was to marry whom was far too important to be left to the vagaries of personal emotions and individual preferences. These decisions entailed rights of succession to high offices, involved the transfer of large amounts of money in the form of dowries and were formalised in treaties with a binding effect in terms of international law. While sudden deaths were incalculable risks, the selection of suitable marriage partners required up-to-date knowledge about the most recent events in the European ruling and high aristocratic dynasties, a thorough familiarity with their histories, and careful projections of the expected consequences of marriage deals for generations to come. Close scrutiny of the health and physical features of candidates was equally important. When Henry VII was in search of a new wife, he dispatched his embassy to the court of Naples and instructed his emissaries to enquire into the physical and intellectual capabilities of a woman under consideration. Among other matters, the emissaries were to find out tactfully whether the women had fresh breath and a healthy complexion. Investigating the health of incumbent and future rulers and their offspring was an often-performed task of secret diplomacy.[28] Yet scores of portraits of unmarried females and males were made for public consumption in the early sixteenth century and later, and still fill art museums in many parts of the world. The portraits owed their existence to the desire to advertise offspring ready for marriage deals and present them in the most favourable light.

Only experienced kin elders had the competence to handle these complex and delicate matters, and Maximilian was the unofficial grand priest of this arcane discipline. He eagerly passed his skills on to his children and grandchildren. Among them, Margaret, Charles, Ferdinand and Mary proved to be his equals.

TEACHER OF A FUTURE EMPEROR: JAKOB MENNEL

Maximilian's *faible* for history is recorded through his intimate relationship with Jakob Mennel, whom he used as a kind of court historian from 1506. Mennel was educated in the 1480s in the then recently founded south German university of Tübingen, from where he received a doctoral degree in law. He used his academic honours to obtain the position of a scribe for the government of the south-west German city of Freiburg, which sent him on diplomatic missions and asked him for legal opinions. Apparently in 1498, Maximilian met Mennel at Freiburg and seems to have been impressed by the rigour of Mennel's scholarship. Ever since the Trier meeting between Frederick III and Charles the Bold, several attempts had been made to provide the Habsburg family with a reliable genealogy. It was the task of this genealogy to support the claim that the imperial dynasty was the oldest, most renowned and most widely connected of all European ruling kin groups. The task was formidable because genealogical records tracing the Habsburgs to periods before the thirteenth century were scarce and subject to controversial interpretations. Maximilian was determined to clear these mists and asked Mennel to travel widely and to search for ancient manuscripts, place-names, tombstones, buildings and other material sources recording the purportedly ancient history of the Habsburgs.[29] Mennel took the imperial instruction seriously and assembled a rich genealogical documentary. The material seemed to support the view that the Habsburgs were directly linked to the Franks, the Huns, the Trojan army and further back to Noah.[30] According to Mennel's genealogical reconstruction, the Habsburgs were indeed the oldest family.

The idea of tracing kin groups to Noah was not new in Maximilian's time. Ninth-century genealogies are on record featuring Noah's name. In the course of the Middle Ages Noah's position as the highest ancestor gained such wide currency in genealogies of ruling families that the practice of awarding to Noah the top position in a genealogy became the target of ridicule. Among others, Aeneas Sylvius Piccolomini, later Pope Pius II, remarked on one occasion that Noah was the ancestor of all humankind and that, consequently, tracing ruling dynasties to him turned rulers and their offspring into ordinary human beings and thus deprived them of all titles to rule. Piccolomini argued that instead of enduring this counterproductive consequence, genealogists in service of ruling families should look out for less prominent figures as focal points of their fancy.[31] However, neither Maximilian nor Mennel were bothered by such quibbles. Instead, they relied on the simple but effective and well-tested method of constructing images of the past where records were scarce.

Mennel did his work well. He made the methodically sound decision to look for the origins of the Habsburgs in the lands of their earliest recorded activities. This area was not Austria but, in terms of modern geography, the triangle of territories across the French–German–Swiss border. This choice led him to link the Habsburgs to one of the core parts of the early medieval Frankish kingdom. Then Mennel constructed the genealogy of the Habsburgs as a branch of the genealogy of the Frankish kings.[32] Like other early medieval rulers, the Frankish kings traced themselves back to the Trojans and to Noah.[33] Mennel provided what Maximilian wanted. In doing so, he followed medieval traditions of origin according to which, in the aftermath of the Trojan War, the Trojan army had dispersed across the world, migrating from Asia Minor to Europe where they appeared as Huns, Saxons, Franks or Hungarians. On the basis of this construction Mennel produced six volumes of a manuscript chronicle of the Habsburg dynasty, narrating the story of alleged Frankish and Habsburg wanderings from the Trojan War to central and western Europe. He submitted the work to Maximilian in 1517 together with a picture index.[34] In his narrative the Trojans-Huns-Hungarians moved further west, where they founded Austria, and then continued to areas west of the Rhine where they appeared as Franks and the alleged invaders of the Iberian peninsula.[35] Moreover, when in the later Middle Ages the Habsburgs moved from the Upper Rhine Valley to Austria, they were merely returning to the ancient lands. Mixing Huns with Hungarians thus helped Mennel provide seemingly solid evidence in support of the Habsburg claim to succession in Hungary. Mennel's narrative supported the view that the Spanish–Habsburg marriage deal was no more than the restitution of the Habsburgs to their long-established ancient rights. The emperor was so pleased with the work that he placed the volumes into the coffin that accompanied him on his journeys. Mennel rose to the position of an imperial adviser on matters of history. When Maximilian felt his end approaching in 1518, he summoned Mennel to his deathbed and asked him to read from the chronicle during sleepless nights.[36]

The history of family relations and genealogies were thus complicated matters. Maximilian knew of their importance and, in 1515, commissioned Mennel to instruct his grandson Charles in history. Mennel wrote an excerpt from his chronicle introducing Habsburg history to Maximilian's heir apparent, drawing on the medieval world picture for his identification of Europe as one of three parts of the inhabitable world.[37] He portrayed the Habsburgs as descendants of Noah and the oldest world rulers of antiquity, whom he identified as Huns and Trojans, and linked them to their purported successors in Roman antiquity and medieval Europe:

> You must know and take into account that, from the time of Noah your first ancestor . . . your line goes and descends through the Trojans and Huns. . . . From these and further persons, who already then held their territories and the government of the world, your ancient predecessors and other kings and princes in your pedigree of Troy and the Huns and the kings of Gaul, Germany and Italy came and descended.[38]

In accordance with his narrative, Mennel addressed Charles in 1515 as 'King of Spain and Hungary, Archduke of Austria, Duke of Burgundy etc.'[39] He did so at a time when Ferdinand of Aragon was still alive, the Spanish succession was an open matter and Maximilian was engaged in mating Charles's brother Ferdinand with the daughter of the Hungarian king. In the same year, Mennel produced a booklet that contained brief references to the Roman emperors and popes as the bearers of traditions of universal rule. At Maximilian's command, Mennel dedicated the booklet to Charles. It reads like an abridged version of the bulky chronicle that Mennel had compiled for Maximilian. Its central feature is the display of the

Habsburg dynasty as the inheritors of the imperial tradition.[40] The abridged works written *ad usum Delphini* fulfilled their purpose. They helped impregnate Charles's mind with the conviction that he was the descendant of the oldest ruling kin group in Europe. The volumes of Mennel's full-length chronicle remained in Maximilian's custody and, upon his death, were passed on to Charles's brother Ferdinand, who kept them in his private library (Plate 4).

TWO

The Stage for the Show:
The Old versus the New World

THE SUCCESSION TO THE SPANISH KINGDOMS (1515–19)

ime flies. At the age of fifteen Charles reached maturity and
assumed the duty of ruling the duchy of Burgundy. He took
office in a ceremony held in the Hall of the Great Palace in Brussels.
Aunt Margaret became his counsellor but continued to assert herself
in Burgundian politics. She selected Charles's advisers so that the
appointed personages were people of her choice. Foremost among
them were Adrian of Utrecht, William of Croy, sieur de Chièvres,
and the aristocrat Jean de Sauvages. Charles, the Burgundian
nobleman, remained in the entourage of Burgundians, who pleaded
for the maintenance of good relations towards their neighbours in
France and England. Thus Maximilian and his daughter Margaret
urged Charles to remain on good terms with Henry VIII, and
Charles had a formal letter sent to England in 1515, declaring his
maturity and assuring the king of continuing friendship.[1] The court
also followed Charles's father in maintaining good personal ties
between the new duke and his lord, the French king. By a lucky
circumstance, a new young ruler had just ascended the French
throne in the person of Francis I, who appeared similar in age and
habits to his high-ranking vassal. Henry VIII was merely a few years
senior to both. For the time being, the Habsburg–Valois rivalry
appeared to be a matter of the past, and the Netherlands, France
and England, the three foremost polities in western Europe, seemed
to be looking forward to a period of peace and friendship. The three
like-minded rulers were seen as a stabilising factor in a volatile
world. They appeared like a triumvirate in need of one another not

merely as partners in peace but also as enemies in war. No one expressed this sentiment better than the English court ideologues who created the motto *Cui adhaereo prae est* (the person to whom I am close is ahead) for Henry VIII, apparently on the occasion of Henry's meeting with Charles and Francis on the Field of the Cloth of Gold in 1520.[2] The motto positioned the English king theoretically as a balancer between the two other rulers although, in practice, Henry would opt for Charles and against Francis on most occasions. In 1514, when Charles decided to revoke the marriage arrangement with Henry's sister Mary, Henry responded by offering her to Francis, but otherwise he remained loyal to Charles.[3] Francis tried to maintain good personal relations with both rulers during much of his reign, though not always successfully. Likewise, Charles hardly hesitated to claim the dynastic prestige he believed he had as the emperor's grandson and heir apparent to the Habsburg dynasty, but to the end of his active life he treated Henry and Francis as his most important partners outside his own dynasty.

For the time being, the advisers arranged matters of high politics for the young duke. Charles attended council meetings without becoming seriously involved. In his ample spare time he cultivated aristocratic decorum, enjoying life at Margaret's court with its traditional Burgundian habits, joining the festivities of the Order of the Golden Fleece over which he presided, and improving his knightly tournament skills. With regard to the last ability, he even received praise from his grandfather, which meant a lot; Maximilian was well known for his knightly skills.[4] Yet the duke's advisers knew well that their protégé's unburdened youth was ending. When Maximilian was winning the struggle over the succession in the Spanish kingdoms, the time for Charles's departure for the Iberian peninsula approached.

The need for departure came sooner than expected, when Ferdinand of Aragon died suddenly on 23 January 1516. Although Charles was the designated successor, the management of the succession was complicated. Charles followed Ferdinand in the crown of Aragon, whereas Castile continued to be under Juana's titular rule. Moreover, during the period of Charles's temporary absence from the Spanish kingdoms, a new regent had to be found for Castile who could also act as interim ruler for Aragon and its dependencies. Government passed into the hands of Cardinal Francisco Jimenez de Cisneros despite his advanced age. Charles's presence in his Spanish domains was urgently required but Margaret's court was wary of sending him away instantaneously. Preparations had to be made, including the selection of his entourage. Although Cardinal Jimenez was asked to make sure that Spanish advisers surrounded the new king, the Burgundian courtiers were unwilling to yield their positions. A Spanish–Burgundian rivalry opened over priority of privileged access to the ruler.

While the preparations for Charles's journey were going on, dramatic events destabilised the Spanish kingdoms. The Cortes of Aragon and Castile together with revolutionary groups of commoners named Germania decided to probe the strength of Jimenez's regency. The Cortes of Aragon demanded their participation in the process of installing the new ruler. The Cortes of Castile requested that Juana's rights to rule should be observed. The revolutionaries aimed at weakening the power of monarchical rulership and, to that end, even appealed to Juana. A delegation visited her at Tordesillas, where she was kept in confinement. She listened graciously to the delegation but did not act. Meanwhile Jimenez fought to restore government control over Aragon and Castile and to enforce Aragonese rule in the western Mediterranean Sea and in the south of the Italian peninsula. He took a strong stand against the Cortes and tried to subdue the Germania. He expanded the naval forces and dispatched a new viceroy to Naples. He appealed to Charles to move to his Spanish kingdoms as soon as possible but could not speed up the preparation process in the Netherlands. Instead, Charles dispatched Adrian of Utrecht as his emissary with the task of suppressing the uprisings.

The cardinal's conundrums became explicit in a memorandum written by Alonso Manrique de Lara, Bishop of Badajoz, on 8 March 1516. Lara was a Castilian who had served Charles's father Philip before joining Margaret's court in 1509. He knew Charles's condition well and advised the cardinal on how to proceed in the succession issue. He began with two observations. The first was that the young king could not speak a word of Spanish. The second was that Burgundian advisers directed Charles. Lara was worried about Charles's lack of knowledge of Spanish because it appeared to indicate that the new king was unfamiliar with the culture and traditions of his subjects and might act against their well-understood interests. The second observation strengthened these concerns as it suggested that Charles's current advisers were neither willing nor able to represent Spanish interests. Straightforwardly, Lara accused Charles's Burgundian entourage of greed and corruption and reported that some capable Spanish aristocrats, surviving from King Philip's time, were being barred from access to the ruler and from participation in his government. In the bishop's opinion, these practices were not only detrimental to Spanish interests but, more importantly, entailed the further evil consequence that the French party at Margaret's court was gaining strength. Eventually, the bishop warned, Charles might accept treaty obligations in favour of French and against Spanish interests.

Lara singled out Chièvres as the strong man representing the French party. He described Chièvres as a Frenchman by birth, through father and mother, as Lara emphasised, and insinuated that Chièvres was responsible for promoting a 'mood of inferiority' in Charles *vis-à-vis* the French king. He expressed his indignation about what he considered as a forthcoming miserable situation in which Charles as a Spanish ruler might sign letters as 'servant and vassal' of the French king. In fact, Charles's Burgundian chancellery arranged for a treaty between Francis I and Charles, signed at Noyon in 1516, according to which Charles would marry Louise, Francis's one-year-old daughter, and pledged to withdraw Aragonese forces from Navarre. The Spanish government saw the treaty as an instrument to tie the Spanish ruler to the French king through dynastic obligations. Although Lara conceded that it was a good thing for both rulers to maintain amicable relations, he insisted that these relations should never be allowed to become detrimental to Spanish interests. He was explicitly critical of agreements that Charles appeared to be willing to sign about the future return of the Spanish part of the kingdom of

Navarre to French control, and demanded that every effort should be made to prevent a personal meeting between Charles and Francis while Charles was on his way to Spain.[5]

A sense of rivalry between the Spanish and Margaret's courts thus led Bishop Lara to demand that Cardinal Jimenez make every effort to further speed up preparations for Charles's journey to Spain. Lara expected that, in the Spanish kingdoms, Charles would be more easily convinced that he had to act in favour of Spanish interests. He had no confidence in Margaret's court and even suspected her of pushing ahead marriage negotiations for Eleanor and Charles that were unfavourable for the Spanish kingdoms. In the bishop's judgement, only Henry VIII appeared as a trustworthy friend.

Yet preparations did not speed up. Eventually, Charles only left the Netherlands in 1517 to travel to Spain by sea. He journeyed in the company of his largely Burgundian entourage. Although the voyage was calm, Charles and his courtiers had to go ashore prematurely, close to the remote spot Viciosa on the coast. The party had to make their way through difficult terrain before they reached Valladolid in November 1518. Thus the new king sneaked into his realms through the back door. Being informed about Charles's arrival, Cardinal Jimenez set off to meet him but fell ill on the way. He was forced to rest and wait for Charles to come. Thanks to the cardinal's rule by iron fist, the Cortes were willing to accept the new king. But revolutionary unrest continued at various places. The government was forced to begin its work immediately. Yet, against these pressures, Charles took time to visit his mother at Tordesillas. He found her and his younger sisters in a miserable condition and decided to establish a small court where Juana could lead a life worthy of the titular queen of Castile. While the king was making his way through the northern Spanish lands, the cardinal died at Roa not far from Valladolid on 8 November 1517, before Charles and his party arrived there. Charles spent the winter at Valladolid, where he received oaths of loyalty from the Cortes of Castile against the pledge not to employ foreigners in his service. He moved on to Aragon in March 1518.

It was a bad start for the new king. Not only were the new and unfamiliar realms in disarray and revolt; family issues were also waiting to be settled. While Margaret was ready to act as his regent for the Netherlands, Charles had yet to accommodate himself with his brother Ferdinand. Now fourteen years of age, Ferdinand had grown up in Spain expecting to spend the rest of his life there. But Maximilian thwarted these expectations with his marriage arrangements of 1515. Hence Ferdinand could no longer stay in the Spanish kingdoms after Charles had arrived there. Maximilian, Margaret and Charles thus agreed that Ferdinand, the Spanish aristocrat, should move to the Netherlands to continue his education at Margaret's court until he could be invested with control over the Habsburg hereditary lands. The castling took place. The Burgundian nobleman took office as ruler in the Spanish kingdoms, and the Spanish aristocrat became available as a ruler in the German-speaking areas.

Moreover, there was indeed widespread disgruntlement at Charles's Burgundian entourage. They were criticised for their habit of big spending that did not appeal to Spanish conventions. Their methods of administration were often felt to be incompatible with the legalism that had established itself as a principle of government in the Iberian peninsula from the fifteenth century. New agencies were established for the purpose of curtailing the influence of Charles's Burgundian entourage, among them the State Council, established in 1521, and the Indian Council, established in 1524. Both councils balanced the impact of the Burgundian staff because jurists trained in Spanish universities as well as aristocrats experienced in government entered them and obtained direct access to the king. Eventually the number of Spanish members in Charles's entourage grew and, with them, the new king's exposure to Spanish traditions and habits. But Margaret dispatched Mercurino d'Arborio Gattinara, whom she knew as an administrator from the time of her marriage with Philibert of Savoy. Charles appointed him to the office of chancellor for the Spanish kingdoms. Gattinara effectively counterpoised the rising influence that Spanish intellectuals and aristocrats were having on Charles.

Based on the solid foundations that Cardinal Jimenez had laid, domestic politics calmed down. Charles could rely on revenue extracted from his Spanish subjects. Surprisingly, the situation in the Netherlands remained smooth. After Charles's departure, Margaret balanced the demands for revenue from her father the emperor and her nephew the Spanish ruler against the often disgruntled and uncooperative estates. The burghers of Ghent articulated their dissent even at the time when Charles was present in the Netherlands. In 1515, when Charles was introduced as the new count of Flanders, the guild of weavers at Ghent protested because Charles was willing to swear the oath of fealty only after the burghers had agreed to a reduction of their autonomy. Charles had some protesters arrested and executed. He issued a decree that prohibited public gatherings and forced office-holders to swear allegiance to it. The burghers of Ghent obeyed but referred to the decree contemptuously as the *calfvel* (calf skin). By contrast, Charles was warmly received at Bruges, where burghers gave him a triumphal entry.[6] In terms of foreign policy, Margaret made lasting efforts to prevent estrangement between Charles and Francis and to boost the friendship between Charles and Henry. She understood, perhaps better than her nephew, that the maintenance of peace in western Europe was a condition for profitable trade in the Netherlands and, further to this, that profits from trade were crucial to the generation of revenue from these provinces. Thus Aunt Margaret and her advisers in the Netherlands pleaded in favour of flexible diplomacy in relations with France and England.[7] By contrast, Charles's advisers in the Spanish kingdoms demanded harsh measures against the French king, whom they often accused of being unreliable and acting in breach of valid agreements.[8]

The dilemma did not wane when Maximilian died on 12 January 1519. After some hesitation and against pleas by his Spanish advisers, Charles decided to announce his candidacy for the imperial office. This meant that he had to seek approval from the seven imperial electors, and he neglected the affairs of his Spanish domains. Charles's campaign turned into a race not only against Francis, who ran as well, but also against Henry, who had not forgotten Maximilian's promise. Like Charles's Spanish advisers, Margaret was opposed to Charles's candidacy. She feared that his rivalry with Francis would have a deteriorating impact on the relations between the Netherlands and France. She thus proposed to nominate a neutral candidate, and her own choice was Ferdinand. Hastily she prepared for his departure to the German-speaking areas. But the Spanish court learned of Margaret's activities and dispatched a stiff note written in Charles's name. In the letter, Margaret was warned not to step beyond the limits of her office as Charles's regent and not to interfere in her nephew's business. Instead, Charles had her informed about his determination to seek election as emperor. Margaret complied and removed Ferdinand from the race.[9] But Margaret's compliance did not reduce resistance to Charles's candidacy in the Spanish kingdoms. His advisers were afraid that Charles as emperor would become involved in many political affairs that were of little interest for the Iberian peninsula and might be detrimental for the Spanish royal coffers. Specifically, they expected that the king would have to leave his domains, again having to entrust government to advisers or to a regent. This expectation materialised soon when, early in 1519, Charles made up his mind to support his candidacy through his own presence in the German-speaking areas.

THE ROMAN EMPIRE AND THE CONQUEST OF THE NEW WORLD

The territorialisation of politics

Centres demand peripheries as their counterparts, and peripheries demand boundaries that not only separate but also interrelate inside and outside. The more centres there are, the more numerous their boundaries must be and the more diversified the political landscape becomes. Centralisation affects the structure of space in territorial polities, the collective identities of the residential population groups and the forms and roles of government.

Throughout the sixteenth century, few territorial polities were rounded off in the sense that they were structured as territorial unities within established boundaries. That is, within a territorial polity, such as the kingdom of France, there could be areas under the government of an external ruler, for example the papal enclaves in Avignon, the Venaissin in central France, and the county of Montbéliard in Burgundy which came under the rule of the duke of Württemberg until 1793. Conversely, there could be territorial polities that were widely scattered across extensive lands, such the areas placed directly under Habsburg rule which extended from the border area towards the Ottoman Turkish Empire to the Netherlands. It was also perfectly normal that territorial polities were carved up into districts for taxation, marked by internal boundaries. Crossing these boundaries implied the obligation to pay customs dues for traders as if they were entering a territorial polity under the control of another ruler. Checkpoints were also erected for the purpose of controlling migrants and curtailing desertion.

On the other side, there were only few sizeable territorial polities which were subjected to the exclusive control of only one ruler or governing institution. That was the case during much of the sixteenth century for the kingdoms of England and Portugal, the core part of the Russian Empire and the kingdoms of Sweden and Denmark, even though the rulers of the last three embarked on expansionist policies. Amid the variegated polities, whose number amounted to more than three hundred all over Europe, the Roman Empire continued with controversial and often-changing boundaries. Towards the east, the boundaries remained poorly defined and gave rise to incessant strife. Towards the south, the empire was in retreat from the rising tide of autonomy in such polities as the republic of Venice. Elsewhere, existing boundaries of the empire became threadbare because territorial rulers inside the empire began to establish their own relations with rulers beyond the recognised imperial confines, and even entered into formal alliances.

Still, the right of hereditary succession to rule over territorial polities prevailed and counterbalanced the otherwise advancing process of territorialisation of rule, although with a declining degree of success. Following the precedence of the so-called Hundred Years War which ended in 1492 in the English withdrawal from France, except for Calais, ever more cases became known in which succession to rule after the extinction of a local dynasty sparked controversy. Thus in the course of the sixteenth century, Maximilian's practice of uniting titles to rule and to overlordship on the grounds of hereditary privileges began to be opposed particularly in southern and western Europe. Nevertheless, Charles continued to use dynastic relations as instruments of imperial policy and made efforts to enforce the principle of dynastic legitimacy. However, at the end of his reign, he admitted that his attempts had failed.[10] Many unresolved cases remained, first and foremost in the empire, such as the controversy over the Prussian succession in Jülich, Cleves and Berg, and these difficulties often resulted from the fact that most of the ruling dynasties in Europe were then so closely affiliated with each other that contending claims emerged and fuelled controversies.

Strengthening the institutional aspects of territorial polities was in the interest of territorial rulers but reduced the viability of attempts to advance universal rule. Territorial rulers were eager to promote institutionalisation because it allowed them to present themselves as the highest ruling agents in the territorial polities over which they were entrusted to rule. In turn, institutionalisation promoted bureaucratisation, and the emergent bureaucracies in service to territorial rulers had to be established in permanent offices in proximity to the ruler's residence. Within these courts, life became highly formalised, with much emphasis on ceremonial and normative behaviour. A special brand of literature emerged whose authors systematised the norms and rules to be observed by the courtiers.[11] Hence the residential capitals of territorial polities grew into administrative centres from which each territorial polity at large was to be controlled. In the sixteenth century, such centralised bureaucratic control remained imperfect in many respects. But the principle that the territorial ruler was to be recognised as the head of a bureaucratic government administrating the public affairs of the territorial polity received widespread recognition.

Foremost among the theorists who supported this principle was Niccolò Machiavelli. In the early sixteenth century, he appeared as the most vocal representative of a theory of government according to which rulers ought to enlarge their competence to rule over land and people, to enlarge the size of the territories under their control and to do so by means of whatever strategies appeared to be conducive to these ends.[12] Since the eighteenth century, Machiavelli's political theory has met with scepticism and he has been accused of ruthlessness in giving morally unacceptable advice to rulers. But Machiavelli did not conclude the most consequential of his political writings without the demand that rulers defend the integrity of the territories entrusted to their control. In this request was implied the further demand that rulers act in fulfilment of the wishes and desires of the ruled and that they do so by safeguarding the ruled against interventions or invasions from outside.

The Roman Empire versus territorial polities

Machiavelli's theory of government thus made explicit the demand that rulers should govern effectively and comprehensively over land and people within a given and stable territory. Executing this demand was only possible on condition that there was only one person or institution in charge of making ultimate decisions over the territorial polity as a whole. This condition could be fulfilled in all territorial polities where an unequivocal hierarchy of aristocratic lords had evolved in the course of the Middle Ages who recognised the territorial ruler as the legitimate holder of supreme power. However, in the sixteenth century, there were few territorial polities where this was unequivocally the case. Within the Roman Empire, it was difficult to decide authoritatively which of the rulers occupied the highest position. There were the emperor, the electors, a substantive number of dukes and earls as well as the free and imperial cities. With regard to these territorial rulers and urban governments, the contest was between proponents of two theories. One group of theorists argued that the empire was no more than a republic of aristocratic lords and that, consequently, the emperor could be the ruler only over the hereditary lands of the family to which he belonged. The other group insisted that, within the empire, the emperor was the sole ruler over all imperial estates.

The first position evolved through attempts to disentangle the right to rule over territorial polities from the person of the ruler.[13] Throughout the sixteenth century, jurists in service to territorial rulers wrote legal opinions regarding the question whether the right to rule over land and people existed as a personal privilege of the ruler or whether it was tied to the land and the population over which it was exercised. These jurists concluded that the right to rule over land and people could only result from the willingness of the population to invest a ruler or a government with the representation of their collective concerns and to relate these concerns to the territory within which the population happened to live.[14] Fourteenth-century ideas of a covenant between the ruled and the ruler[15] resurfaced and promoted the conclusion that only one personal ruler or governing institution could act as the representative of the collective will of the population. However, the population could only be understood as a partner in the covenant with a single ruler if it lived in united territories with clearly demarcated boundaries.[16] Jean Bodin cast these views into a technical term that has remained in use ever since. He identified the sole and exclusive ruler over a territory as the 'sovereign'. Neither the word sovereignty nor the subject matter was new. The Latin word *suprematus* and its vernacular renderings, such as Old English *sovereyn*, were in use during the thirteenth century, together with vernacular terms such as German *oberkait*. In its application to the empire, the theory of sovereignty confirmed the position that the Roman Empire was not and could not be a territory of its own and that, consequently, the emperor was not a sovereign. Thus the theory placed Charles in a dilemma. He could claim to be sovereign of the Spanish kingdoms with the argument that he was the sole territorial ruler there and that Spanish aristocrats had accepted him as their ruler. But he could not at the same time claim to be overlord of the Spanish kingdom in his capacity as Roman emperor. As Spanish ruler, he was in control of the Spanish overseas territories. As Roman emperor, he was practically confined to rule over parts of Europe. The medieval theories of universal rule that Maximilian could still use to claim the position of a suzerain of the world were reduced to fanciful dreams.

If the emperor had any role to play in the world at large, he was obliged to act as the divinely willed bringer of peace. Yet theorists as well as practical political decision makers were familiar with the paradox that the promotion of peace was difficult without maintaining the ability to issue serious military threats.[17]

Theorists of the rival group defended the Roman Empire as a territorial polity of its own to which the same definitional elements ought to be applied as to territorial polities.[18] These theorists claimed that rule over the empire did not come into the hands of the emperor as a personal gift through hereditary succession, but that it was handed down to him through divine grace. Consequently, these theorists limited the rights of territorial rulers within the empire to the territories placed under their control and subjected them to the ultimate sovereignty of the emperor. Likening the rule of the emperor to the authority of the housefather in the tradition of St Augustine,[19] they concluded that the imperial estates had no right to stand up against the emperor. According to these theorists, Charles was unequivocally sovereign of the Roman Empire but the empire itself was no longer universal.

In summary, throughout the sixteenth century, rulers emerged at the centre of bureaucracies that began to place themselves in charge of controlling the public affairs of territorial polities. Most of these rulers were monarchs who assembled in their courts administrative specialists, many of whom were trained in jurisprudence. They centralised public affairs in their courts which, in turn, developed into central places of territorial polities. The centralisation became architecturally explicit in new spacious palaces that the territorial rulers had built for themselves, their families and dependants as well as the growing numbers of courtiers. These palaces differed sharply from the medieval castles that had been secluded from the physical environment by their walls. Architects demanded that palaces should be built so that their inhabitants could overlook the open landscape.[20] Building them was a costly and time-consuming process which only territorial rulers, a few high-ranking aristocrats, senior church officials and wealthy members of the urban patriarchates could afford. Lesser aristocrats whose funds were limited remained confined to their medieval castles and responded with confessions of envy to the lavish palaces which, to them, appeared as manifestations of luxury.[21] The newly built palaces were not only open to the landscape but conformed to simple though stern geometrical shapes in which symmetries and centralisation achieved paramount significance. The geometrical patterns extended through the formal gardens into the physical environment in the vicinity of the palaces. These patterns were expressions of a wider-ranging human desire to control the physical environment and subject it to a human-made symmetrical order.

Moreover, the central position of the palaces as the courts and administrative centres became manifest in the geometrical structuration of the territorial polities. Here, the main instrument was the building of roads. Territorial rulers, such as King Henry VIII of England, began to supervise the building and repairing of roads, which they considered to be vital for commerce in the polity at large.[22] The more the ruler's administrative centre grew to become a residential capital, the more the road networks were focused on the centre. In the course of the sixteenth and seventeenth centuries, several miles discs were printed showing distances to and from major cities, such as London, Augsburg or Nuremberg. For an entire polity, one such network is shown in the frontispiece of John Ogilby's *Britannia* of 1675.[23] The picture shows a map of England in which the most important roads connect peripheral places with London and terminate at the outward boundaries of the kingdom. A similar map had already been printed in 1502 by Erhard Etzlaub for the purpose of describing pilgrims' roads to Rome.[24] The map places the south with Rome at the top and gives pictorial instructions on how to find and cross the major Alpine passes into the Italian peninsula. Etzlaub's map does not feature administrative boundaries, but portrays Europe as permeable. It characterises Rome as the final destination for pilgrims from Europe north of the Alps, but not as the administrative centre of a territorial polity.

Indeed, sixteenth-century cartographers made growing efforts to display the world as an assemblage of territorial polities. In 1537, John Putsch (Bucius) of Innsbruck created the first image of Europe as a virgin whose body consists of the names of territories.[25] The map was first printed in Paris and reappeared in many editions of Sebastian Münster's *Cosmographia* between 1544 and 1628.[26] It was also included in the Czech version of Heinrich Bünting's *Itinerarium sacrae scripturae* of 1592.[27] Moreover, in 1587, Abraham Ortelius created a much-imitated cartographical image of the world where the continents were filled up with names of territorial polities and allowed for no blank spaces. Only some mythical Arctic lands and the hypothetical Fourth Continent were allowed to feature without names, but they did so as unknown lands. This cartographical image was reflected by the growing number of handbooks containing verbal descriptions of the existing territorial polities by continents.[28] The descriptions were comparative and touched upon aspects of the physical environment, natural resources, production, trade and other economic activities, customs and habits, government and armies as well as history. Such comparative surveys had already been composed in the fifteenth century,[29] but their focus on territorial polities was new in the sixteenth century. Like the world maps, the handbooks presented the world with its territorial divisions rather than as the theatre of universal rule (Plate 10).

The New World

While the Habsburg–Spanish family of rulers was being established and Charles began to rule over the Spanish kingdoms, dramatic changes of the world picture occurred when an apparently 'new world' came into the sight of European mapmakers and rulers. The phrases *orbis novus* and *mundus novus*, meaning new world, were already part of Columbus's vocabulary and appeared elsewhere in the 1490s. But the meaning of the words *orbis* and *mundus* varied. In the terminology of Columbus, his contemporaries and the reporters on his voyages, they related to the island worlds in the ocean west of Europe and Africa, and contained nothing suggestive of the claim that Columbus may have visited parts of a new continent separate from the land mass shown in medieval world maps. Other references to these western island worlds visited by Columbus and his contemporaries were cast in words and phrases such as *terra, terra firma* or *continens*, meaning land or continent. Again, none of these references supports the claim that the navigators traversing the ocean in the 1490s and early 1500s had a vision of America *avant la lettre*. Instead, the *orbis novus, mundus novus*, the *terra nova, terrae* or *terrae firmae* or the *continentes* mentioned in the reports, descriptions and maps on the voyages of Columbus and his contemporaries were merely various expressions for the same kind of geographical phenomena, namely certain islands which were larger in relation to other islands in their vicinity.[30] Such terminology is by no means uncommon. In the Japanese archipelago, for example, the largest of the Ryûkyû Islands is known as Okinawa Hontô, that is Okinawa Main Island, and the largest island of the entire archipelago is Honshû, the main land. Hence there is little excitement enclosed in these phrases, as they simply reflect the fact that the island worlds in the ocean were believed not to have been known to European geographers during antiquity and the Middle Ages. Insisting that these island worlds represented an *orbis novus* or the like was nevertheless an admission that the medieval world maps had been imperfect and, moreover, an explicit criticism of the geography of antiquity. The criticism was primarily targeted at the cartographic work printed under the name of Ptolemy at the turn of the sixteenth century. Against this background, references to the *orbis/mundus novus* reflected the pride of the navigators who had not only proved that Ptolemy was empirically wrong but could claim to know more than the celebrated sage of antiquity and the makers of medieval world maps.

The most consequential use of the *orbis/mundus novus* phraseology occurred in a report on the voyage conducted by Alvares Cabral in 1500. The report was first published in the form of a letter addressed to the Medici in Florence by one Amerigo Vespucci in 1503.[31] Vespucci was a member of Cabral's crew. In his report, he described aspects of the coastlines of what is north-east South America in present geography. Vespucci was a skilful writer and gave an impressive account of the voyage that became a bestseller pamphlet. Vespucci used the phrase *mundus novus* in the title of the pamphlet and thereby did much to spread the use of the *orbis/mundus novus* phraseology. However, Vespucci made no attempt to identify as a separate continent the growing number of islands and *terrae firmae* coming in sight of the European navigators. Instead, he shared Columbus's perception that the island worlds were located in a previously unknown part of the ocean.

By the middle of the first decade of the sixteenth century, the number of accounts on the western voyages became substantive enough to attract the interest of cartographers. The school of intellectuals at St Dié in Lorraine, whose members were devoted to the study of Ptolemaic geography, seem to have eagerly absorbed the incoming news in attempts to fit the island worlds into cartographic world pictures. Fortunately for them, Alberto Cantino, an Italian agent working in Lisbon for the Duke of Ferrara, seems to have had access to the inner circle of Portuguese scholars and mapmakers and brought with him the results of the Portuguese voyages. The map stands in the tradition of the late medieval portulans or sea charts and lists a large number of coastal points in Africa, South Asia and the island worlds of the ocean. It displays in considerable detail the coastlines of what are southern Africa, south-west India and north-east South America today. The St Dié scholars, most notably Martin Waldseemüller,[32] knew Vespucci's work and must have had access to Cantino's map, for they produced their own map in 1507 which represents north-east South America in exactly the same shape as the Cantino map. Consequently, the Cantino map and the St Dié map both agreed on allowing unrestricted passage from Europe to Asia through what they described as island worlds in the ocean. Moreover, the tri-continental landmass of Europe, Asia and Africa formed the centrepiece in these maps. But they also reflected important innovations. Most significantly, they vastly extended the share of the earth's surface that they displayed as covered by water. The narrow strip of water which had separated Europe and Africa from Asia in maps modelled on medieval world maps gave way to vast stretches of oceanic waters into which numerous islands and *terrae firmae* were interspersed. The St Dié mapmakers thus

45

embedded the tri-continental landmass into widely diversified oceanic waters through which unrestricted trespass was possible. The St Dié map makes the craving for novelty of its authors even more explicit through the pictures and inscriptions on its margins. On the upper margin it depicts images of Ptolemy and Vespucci facing each other. Ptolemy is introduced as the sage of antiquity whereas Vespucci comes along as the discoverer of the New World. The most significant innovation of the map relates to the nomenclature. The St Dié mapmakers inscribed the name 'America' into the largest item in the island worlds between Europe and Africa on the one side and Asia on the other, thereby replacing the previous use of such names as *Terra Sanctae Crucis*.³³ The process of renaming the *Terra Sanctae Crucis* into America began with the St Dié map that placed the name 'America' into the eastern part of the *terra* described by Vespucci and set this *terra* apart from the area which he portrayed as having been discovered 'by command of the King of Castile'. Thus the St Dié scholars differentiated areas in accordance with the stipulations of the Tordesillas treaty but did not insert the demarcation line. For the text of the inscription about the area associated with the 'King of Castile', the mapmakers drew on the Cantino map. Yet Waldseemüller did not insert the name 'America' into his edition of the work of Ptolemy, which appeared in Strasbourg in 1513. Instead, he used the formula *terra incognita*. Nevertheless, the Strasbourg printers Johann Adolph Muehlich (= Johann Adelphus) and Johann Grüninger, as well as the cartographer Johann Schöner for his globe of 1520, used the St Dié terminology. Muehlich–Grüninger inserted an area identified as *nüwe insel oder welt* (new island or world) into the far western part of their global map, placed it 'next to Europe and Africa to the outside and the sunset', and maintained that it should 'be named America after its discoverer'.³⁴ Other reporters on the 'discoveries' followed the St Dié school and distinguished between the island worlds and the *terra* visited by Columbus on the one side and Vespucci on the other. Or they mentioned Columbus as the discoverer of many islands but derived the name 'America' from the name of Amerigo Vespucci and described it as the fourth 'part of the world that was discovered in the year 1497'.³⁵ In view of the fact that Amerigo Vespucci appears as the discoverer of this part of the world in the same map, it is difficult to deny that the St Dié mapmakers derived the name for the area from Vespucci's given name.

Apart from these grand maps of the entire earth, there were sketches of details or parts of the *mundus novus*. The best known is the portulan map drawn in 1500 by Juan de La Cosa, who was a member of Columbus's crew.[36] La Cosa's map shows a solid land together with the island world which the Columbus expeditions had visited during the fifteenth century, and the distance between Europe and this island world. It is a display of the navigatory accomplishments of Columbus and his crew without an attempt to interconnect the results of the expeditions with some picture of the earth as a whole. The same kind of practical task seems to have been behind three small maps showing areas visited during Columbus's voyages. Columbus's brother Bartholomew appears to have sketched them although they are extant only in a report written by the Venetian Alessandro Zorzi.[37] The maps illustrate the achievements mainly of Columbus's third voyage, which reached the northern shores of what is the South American continent in present geography. One of the maps displays this area as an island, names it 'MONDO NOVO' and places it in proximity to Asia. It is known from reports on Columbus's third and fourth voyages that, on these occasions, he believed he had reached waters close to the Ganges River. Another map of the world west of the first one shows the eastern and southern coasts of Asia and identifies the seaway south of Asia in the Ptolemaic tradition as INDICVM MARE (Indian Sea) and once more in accordance with the medieval world maps as OCEANVS INDICVS (Indian Ocean). The small maps confirm Columbus's continuing belief that he was travelling in Asian waters and that eastern Asia as well as southern Asia were accessible from Europe by a westward voyage. However, like the La Cosa map, they fail to integrate this area into the geographical context of the entire earth. That is to say that, during the first decade of the sixteenth century, neither the cartographers and other intellectuals who were studying the world picture, nor the Portuguese and Spanish rulers as the organisers of the oceanic expeditions and other practical political decision makers elsewhere in Europe saw any urgency to depart from the conventional perception of the world as a tri-continental landmass. Nevertheless, they did attribute a larger share of the surface of the earth to water.

New oceans

The waterway known as the 'Indian Sea' on Ptolemaic maps[38] and as 'mare Occeanum' in fifteenth-century geography[39] attracted much attention in the early years of the sixteenth century. The waterway had been the theatre of a trading network for five hundred years at the time when Vasco da Gama arrived there in 1498. It connected Japan and China with the East African coasts and was maintained by the cooperation of merchant mariners from Japan, China, the South-east Asian archipelago, south-west and north-west India as well as the Arabian peninsula. The Portuguese merchants appeared in this waterway initially as competitors to Arab Muslim merchants. They tried to put Muslims out of business and thereby demonstrated their willingness to continue to adhere to the crusading rhetoric of the Middle Ages.[40] Da Gama's first attempt at Calicut failed, but Portuguese sailors subsequently resorted to military violence. Vasco da Gama returned as viceroy of India on his second expedition from 1502 to 1505 and was succeeded by Afonso d'Albuquerque, who arrived in South-east Asian waters in 1509. With the sack of Malacca by Albuquerque's troops in 1511 and the withdrawal of the local sultan from the place,[41] the Portuguese placed themselves in control of a strategic spot, which allowed them further penetration into the South-east Asian archipelago and the Chinese Pacific coast. Yet the costs of the conquest were high. Malacca, which had been a thriving market during the fifteenth century, sank into obscurity as the Portuguese expansion encountered fierce opposition from Muslim and other traders. This opposition forced the Portuguese King Manuel I to commission the building and maintenance of fortresses on the spots in the South-east Asian archipelago where Portuguese merchants were doing business.

Activities were also advanced towards the ocean in the west. Upon departure for his fourth voyage, Columbus received a letter from the Spanish rulers addressed to Vasco da Gama, who was known to operate in Asian waters at the time.[42] The letter records that the Spanish rulers shared Columbus's belief that the expedition was to head for the eastern coasts of Asia. It also shows that the Spanish rulers were worried about a structural defect in the Tordesillas treaty of 1494. The treaty had demarcated the Portuguese and Spanish zones of influence only along a longitude west of Europe and Africa but had not specified where the eastward Portuguese and the westward Spanish expeditions were to end. Spanish worries resulted from the increasing Portuguese activity in the oceanic waters, seen as stretching between Asia and Europe. The sheer size of the oceanic waters seemed to demand considerations about a second line of demarcation east of the Asian coasts.

The defective character of the Tordesillas agreement became even more disturbing once Vasco Nuñez de Balboa established with certainty in 1513 that there was a land bridge west of Columbus's island worlds and came in sight of a further ocean after he had crossed this land bridge of Panama westwards. The most frequent early name of this ocean, now known as the Pacific, was *Mar del Sur*, the Southern Sea. This naming of the ocean west of Columbus's island worlds reflected the view that this was the ocean at the southern end of which a vast, as yet unknown, continent was expected. Thus efforts were deemed necessary to penetrate further into the Southern Sea and to determine the share that the Spanish rulers would be able to claim for themselves from the hypothetical Fourth Continent.[43]

The first author to make extensive use of the *orbis/mundus novus* concept and to make efforts to adjust the conventional world picture to the results of the expeditions was the Spanish scholar Peter Martyr d'Anghiera, who began to report on the Columbus voyages in 1493 and whose work first appeared in print in 1516. Anghiera appears to have had access to sources on the voyages and presented detailed accounts of Columbus's activities in the island worlds. He used the phrase *terra nova* as a reference to the island world visited by Columbus.[44] Anghiera also plunged into theoretical debates attempting to fit the Columbian island worlds into the conventional world picture. His use of the phrase *terra nova* made it explicit that he was convinced that Columbus had travelled to previously unknown places in the ocean.

As Spanish ruler Charles was thus pressured to continue the westward expeditions. The ongoing Portuguese expansion in the Asian waters where Canton was reached in 1517 was a constant source of worries on the Spanish side, particularly as news about the profitable Spice Islands in the south-east Asian archipelago within or close to the Southern Sea was confirmed. In 1518, a committee presented Charles with the proposal for a westward voyage around the southern end of the Spanish island worlds. The proposal included the demand that the full southern extension of the *terra firma* be determined: it was named 'America' by some cartographers but was called 'New Spain' by the Spanish administration. If the Spanish expedition could find a passage south of the area that Cabral had claimed for the Portuguese kings, seaborne access to the Southern Sea and the Spice Islands therein would become possible under Spanish control. The proposal thus drew on the expectation that the *terra firma* first visited by Portuguese mariners in 1500 might have a substantive south-western extension.

Charles accepted the proposal and entrusted the command for the expedition of four ships to Fernand de Magellan, a Portuguese by birth and a navigator with experience of the ocean.[45] The expedition was launched in 1519, eventually reached the southernmost tip of the *terra firma* in 1521 and then continued westwards into the Southern Sea. The passage which Magellan used, and which ever since then has borne his name, was not understood to separate the *terra firma* from a few islands scattered in its south.[46] Instead, the land which the expedition recorded to be south of the passage was taken to represent the northern fringes of the Fourth Continent and came to be named *Terra Magellanica*. Maps of the seventeenth century still displayed a vast stretch of land extending southwards from the route which Magellan found on his voyage west of the *terra firma* of 'America' or 'New Spain'.[47]

The transformation of the European world picture

In 1521 Magellan was killed in a skirmish on Maketan in the group of islands later referred to as the Philippines, but the expedition continued westward. That it did so was unequivocally a breach of the Tordesillas treaty. Nevertheless, the expedition continued unmolested, and one ship returned to Spain in 1522. The expedition thus firmly revealed the deficiency of the Tordesillas arrangements and solicited the demand to supplement this agreement by a further agreement on a line of demarcation along the Asian coasts. Thus the Magellan expedition was as crucial in economic terms regarding trade in spices as it was in political respects concerning control over the Southern Sea and the hypothetical Fourth Continent. But its intellectual significance was even higher; it stimulated efforts to represent the earth as a globe with as many details as possible. Such efforts had already begun with Behaim's globe of 1492. The St Dié mapmakers produced a map in 1507 which showed several gores thinning out towards the top and the bottom. In this way, it became possible to print a globe on paper, then to cut out the vacant space in between the strips and to glue the strips together into a globe.[48] At the same time, the St Dié mapmakers tried out a further solution to the problem of representing the three-dimensional shape of the earth on a two-dimensional printed map. This solution consisted of printing two global hemispheres next to each other and joining them together through a continuing equatorial line. This attempt had been included in the upper margin of the large world map of 1507 between the figures of Ptolemy and Vespucci.[49] Giovanni Contarini attempted a third solution in 1506.[50] In striking similarity to the Zorzi small maps, Contarini showed Columbus's island worlds in proximity to Asia and projected the earth in a fan-like shape in which the size of the earth had visually been reduced from 360 degrees to 225 degrees. Contarini did this by cutting the Asian continent in the upper part of his map, suggesting that viewers should join the parts together in their minds. But this projection had the grave disadvantage of enforcing distortions of distances so that the purported easternmost tip of Asia came to be placed in proximity to northern Europe. Johann Stabius and Albrecht Dürer pursued a further possibility by command of Emperor Maximilian I in 1515. Their two-dimensional map shows the earth as a globe in one single picture. Dürer imagined that the viewer would understand that the right and left margins of the globe were to be joined at the virtual back of the map. As in the St Dié map of 1507, Stabius and Dürer placed the east coast of Asia on the far right and the island worlds of the ocean on the left margin of their map.[51] But this style of projection became possible only at the expense of certain distortions of locations depicted on the left and right margins. Hence these projections were unsatisfactory and had no successors.

During the third decade of the sixteenth century, several further attempts were made to manufacture more elaborate three-dimensional globes and to reduce the distortions of two-dimensional global maps. Johann Schöner composed a detailed globe in 1520 for which he relied on the St Dié world map of 1507.[52] In 1530, Peter Apian tried to refine the Stabius–Dürer projection and experimented with a heart-shaped projection.[53] Apian drew his map symmetrically on either side of a central line separating the eastern and the western hemispheres and cutting through western Asia in the middle of the Caspian Sea in the same way as the Ptolemaic maps had done in the later fifteenth century. Apian followed the St Dié mapmakers in juxtaposing Ptolemy and Vespucci, separating Asia from the island worlds in the ocean and printing the name 'America' for these island worlds in the left margin of the map.

Subsequently, depictions of the earth as a globe became standard illustrations in geographical and cosmological works.[54] These global projections made it mandatory for cartographers to know the distances between the points mentioned in the maps and to do so without more than necessary distortions. At the time, this theoretical demand met with serious obstacles, as nautical knowledge did not suffice to determine locations unequivocally. Specifically, problems emerged with regard to Marco Polo's description of Zipangu.[55] In the fifteenth century, Zipangu was displayed somewhere in the vicinity of the Asian coast; hence its association with Asia had been taken for granted. However, when the island worlds in the ocean turned out to be part of an extensive *terra firma* dividing the ocean, the location of Zipangu became a bone of contention. The principal decision that cartographers had to make was whether they should follow Columbus, who had believed he was close to Zipangu,[56] and place the island in the oceanic waters between Europe and the island worlds that Columbus had visited. Alternatively, they could take the view that Columbus had been mistaken in his search for Zipangu and would then have to place the island in the oceanic waters between Asia and the island worlds visited by Columbus. Early sixteenth-century maps display a wide variety of choices, from identifying Zipangu with Yucatan or Cuba to locating it midway between 'America' and Asia.[57] Only in 1569, after Portuguese sailors had reached Japan, did the Dutch geographer Gerhard Mercator explicitly identify Zipangu with Japan, but added that the island was also identical with the mythical gold island Chryse known from Greek mythology.[58]

Moreover, all sixteenth-century world maps concurred in giving a great deal of space to water covering the surface of the earth. As a rule, maps displayed open seas, namely waterways, without physical or otherwise noteworthy restrictions of sea-borne access. This convention was underlined by representations of Europe as the only continent open to the sea. A remarkable piece of pictorial evidence for this perception is recorded in a world map printed in Basle in 1532. The map is part of a cosmological description by Simon Grynaeus but was made by Hans Holbein the Younger, the celebrated artist based at Basle. Holbein added to the map a sequence of scenes representing the three continents and the *mundus novus* and placed them on the margins of the map.[59] For these representations, Holbein relied on stereotypes current at the time. Pictures of hunters in purportedly Persian dress stand for 'Asia', wild animals for 'Africa' and cannibals for 'America'. Whereas images of land dominate in these three pictures, 'Europe' is shown as a stretch of coastal land overlooked by a large building of which two columns are visible. The latter stereotype promoted the image of access to the open sea. Hence, in the view of sixteenth-century intellectuals, Spain was facing the ocean and the king of Spain was the ruler of the ocean waves. Charles and his entourage shared this view. Apparently during the preparations for his departure from the Netherlands for Spain, the Burgundian court invented the motto PLVS VLTRA for the new king. Literally translated it meant 'Still further' and responded to the medieval Dantean formula 'Non Plus Ultra' (no further). Charles's motto was abundantly successful. He campaigned with it for the imperial election and continued to use it to the end of his life. The motto was often combined with two columns symbolising Hercules' pillars or the westernmost part of the inhabitable world according to the world picture of antiquity.[60] In accepting this motto Charles demonstrated his willingness to look west and search for new horizons beyond the ocean.

Spanish crusaders in the New World

In the early phase of his reign, Charles associated the motto with the legacy of medieval universalism and applied it to a world picture from which the New World had been absent. Yet his Spanish administrators took an alternative viewpoint that positioned the New World as a Spanish domain. This alternative view had already been made explicit in the so-called *Requirimiento*, which was drafted in 1512, probably by Juan Lopez de Palacios Rubios, legal adviser to Ferdinand of Aragon.[61] This document was to be read aloud to Native Americans before the beginning of military action. It demanded that all human beings should subject themselves to the power of the pope of Rome because the pope had received his power directly from the divinity. The pope was supposed to have requested assistance from the Spanish rulers for the purpose of converting Native Americans to Catholicism. Should they resist, they were to receive harsh treatment and be converted by force.[62]

While world rule was incompatible with this world picture, designs for conquests of overseas polities could still be clad in the quest for world-empire. Hernán Cortés played with this idea when he left the island of Hispaniola (Haiti) in 1519 and launched an unauthorised military campaign. From its very beginning the goal of his campaign appears to have been nothing less than the conquest of the Aztec Empire in what today is Mexico. Instead, he was instructed by the appointed governor of the Crown, Diego Velázquez, to search for Spaniards who had been missing and were believed to have been taken as prisoners by Native Americans. Moreover, he was commissioned to obtain information about the solid lands in the vicinity of Hispaniola.[63] But Cortés seems to have been determined to ignore his instructions and to become a famous conqueror. Yet he scrupulously followed legal procedures. He had the *Requirimiento* read out in full at the beginning of the campaign and employed a public notary to observe and certify the legal act. In the course of the conquest he then combined the ruthless use of martial arms with the build-up of a legalistic theory capable of justifying his military actions. The theory consisted of the claim that Cortés had ignored Velázquez's instructions for the benefit of the emperor and had helped to aggrandise imperial power. Because Cortés defied his instructions he had to be prepared to appeal directly to Charles if he succeeded as a conqueror. Only Charles himself could relieve Cortés from the odium of having been a traitor. Indeed, Cortés's legalistic defence was eventually successful when Charles exculpated him.

Hindsight makes it easy to appreciate the full scale of the risk Cortés had to face under these circumstances. But these dimensions are such that it would be unrealistic to assume that Cortés had a grand strategic design covering all major possible eventualities of the campaign. Instead, lack of contemporary records from the very beginnings of the campaign renders difficult any assumptions about the strategies that Cortés may have had in mind upon his departure. It seems more appropriate to surmise that Cortés continuously advanced his strategy and adapted it to the changing situation on the spot. This assumption remains possible even in the light of retrospective records written by Cortés himself. In these texts, namely the five reports (*cartas*) which he sent to Charles as emperor, Cortés made substantive efforts to present himself as the chosen man of great vision. Thus he habitually attributed unexpected success in battle to divine intervention in his support, and frequently claimed that it was through his perseverance that he was capable of eventually accomplishing success.[64] But these reports are skilfully styled rhetorical letters composed to construe the campaign as a legitimate series of well-designed actions in execution of divine will and for the benefit of the emperor. Therefore, they are sources for the image that Cortés wanted to disseminate about himself and in his own defence, but they contain no clues to his initial attitudes, perceptions and goals. The implication is that Cortés's reports must be read critically with an eye on the differences that may have existed between his primary motives (about which little can be known) and the retrospective image produced for consumption in Spain.

Nevertheless, Cortés's reports are relevant to Charles's strategies for empire because Cortés drew on a specific theory of empire in defence of his conquest. In the first two reports, he defended his conquest on the grounds that the Aztec Empire had once been part of the Roman Empire. In the second report, he described Moctezuma's arrest and boasted that his action would allow Charles to style himself emperor of the areas of which Cortés appeared to be in control and that Charles could do so by the same divine right that had granted him title to rule over the 'Empire of the Germans'.[65] In the same report, Cortés recorded a speech that he claimed Moctezuma had delivered during a series of meetings with Cortés in the capital. Moctezuma is made to say that some of his Aztec forefathers had left the land after some strife and that, since then, local customs and rules had changed fundamentally. According to Cortés, Moctezuma identified the conqueror as the descendant of those forefathers. In his own view, Cortés was thus doing no more than restoring the rule of the Roman emperor to the solid lands in the ocean.[66]

The alleged speech is only on record in Cortés's report. This report is unlikely to be a faithful account of Moctezuma's negotiations with Cortés as the Aztec ruler is credited with knowledge of features of Christian tradition with which he cannot have been familiar. It is therefore unlikely that Moctezuma's speech, provided it took place at all, contained the elements that Cortés chose to place in Moctezuma's mouth. Cortés rather seems to have drawn on a fourteenth-century political theory that he used to reconcile the existence of particularistic polities with traditions of political universalism. It is contained in tracts on the validity of Roman law as the law of empire written by the legist Bartolus of Sassoferato. Bartolus faced the difficulty of having to explain how the Roman Empire could exist as a universal empire in view of the multitude of secular polities under the rule of their own specific law. He developed a casuistry which defined four different categories of groups and legal frameworks: the first referred to groups living under Roman rule and under Roman law, the second to groups living under Roman law but not under Roman rule, the third to groups living neither under Roman rule nor under Roman law but being of Roman origin, and the fourth to groups living neither under Roman rule nor Roman law and not being of Roman origin. For the fourth category of groups, Bartolus postulated the existence of some freedom privilege that a Roman emperor had issued in the more remote past.[67]

Cortés operated with the third of Bartolus's categories. The second report in which this argument was used was crucial for Cortés in his bid to obtain recognition as the conqueror and royal governor of the former Aztec Empire. He could have known Bartolus because he had familiarised himself with legal matters while still in Spain and had acquired practical administrative experience during his stay in Hispaniola. It has been shown that in preparing his reports Cortés used legal sources of various traditions, among them the thirteenth-century *Siete Partidas* of King Alfonso X of Castile, even though there is no certainty that he had direct access to an original version of this text. Likewise, there is no certainty that Cortés's recourse to the legist tradition of universalism helped him to win eventual vindication. However, the fact of the matter is that Charles decided to retain Cortés in his position and to leave him unpenalised although he dispatched a number of administrators under royal supervision to keep him in check.[68] Thus Cortés cannot have been completely mistaken about the effects of his recourse to the legist justification of universal rule.

In addition, Cortés received further arguments in his support through the ideology of mission. These arguments drew on the crusading ideology. It implied that it was, first and foremost, the emperor's task to spread Christianity, if necessary through military means, and to subject 'infidel' adversaries of the Christian religion to Roman rule. The ideology was old. It can be found as early as the ninth century, when Saxon hagiographers defended Charlemagne's wars against the Saxons with the argument that he had legitimately used force to convert the Saxons.[69] In principle, every Christian ruler had the task of defending and spreading Christianity according to this ideology. Yet the rulers at the helm of the Roman Empire, if there were any, had to do so in the first place. Charles inherited from his grandfather the obligation to conduct crusades against the Ottoman Turkish Empire.[70] Charles also took over the legacy of the Spanish *reconquista*, which obliged him to permit and even support acts of conquest against non-Christians. In the course of the Middle Ages, traditions of the *reconquista* had become associated with the legend of St James the Apostle, whose central place of veneration developed in Santiago de Compostela and who was commonly labelled the 'Matamoros', the killer of Moors. Early in the sixteenth century, St James became the 'Mataindios', the killer of Native Americans. Sculptures feature him on the back of a horse triumphant over an 'Indio'.[71] In his description of the conquest of Tenochtitlan, Bernal Diaz del Castillo, one of the *conquistadores*, reported that Cortés's troops frequently invoked help from St James in the course of the battle.[72]

There are numerous further instances showing that the Spanish administration regarded the conquest of the New World as a crusade. One is that the Crown reserved for itself the use of 20 per cent of the spoils, which is the standard share claimed for the organisers of crusades.[73] Monks such as Matías de Paz[74] and soldiers such as Martín Fernández de Enciso[75] agreed that the conquests were just. This was traditional crusading rhetoric. Pope Gregory VII had already announced benefits for participants in crusades[76] and similar announcements were repeated in the fifteenth century in papal bulls.[77] A version of the text of an alleged speech by Cortés was included in Ginés de Sepúlveda's *History of the*

Conquest. In this version, Cortés is even supposed to have referred to the *Requirimiento* and to have argued that it was his duty to continue the war because of the obstinacy of the Native Americans. Cortés is supposed to have said that, after the reading of the *Requirimiento*, the Native Americans knew what their fate was going to be and that if they chose to resist their conversion, force would be applied.[78] There were thus differences in detail regarding the use of the crusading ideology between Cortés's report and later versions. But the bottom line of the argument was the same on either side: the conquest was displayed as a crusade for the purpose of extending the Roman Empire to the boundaries of the globe.

In his campaign for the conquest of the Inca Empire in what is today Peru, from 1531 to 1533, Francisco Pizarro employed similar tactics, using the crusading ideology in defence of his actions; he obtained a royal charter investing him as governor of Peru. He denied Native Americans the moral status of human beings and put down rebellions remorselessly. Pizarro could rely on theorists who rejected the applicability of natural law to Native Americans and took the view that Native Americans did not have the moral status of human beings. Among these theorists was the cleric Domingo de Betanzos, who believed that the only option for Native Americans was to go to hell. Indeed, in 1529, even Pope Clement VII requested that Charles should make sure that force should be used if Native Americans strongly resisted their conversion.[79] In the 1530s, however, the Catholic Church was beginning to take a different position. When Pope Paul III came under the influence of Dominican missionaries – who had acted in defence of Native Americans since 1511 – he issued a bull in 1537 in which he demanded the respect of natural law *vis-à-vis* Native Americans, their treatment as good human beings and assurance of their freedom.[80] Moreover, the pope now insisted that Native Americans should be converted without the use of force. Against the verdict by the pope Charles accepted Pizarro's attitude in 1537 when he declared a papal edict as void for the Spanish kingdoms. At Charles's request the pope revoked the edict.[81] But the crusading strategy had its flaws. This was first and foremost because it relied on the acceptance of some papal privilege to invest rulers with the right to conduct missionary efforts. The Portuguese kings and Spanish rulers of the fifteenth century could accept this papal privilege but it was problematic for the emperor. If the emperor was a universal ruler, the pope could not invest him with rights to rule as, in this case, the emperor would recognise the supremacy of the pope.

In summary, strategies to refurbish universal rule as the guiding imperial ideology were no longer viable. Not only were the advocates of universal rule plagued by the deficiency of their arguments; they found no means to stem the rising tide of territorialisation. However, the pluralism of territorial polities did not render universalism dispensable. On the contrary, no single series of events revealed more dramatically the necessity to consider humankind as a whole than the activities of the *conquistadores* in America. Mission made sense only on condition that humankind embraced every human being in moral respects. This was a principle of natural law that stood against the use of military force for missionary purposes. As Thomas Aquinas had identified natural law as divine law, it was in the world as part of the creation and not in need of human-made institutions for its enforcement. The missionaries who began to work in the islands and solid lands in the ocean under Spanish rule in the early sixteenth century accepted Aquinas's position and turned against Cortés and his successor *conquistadores*. They also acted in accordance with the papal bulls demanding the conversion of Native Americans. First and foremost among them was Bartolomé de Las Casas, who devoted much of his long life to the missionary task. He arrived in Hispaniola in 1502, became active as a preacher in 1510, joined the Dominican Order in 1522 and headed the missionary bishopric of Chiapas in Mexico to 1551. Against Cortés, Las Casas used missionary ideology to induce Pope Paul III to speak out against the abuse of Native Americans.[82]

DIVIDING THE WORLD?

Did anyone divide the world at the turn of the sixteenth century? During the protracted period of their penetration into oceanic waters, the Portuguese and Spanish rulers mostly followed a policy of the diplomatic accommodation of rival claims. The Alcacovas treaty of 1479 marked the first agreement on a line that purported to regulate access to the ocean strip west of Europe and Africa. The line agreed upon at Alcacovas ran westwards from the coast north of Lisbon. It allowed Spanish ships to ply the ocean in the northern hemisphere and reserved the southern hemisphere to the Portuguese. Yet Spanish ships continued to have access to waters west of Africa around the Canary Islands, which were under Spanish control. Columbus's return from his first voyage sparked hectic diplomatic activity because he landed at Lisbon, that is, south of the Alcacovas line, and thereby acted in breach of the treaty. The Portuguese king used the opportunity to have Columbus interrogated by the experienced sailor Bartolomeo Diaz. Diaz was the leader of the Portuguese crew that first reached the Cape of Good Hope in 1488. Through Diaz, the Portuguese court obtained first-hand knowledge about the trans-oceanic voyage that the Spanish rulers had authorised in the previous year.

It soon became clear that the Alcacovas line was far from ideal because it left its western end unspecified.[83] This deficit mattered because Columbus's voyage put on record that the distances he had covered across the ocean were in excess of what had been taken for granted in medieval cosmography. Thus the two parties had two choices: they could renegotiate the bilateral Alcacovas treaty to the end of extending the line westward, or they could make a new treaty. Both parties agreed to do the latter and to involve the Catholic Church during the negotiations. Throughout the fifteenth century, the Catholic Church was an actor in the organisation of the Portuguese expeditions and the Spanish *reconquista*, at times appearing behind the scenes. Up until the 1450s Henry the Navigator sought and obtained privileges from the popes legitimising the Portuguese southward advance along the African coast in the terms of a crusade.[84] After Henry's death in 1460, Alfonso V, John II and Manuel I obtained further privileges or received confirmations of previous privileges from Sixtus IV, Innocent VIII and Alexander VI.[85] Spanish rulers down to

Ferdinand of Aragon and Isabel of Castile sought and obtained papal crusading bulls and edicts authorising them to continue the *reconquista*.[86] Hence both sides customarily approached the popes as umpires of their rivalries and as an authority that was held to be able to grant missionary rights over people beyond the confines of Europe. The longer the Portuguese–Spanish rivalry lasted, the more both sides felt compelled to use bulls and edicts emanating from the papal chancellery, with the aim of delineating areas over which they intended to exercise their own control. The chancellery issued bulls and edicts that they designed as investiture privileges but not as donations, even though the legitimacy of issuing such privileges was contested.

Foremost among the early sixteenth-century scholars who questioned the papal right to issue investiture privileges was Cardinal Tommaso de Vio from Gaeta, who called himself Cajetan. In his comments on St Thomas Aquinas's *Summa Theologiae*, Cajetan followed Bartolus of Sassoferato in dividing non-Christians into three groups: people who did not live according to the rules of the Christian faith but had once been under the control of the Roman emperor as a Christian ruler; people who lived elsewhere under the control of a Christian ruler; and people to whom neither category could be applied. Cajetan concluded that the people visited by Columbus belonged to the third category and could therefore not be rightfully subjected to the control of any Christian ruler; nor could competence to govern them be legitimately allocated by the pope.[87] Cajetan was uncertain about what the legal status of the New World was. He assumed that Popes Nicholas V and Alexander VI had not had a legal title to act as arbiters between the rival rulers of Portugal and Spain. He did so on the grounds that the ocean and the islands as well as the solid lands were areas outside the tri-continental landmass. They could not fall under the lawful control of the popes because there were islands in the ocean, such as the British Isles, which obviously did not come under papal rule. Cajetan concluded that while the islands and solid lands in the ocean did not indeed belong to the Old World, they did not acquire the status of a *terra nullius*, a no-man's-land, because they were inhabited. Columbus's islands and solid lands fell under control of no one other than their inhabitants. He thus argued that they could neither be the target of rightful conquest nor the object of papal adjudication. Instead, he argued in favour of the principle that Native Americans were by nature free and thereby had the inalienable right of self-rule. By these standards, the European conquest and occupation of America could not be founded on any lawful grounds but resulted from nothing other than the application of physical force. Cajetan was not alone in setting the tri-continental Old World as the theatre to which Roman emperors were confined for their actions. Erasmus of Rotterdam also took this view in 1517 when he denied universal rule to the emperors and identified Christ as the sole ruler of the world.[88] These theories thus turned the conquest into an undeclared war fought by Europeans against Native Americans for morally indefensible reasons.

In the view of Columbus and the Spanish rulers, the Spanish–Portuguese rivalry mattered more than these intellectual objections. Manifestly, the trans-oceanic expeditions were directed at 'islands and firm lands' that lay south of the Alcacovas line and in waters far west of the Canary Islands. The Spanish rulers accepted this fact in a letter to Columbus, dated 5 September 1493. In their letter, they admitted that the newly found 'islands and the firm lands' were located in a part of the world to which the Spanish side had no access by the stipulations of the Alcacovas treaty.[89] Thus, Columbus's voyage reopened the potential for military conflicts between the Portuguese and Spanish kingdoms. This potential had caused great concern to the Portuguese kings throughout the fifteenth century and they remained fearful that, after the occupation of Granada, the Spanish rulers might continue the *reconquista* into Portugal. Unfortunately for the Portuguese, the newly elected pope Alexander VI had strong kinship ties to Aragon and Castile, whereas many of his predecessors as far back as Celestine III at the end of the twelfth century had tended to support Portuguese causes. Indeed, Alexander's chancellery responded favourably to Spanish requests for new privileges concerning the

Columbus voyage and hurried to confirm the Spanish position that the newly found 'islands and firm lands' stood of right under Spanish control.[90] The wording of the edicts in the name of Alexander VI followed fifteenth-century conventions. They agreed with Columbus's demand that the Spanish rulers were to be invested with the right to control the 'islands and firm lands' and that the latter were required to shoulder the burden of spreading Catholicism there. The Spanish concluded that Alexander's edicts identified Columbus's voyages as the beginning of a trans-oceanic crusade against non-Christian populations, although the edicts neither justified nor stipulated military conquest.

Alexander's intervention was disturbing for the Portuguese. Heavily involved at the time in the continuing expeditions along the African coast, King John II had neither reason nor title to approach the pope in his own right, because the Portuguese southward advance had already been sanctioned. Moreover, John was preoccupied with preparations for an alliance with presumed or actual Christian rulers in Africa and Asia and thus saw no possibility of supporting westward expeditions in addition to those following the African coasts. It was therefore a matter of expediency to find a diplomatic arrangement with his rivals in the Spanish kingdoms. The Spanish rulers were not disinclined to enter into direct negotiations because, from their point of view, the Alcacovas line had to be supplemented in accordance with Alexander's edicts. Negotiations eventually began in Tordesillas in 1494. While Alexander's delegate was present on the spot, the pope neither intervened nor intermediated in the course of the negotiations.

The treaty agreed upon at Tordesillas in 1494 stipulated a change of the oceanic line that had been recognised since 1479.[91] The new line ran from the north to the south poles at a longitude of 370 nautical miles west of the westernmost Azores. It allocated access rights for the western hemisphere to the Spanish side while the Portuguese side was confined to the eastern hemisphere. Accordingly, Portuguese ships could continue their expeditions along the African coast without molestation from Spanish competitors, and Columbus was entitled to continue to search for 'islands and firm lands' in the far West. Close contemporary maps display with some rigour efforts to differentiate between the Portuguese and Spanish zones on the newly emerging American continent. Thus the so-called Cantino map of the early sixteenth century showed a demarcation line following the stipulations of the Tordesillas treaty.[92] There are also verbal descriptions, such as the one contained in a map of 1519. This map, which was preserved in the monastery at Bretten (Bavaria), features inscriptions on the land representing the north-eastern coast of South America. The inscriptions read 'all the land discovered by Christopher Columbus for the King of Spain' in the western section and 'all the land called "Land of the Holy Cross" of the King of Portugal' in the eastern section. It was with reference to these descriptions that the governor of Española, Zuazo, made the remark in a letter to Charles in 1518 that the world was being divided between the Portuguese king and the Spanish majesty like an orange.[93]

While the Tordesillas line was thus respected, problems of legitimising the ensuing conquests arose. In the understanding of the Spanish rulers the papal demand for missionary activities implied that the populations on the newly found 'islands and firm lands' had a choice of either accepting Catholicism or facing extinction. Yet neither the pope nor the Tordesillas treaty partitioned the world or established suzerainty rights over 'islands and firm lands' in the ocean. Neither did the pope donate land to the Portuguese and Spanish rulers, nor did he claim any overlordship over monarchs in Europe or elsewhere in the world.

However, Martín Fernández de Enciso, a military man and commentator on Cortés's conquest, went a step further. He described the ongoing Spanish conquest of America within the topology of the biblical exodus and thus created the image of America as the Promised Land. At the same time, Enciso justified the conquest as a crusade against people who, he claimed, were venerating idols and were incapable of keeping peace. Moreover, Enciso reasoned that the divinity had donated their lands to the Spanish rulers in the same way that Israel had been given to Moses and his people. In Enciso's perception the Spanish *conquistadores* were bringers of peace with divine support, and they were treating the Native Americans merely as Joshua had treated the Canaanites. The argument continued to be traded among the Spanish soldiery into the 1560s on many occasions when there was a need to justify brutalities committed against Native Americans.[94] The earliest explicit piece of evidence that the Spanish courts understood the provisions of the papal edicts of 1493 as a donation in the sense of Roman law is extant in Rubios's work. Rubios derived what he understood as the papal capacity to 'donate' islands in the ocean from the papal claim for divinely willed universal rule. This claim, he knew, had been articulated from the time of Pope Innocent III at the turn of the thirteenth century. Rubios regarded these islands as located outside the *mundus*, which he identified as the area under the control of the emperor. With respect to these islands he employed the Latin word *donatio* in the sense of the transfer of the power to rule over land, as laid down in Justinian's civil code.[95]

Nevertheless, the Tordesillas treaty was a bilateral agreement and thus not binding for other rulers and their subjects. English merchants, mainly from Bristol, had a long record of penetrating westwards into the ocean from 1481 at the latest.[96] Sailors from Italy and France soon followed Columbus across the ocean. None of these sailors was willing to accept Columbus's position that the stipulations of the Tordesillas treaty closed access to the western ocean to everyone not holding privileges from the Spanish rulers. As ruler over the Spanish kingdoms, Charles was hard pressed to effectively end the ongoing competition between Spanish and non-Spanish sailors plying the ocean. But he left the issue pending. On the one hand, he was criticised in 1544 for an agreement made with Francis I that could be understood as allowing French sailors unrestricted access to the ocean.[97] But Charles did not respond to the criticism. On the other hand, his sister Mary declared laconically in 1554 that the ocean was free, and Charles remained silent as well.[98] In a way, his motto PLVS VLTRA (still further) suggested that he was inclined to the latter position.

Hence, no one divided the world at the turn of the sixteenth century. Maximilian was the great promoter of the unification of rule in Habsburg hands. In 1503 he had insisted that merchants from the German-speaking areas ought to be willing to go as far as Calicut in India to do business.[99] On Maximilian's mental map, Calicut represented the far eastern end of the world and Columbus's 'islands and firm lands' stood for the far west. In proclaiming himself imperial suzerain over the Portuguese and Spanish ruling dynasties from 1507, he emphasised his determination to expand imperial rule as overlordship to the boundaries of the then known world. Charles took over Maximilian's heritage in his bid for election to the imperial office in succession to his grandfather. However, Charles's strategies to refurbish universal rule as imperial overlordship over the most expansive European dynasties were no longer viable after Maximilian's death. Charles could accept papal privileges in his capacity as the ruler of the Spanish kingdoms. But he could no longer do so once he had become emperor. Hence the advocates of universal rule not only found no means against the rising tide of territorialisation but were also at a loss to cope with the widening scope of oceanic waters that had to be recognised as covering the largest part of the surface of the earth. Philip Melanchthon, Charles's supporter in the German-speaking areas at the time of the imperial election, eventually took the view that the notion of universal empire should remain confined to areas that had been under the sway of the Roman emperors of antiquity.[100] Therefore, Charles had no choice other than to accept the de-territorialisation of universalism and to untie the Roman Empire from the traditions of universal rule.

THREE

Enter the Peace-bringing Ruler: the Making of an Emperor (1519–21)

ELECTING A NEW EMPEROR

Money makes the world go round. As ruler of the Spanish kingdoms and the Netherlands Charles had to find his way between the Scylla of demands to promote the unity of the kingdoms and the Charybdis of requests to grant autonomy to the Netherlands with their self-governing urban communities that were engaged in production and trade. In the Spanish kingdoms, only a stable and smooth but strict and law-enforcing administration based on good governance could generate the revenue that was essential for the continuation of overseas expansion and the rigorous pursuit of Spanish foreign-policy interests in Europe, specifically *vis-à-vis* France. In the Netherlands only government by consent allowed the ruler to take his share of the available financial resources. Balancing these mutually exclusive goals was a difficult task, as Charles realised after he had moved from the Netherlands to the Spanish kingdoms. For the time being, he relied on Margaret's skills when it became necessary to persuade the often-disgruntled estates in the Netherlands to accept additional tax burdens. Yet tougher choices lay ahead of Charles as he was campaigning for his election as emperor. Whereas he had succeeded in the Netherlands and in the Spanish kingdoms by the right of inheritance, the election in the Roman Empire was considered to be free in the sense that it was the privilege of the electors to determine who the next emperor was going to be. The campaign for the imperial office was not merely a battle of arguments but also a contest about the capability of the candidates to mobilise lavish funds to be paid to the electors and the parties supporting them.

The politics and economics of making an emperor

In addition to the desire for money, the need to avoid a long vacancy of the imperial throne added to the pressure. Maximilian died unexpectedly after a short illness in the midst of much unfinished business. As late as in September 1518, we find him engaged in preparations for a crusade against the Ottoman Turkish Empire. To the Augsburg imperial diet (June to October 1518) he presented his strategic plan for the conquest of Istanbul through a pincer movement by sea and by land. He used the gathering as a platform for positioning himself as the leader of this crusading army, with which he hoped to restore imperial rule in the East.[1] But the responses from the estates were lukewarm, and Maximilian left Augsburg for Vienna in a mood of despair. He had outlived many of his formidable rivals, like Ferdinand of Aragon, but was unsure whether he would have enough time to accomplish the grandest of his goals. He employed several of the most famous artists of his time, among them Hans Burgkmair,[2] Albrecht Dürer[3] and Albrecht Altdorfer,[4] and asked them to design and manufacture long series of large propagandistic pieces of art. He hoped to use them to establish and promote his everlasting glory as conqueror of the Ottoman Turkish Empire and successful crusader.[5] Even while at Augsburg and in the following months he sent a flurry of messages to the artists pressuring them to speed up their work. He reported optimistically to Margaret that the work was proceeding well.[6] The messages convey the impression that Maximilian felt his end approaching without imagining that it was to come immediately. Thus in all his business he neglected his most important task, namely designating his successor, although he received confirmation from some electors at Augsburg on 1 September 1518 that they would cast their votes in Charles's favour.[7] But this confirmation merely revealed that the succession was contested.

While journeying eastwards from Augsburg Maximilian fell ill and rested at the small town of Wels in what is today Upper Austria. It was probably Mennel who drew up a text on 30 December 1518 that was written as Maximilian's last will. Maximilian may have dictated it. The will displays Maximilian as exclusively concerned with his own memory, giving orders about the arrangement of his tomb and the distribution of his property.[8] The issue of imperial succession had vanished from the emperor's mind.

The emperor's death at Wels on 12 January 1519 was reported immediately and superseded all other issues on the political agenda within the empire and elsewhere in Europe. As Charles decided to enter the election campaign against the pleas by his Spanish advisers and found no more than reluctant support from Margaret, he could rely neither on Spanish revenue nor on funds from the Netherlands to finance the campaign. Therefore, the campaign strategy had to accomplish two related goals in turn. The first was to generate funds from sources within the empire in support of Charles's candidacy. The second was to use the money to the end of rallying all electors behind Charles. As he had to seek a unanimous vote the threshold was high.

In pursuit of the first goal Charles tried to combine the quest for new horizons expressed in his motto PLVS VLTRA with an appeal to a sentiment that has been called proto-nationalism (Plate 5).[9] It was widespread in the early sixteenth century, specifically in the Italian peninsula, the German-speaking areas, including parts of the Netherlands, the Spanish kingdoms, England and France. It can be traced in expressions of the appreciation of and care for the grammars of standard languages, such as English, German, French or Italian. Grammarians took the view that these standards should be spoken uniformly by large population groups with purportedly common traditions, past experiences and continuing institutions.[10] The sentiment also emerged from the willingness to make manifest and codify dress habits among population groups believed to speak the same language.[11] It was finally reflected by the popularity of a historiography whose task it was to assemble and transmit the purportedly common group-bound traditions and past experiences in connection with institutions that were held to have continued from the remote past to the present of the sixteenth century.[12] Proto-nationalism differed from nineteenth-century nationalism in that it was not drawn on race or other genetic indicators of collective identity. Instead, proto-nationalism dwelt on climate theories suggesting that residence shaped 'national character';[13] hence its emphasis on dress as a distinguishing feature.[14]

Charles's proto-nationalist ticket and the election campaign

In his campaign against Francis I, Charles utilised proto-nationalism by drawing on the popularity of his deceased grandfather in the German-speaking areas, and displaying his ties with the Habsburg dynasty. He emphasised that he was born archduke of Austria, then a core imperial estate. He claimed that he could speak and write German, promised to safeguard the privileges and liberties of the German nation to whom, he said, the Roman Empire had been transferred,[15] and pledged to defend peace and law in the empire.[16] He thus positioned himself as the guardian of unity and peace. Charles's proto-nationalist propaganda helped draw bankers mainly from southern German and northern Italian cities to his side, on whom Maximilian had already relied. Specifically, the Augsburg trading house of the Fuggers decided to invest in Charles's campaign, hoping to obtain favourable privileges in return. Being able to utilise Fugger funds, Charles was in a position to approach the still-reluctant electors with offers to settle some of their bills. For example, he could promise to donate the amount of 32,000 guilders to the Elector of Saxony for debt relief. In his summary cost balance of 1520, the Augsburg merchant John Lukas did not forget to add that the Elector of Saxony took the money only for this purpose and not for the settlement of any private bills. Likewise, Count Palatinate Louis was offered 8,000 guilders for the consolidation of his rule in Alsace and a further 30,000 guilders as compensation for previous military expenditures. The three ecclesiastical electors of Mainz, Cologne and Trier received 103,000 guilders, 40,000 guilders and 22,000 guilders respectively 'for their own person'. The phrase may imply that the money was given to them in their capacity as religious leaders, that is, as a donation to the archbishoprics, rather than for purposes of governing the electorates. There were further offers to imperial estates in the entourage of the electors as well as to some lesser-ranking aristocrats serving as makers of public opinion. Only the margrave of Brandenburg was left with the minimal gift of 100 guilders because he remained approachable by the French side to the end of the race. Lukas listed even Swiss recipients of donations, although the Swiss Confederacy had received an imperial pledge of non-interference in 1499.[17]

The distribution reveals the strategy of drawing electors into Charles's camp as early as possible in the course of the race. Charles tried to oblige them to cast their votes in his favour on the basis of financial assistance to their own fiscal, military and administrative policies as well as court expenditures. He also wanted to promote a 'we-feeling' among the imperial estates on both sides of the Alps. His financiers had detailed knowledge of the financial situation of the electors and their parties.

King Francis I, the second contender, also contributed donations. Charles complained that Francis's donations were formidably high. He used this argument to squeeze further funds out of his creditors. However, Francis drew mainly on French sources, with the implication that his insight into the financial needs of the electors was limited. Instead, his contributions were more straightforwardly directed towards the goal of buying votes when political arguments in support of his bid for election appeared to be too weak. In his political propaganda Francis emphasised the status of the Roman Empire as a universal polity in confinement to the Old World of Asia, Africa and Europe and pointed out the necessity of electing the most capable ruler for this universal polity. He also claimed that he was most successful as a mediator in European politics and crusader against the Ottoman Turkish Empire. He attacked Charles for being an inexperienced warrior and promised to be the better helmsman for the empire. Further to this, he argued that the French and the Germans had once been united under Charlemagne's rule and that he was the most suitable successor to Charlemagne. He alluded to the myth of Trojan descent and insisted that he was successor to the Roman emperors of antiquity, thereby implying that he had inherited their moral virtues. In a highly original interpretation of

Roman imperial history, he identified these qualities as Augustus's good luck, Titus's humaneness, Nero's clemency, Trajan's honesty and justice, Constantine's spirituality and Theodosius's clemency. In conclusion he repeated the observation that the Germans and the French had common roots and mentioned that the name of the French was derived from that of the Franks. Frankfurt (where the election was scheduled to be held) received ample praise as the city of the Franks and the best imperial city of the German-speaking lands.[18]

Francis had his propaganda designed to contradict Charles's. He argued that a candidate's ability to provide good government was more important as a criterion of eligibility than his dynastic privileges. He demanded that the commonality of past experience should be valued higher than the present divisiveness of proto-nationalist sentiment. He appealed to a conventional interpretation of universalism that associated the Roman Empire with the tri-continental *ecumene* and insisted that the imperial office was accessible to all Christian rulers. He positioned the Roman Empire as the major power base against the Ottoman Turkish Empire and posed as a model crusader. Thus Francis's propaganda was informed by traditional doctrines of universalism, whereas Charles's rhetoric made appeals to the new proto-nationalist creeds.

Seeing that high risk and big business were involved in the imperial election campaign, Henry VIII, the third candidate, withdrew from the race.[19] But some imperial estates remained dissatisfied with the choice between the French and the Spanish king and, as the last resort, requested that Frederick the Wise, duke of Saxony and the most senior elector, should run himself. The request was put on the agenda late in June 1519, shortly before the electors were scheduled to meet at Frankfurt to cast their votes. But Frederick, then aged 56, declined on the grounds of old age and pledged loyalty to Charles. Scholarly suggestions that Frederick was actually elected and then forced to abdicate in Charles's favour are unfounded speculations.[20] Instead, the choice remained between Francis and Charles. Realising that his colleagues inclined to the latter, the margrave of Brandenburg eventually gave up his resistance and opted for Charles, with reservations about the candidate's qualifications. The voting took place on 28 June 1519 in accordance with the conventional procedure. Each elector cast his vote in an open confession and in an established order. The archbishop of Mainz performed the duties of the master of the ceremony, asking the archbishop of Trier to go ahead. The archbishop of Cologne, the king of Bohemia, the Count Palatinate, the duke of Saxony, and the margrave of Brandenburg followed before the archbishop of Mainz finally stated his opinion.

Charles was elected king of the Romans, which meant that he was entitled to seek coronation as emperor by the pope. Like Maximilian, Charles received the status of emperor elect together with the position of king of the Romans. A coronation ceremony was arranged at Aachen to sanction his election, of course without the involvement of the pope.[21] In the meantime, a wave of public celebration swept across the German-speaking areas. Charles was hailed as a new saviour, defender of the Christian faith and unifier of the world. Even Martin Luther praised the new ruler as the long-desired reformer of the Church.[22] Moreover, inhabitants of the south German cities welcomed Charles as the bringer of peace, pledged loyalty to him and greeted him with bonfires.[23] His appeal to proto-nationalism fell on fruitful soil. Yet Charles was soon to disappoint the exultant welcome because his proto-nationalist ticket was incompatible with the tasks he had to face at the helm of the empire.

The politics of the new emperor

There were thorny legal issues involved in the imperial election. They resulted from the excessive number of ruling offices and titles to rule that Charles united in his person. Like his father he ruled over Tournai, Artois, Picardy and Flanders not in his own right but as the holder of French fiefs. As titular duke of Burgundy he claimed control over territories over which the king of France actually ruled. Had Charles ever restored himself to actual control over Burgundy he would have succeeded his father once more as the French king's vassal. As archduke of Austria, he had never visited his inherited lands and was thus completely unknown to his subjects there. As the lord of the Netherlands he was equally remote. As the ruler of the Spanish kingdoms, he was journeying in far-away lands. Emperors were itinerant anyway because the empire had no official residential capital. But Charles had to aggravate this deficit by his obligation to keep his visits to the empire brief and return to the Iberian peninsula as soon as possible. In order to relieve himself of some of these many duties Charles was forced to pass some of his offices on to regents. The case of the Netherlands was easiest. Having learnt her lesson, Aunt Margaret accepted her nephew as her suzerain and confined herself to preventing decisions that she and her advisers regarded as unfavourable to the Netherlands. Control over Burgundy, however, continued to remain a dilemma. If any appearances of vassality to the French king were anathema to the Spanish ruler, so much more were they to the holder of the imperial office. As emperor elect, he could only be restored as reigning duke of Burgundy if the French king ceded suzerainty over the duchy. Francis I would not even consider this request, nor would Margaret support it. But if Charles let Burgundy go he would give away Habsburg hereditary rights, thereby weakening his position as the leader of the Habsburg dynasty. Charles decided to leave the dilemma pending and hoped for a solution through future marriage projects. Two of his sisters were still unmarried and his elder sister Eleanor, currently married to the ageing Manuel of Portugal, would soon be available for a new marriage arrangement. For the time being, Charles terminated the pro-French policy that Margaret and her advisers advocated.[24] The rift between himself and Francis over the imperial election was merely one facet of a more fundamental controversy about the integrity and sovereignty of the French kingdom. Questions about the control over territories, such as Burgundy, the duchy of Milan, the kingdom of Navarre and some Flemish provinces, were at the bottom of the rivalry between Charles and the French king, who considered these areas to be legally his domain.

The imperial election race also widened the rift between Charles and Henry VIII. Already Charles's dissolution of his betrothal with Mary, Henry's sister, and her subsequent marriage to Louis XII of France had estranged the two rulers and pushed Henry to the French side. The new friendship allowed Francis to pose as an intermediary in European affairs, to Charles's disadvantage in the imperial election campaign. Again, Margaret advocated the improvement of relations with Henry. Fortunately, Henry had a daughter by Catherine of Aragon, another Mary, who was born in 1516. Margaret and Henry considered the girl to be a suitable match for Charles, once she had grown to maturity.[25] The marriage would not only help overcome the rift between Henry and Charles, but also restore Charles's prospects of establishing the Habsburgs as future rulers over England and settling the pending controversy over reimbursement of the dowry that Henry had paid to Charles for his sister Mary. Margaret's arrangements proved successful. A treaty was signed on 25 August 1521 according to which Charles would marry the younger Mary upon the completion of her twelfth year. The treaty stood under the proviso that the marriage could not be concluded if Henry died without a male heir and Mary succeeded him. It also obliged Henry to pay a dowry of 400,000 gold escudos and stipulated that Charles must give to Mary an annual dower of 50,000 gold crowns. Charles was also bound to repay the dowry if he refused to marry Mary.[26] To finalise the deal Charles accepted Margaret's advice and decided to stop in England for a visit on his return from the empire to the Iberian peninsula after he had received his coronation as king of the Romans.

There were three further issues that Charles hoped to resolve before returning to his Spanish realms. The first was related to control over the Habsburg hereditary lands, the second to the government of the empire and the third to Luther's reform movement in the Catholic Church. With regard to the first issue Charles once again followed Margaret's advice and installed his brother Ferdinand as archduke. The choice made sense, given the possibility of Ferdinand's succession to Louis of Hungary and Bohemia if the king remained without offspring. Thus Ferdinand was transferred to the court in Vienna where he took office in 1522.[27] The second issue arose from a demand that Charles received in 1519 concerning the installation of a permanent government for the administration of the empire. The intention behind the demand was easy to recognise, namely to transfer control over the empire from the emperor to the imperial estates. Charles was apprehensive of the driving force behind the demand and stood against it. He did so with success. An agreement was reached that the imperial government should be in power only while the emperor was absent from the empire. This agreement was beneficial for Charles as it left it to him to decide when he wanted to become directly involved in imperial affairs.[28] Charles thus forced the estates to give Ferdinand a key role in the imperial government and succeeded in positioning himself at the centre of a network of dynastic relations with his closest relatives. Rulers of Habsburg kin thus controlled the empire, the Spanish kingdoms, the Netherlands, the Habsburg hereditary lands, the Spanish overseas dependencies, much of the Italian peninsula and the islands in the western Mediterranean Sea. They also held options to rule over France, England, the Scandinavian kingdoms, Hungary and Bohemia. Charles's initial decisions at the helm of the empire display him as a faithful executor of the legacy of Maximilian's dynastic policy.

However, the third issue challenged Charles's capability as a manager of imperial affairs. It was a tough decision that alienated many of his erstwhile supporters. The decision became necessary in consequence of the movement that Dr Martin Luther's reform initiative of 1517 had sparked. Luther, an Augustinian monk trained as a theologian and preacher in the castle church of Wittenberg in Saxony, argued in favour of principal reforms in the Catholic Church for the purpose of deepening the religious faith of his fellow Christians. Initially, after being informed about the growth of Luther's movement and at the behest of his father confessor Jean Glapion, Charles seems to have been inclined to accept some of Luther's arguments. First and foremost, Charles was willing to consider Luther's demand that the Church leadership should end its evil practices, such as the granting of letters of indulgence. But

Luther's reformist zeal[29] antagonised many holders of high church offices who feared that giving in to his demands would undermine their authority. Thus they grew increasingly wary of the rhetorically powerful monk and began to class his teachings as heretical. Early attempts to channel his reform movement into due processes in accordance with established church procedures failed by 1519, and the Church appealed to the new emperor to help to settle the issue. The main reason for the failure of attempts to accommodate Luther was that, at the time, the Church took into consideration merely one solution, and that was the suppression of Luther's movement. Consequently, the pope issued the demand that Luther was to be banned as a heretic without further debate.

Charles agreed to use the imperial diet of Worms, to be convened in 1520, as the occasion for the settlement of the so-called 'Lutheran heresy' before his return to the Spanish kingdoms. From Charles's point of view, the only thinkable solution was to execute the papal demand and suppress the heretic movement. By contrast, Duke Frederick of Saxony, in his capacity as the territorial ruler in charge of the execution of the envisaged ban against Luther, pleaded in favour of allowing Luther to explain his demands. He therefore requested that Luther be summoned to the diet to state his case under the assurance of safe conduct. Other imperial estates supported Frederick's plea, thus taking issue with the papal demand to condemn Luther straightforwardly. Eventually, Luther appeared at Worms, in 1521 to be heard by the diet in Charles's presence. There were two hearings. During the first hearing on 17 April 1521 Luther was asked to revoke his demands. He requested one night for consideration and reappeared on the following day.[30] During the second hearing he refused to revoke his demands, thereby obliging Charles to respond. Charles had to do so in his capacity as defender of the Catholic Church. On 19 April 1521 Charles signed a document that he had written by himself and in which he declared himself to be Luther's perennial enemy and refused to hear him any further. Charles's reply came out in the form of a statement of principles for which he drew on the dynastic traditions in which he stood:

You will know that I descend from the most Christian emperor of the honourable German nation, from the Catholic kings of Spain, from the archdukes of Austria, the dukes of Burgundy, all of whom were faithful sons of the Roman Church to their deaths, always defenders of the Catholic faith, the holy ceremonies, laws, directions and the holy customs, to the honour of God, the augmentation of the faith and the salvation of souls.

After their departure from the world and due to their inherited rights, they have handed down upon Us the said holy Catholic obligations to live in accordance with them and to die after their example. Up until here and now, We have lived according to these obligations as true imitators of these predecessors and with the grace of God.

For this reason, I am determined to continue everything that the said predecessors and I myself have preserved up to this hour. . . . For it is certain that a single friar has erred with his view which he has turned against all Christendom of the past one thousand and more years as well as of the present. If his view were true, all Christendom would always have erred and would still do so today.

For this reason, I have decided to invest everything into this matter, my kingdoms and territories, my friends, my body, my blood, my life and my soul. For it were a great disgrace for me and for you, this honourable and famous German nation, as we are destined to be defenders and protectors of the Catholic faith, if, in our time, not just a manifest heresy but even a suspicion of heresy or some other impediment of the Christian religion were to remain in the hearts of human beings after Us, to Our perennial disgrace and the perennial disgrace of Our successors.

And after we have listened to the stubborn response which Luther gave in the presence of all of us yesterday, I herewith declare to you that I regret having hesitated so long to act against the said Luther and his wrong doctrine. And I am strongly determined not to hear him any further. On the contrary, I want him to return in accordance with the wording of my previous mandate and in observation of safe conduct but without preaching or instructing the people in his evil doctrine and without desiring to provoke popular resistance.[31]

Charles's arguments reflected Maximilian's dynastic attitudes. He placed himself at the helm of the Roman Empire as a universal empire and described himself as the personal holder of hereditary rights to rule. He viewed these rights in terms of obligations conferred upon him through hereditary succession. He was determined to act in fulfilment of these traditional obligations and not in execution of the *ad hoc* mandate which the pope had issued against Luther. This fundamentalist position left Charles no choice but to ban Luther and to subject the territorial rulers supporting him to imperial jurisdiction. Moreover, Charles came under the influence of conservative Catholics who feared that Luther would revoke essentials of Christian theological dogma. Therefore he felt pressured to request that Luther's written works no longer be printed and that available prints be destroyed so as to prevent the dissemination of Luther's doctrine.[32] However, the threat itself already disclosed the weakness of the imperial position. For the emperor had to rely on the imperial estates to enforce the ban. If no concerted action against Luther took place, the empire would be split. Dissenting territorial rulers could then elevate themselves into a position where they competed with the emperor as defenders of the faith, even though what they defended was no longer Catholicism. The decision was a crucial one. It soon became clear that Charles did not have the means to enforce the ban throughout the empire and elsewhere in Europe. In consequence, the emperor lost his position as the sole defender of the faith. His support of Catholicism meant in practice that the position of those territorial rulers within the empire who continued to support Luther and his fellow Protestants was strengthened.

From Worms Charles moved on to the Netherlands and left for the Iberian peninsula via England in 1522. His second meeting with Henry VIII was joyous.[33] The imperial government took office as his regent. Ferdinand and Margaret emerged as loyal though by no means subservient lieutenants. Henry, Francis and the pope were difficult partners – at times the emperor's friends, at times his enemies. While Cortés conquered the Aztec Empire in Charles's name, Ottoman Turkish troops advanced further northward through the Balkans towards Hungary and further westward to the Mediterranean Sea. The young emperor had a long way to go to accomplish his grand goal of bringing peace to the world.

PEACE VERSUS THE PURSUIT OF POWER

Two peace strategies were competing with each other in the early sixteenth century. One was contained in the legacy of medieval universalism; the other was informed by the ethics of Renaissance humanism. Charles obtained knowledge of late medieval universalism through his learned chancellor Mercurino Gattinara. Whether he was familiar with the ethics of Renaissance humanism remains uncertain.

Political theorists of late medieval universalism like Dante took for granted the Augustinian theological doctrine[34] that peace was to be ascertained or restored within the Roman Empire as the divinely willed universal polity.[35] Augustine argued that the Roman Empire as the last of the four world empires would continue to exist as long as it remained a Christian empire. He believed that the divinity would not allow the world to come to its end as long as Christianity prevailed. In his work on monarchy, Dante drew on Augustinian hopes when he used the expedition to Rome of Emperor Henry VII to project a scenario for the accomplishment of peace through the rule of the Roman emperor as the envisaged universal ruler. Dante argued that the emperor was the sole source of law and the eventual guardian of peace. In his projection the maintenance of peace within the Roman Empire was a contribution to its stability, and the quest for universal rule was a means to safeguard the world. According to Dante's theory, then, the highest, most urgent and most rewarding task of the Roman emperors was the promotion of peace. Universalism as the quest for rule of the tri-continental *ecumene* and the quest for peace in the Old World complemented each other like the two sides of the same medal.

81

Dante's political theory resurfaced in fourteenth-, fifteenth- and early-sixteenth-century political thought, namely in works by Engelbert, the learned abbot of the Styrian monastery of Admont, Aeneas Sylvius Piccolomini, later Pope Pius II, Hermann Peter of Andlau, Antonio de Rosellis and Miguel de Ulcurrum. In the first half of the fourteenth century, Engelbert and Piccolomini wrote treatises on the future of the Roman Empire and articulated Dantean hopes.[36] In *c.* 1460 Hermann Peter of Andlau, professor of canon law at the University of Basle, published a treatise on the tasks of emperors. In this treatise he turned the quest for peace into an issue of practical administration and demanded that the emperors guarantee the safety of road travellers as an element of what might be called 'human security'. His fellow canonist Antonio de Rosellis from Arezzo explicated Dante in defending the view that the emperors received their legitimacy directly from the divinity to accomplish their task as bringers of peace in the universal empire.[37] In his book published in 1525, Miguel de Ulcurrum, jurist and protégé of Adrian of Utrecht, took a more theoretical approach again. He portrayed the emperor as the guarantor of world order, the source of peace, the King of Kings (*Rex Regum*) and originator of the law of nations as the supreme law (*lex legum*) in the world.[38] Ulcurrum, then member of the Council of Navarre, dedicated his work to Charles.

Gattinara knew Augustine's theology well and owned a version of Dante's book on monarchy and used it to advise the recently elected emperor.[39] In a memorandum dated 12 July 1519, Gattinara took up Dante's vision but expanded it to the boundaries of the globe. He urged Charles to perceive himself as the true successor of Charlemagne. Having with divine help subjected more territories and populations to his lawful rule than his distinguished predecessor and namesake, Charles ought to make efforts to become the pastor for the entire world, Gattinara declared. Charles should do so by confessing the Catholic faith and by promoting the Christian religion to the end of accomplishing the 'good universal peace'. Moreover, Gattinara requested that Charles should respect and augment the heritage of his forefathers and that he should employ wise and conscientious advisers. Furthermore, Charles should administer justice truly and fairly and should follow the example of Emperor Justinian, the great codifier of law, and act as the world's legislator. In this way, Gattinara insisted in Dantean fashion, Charles would become the sole source of equitable laws in the entire world. While an essentially bellicose human nature would encourage people to fight when no powerful ruler was available, Charles's justice and fairness would be recognised as advantageous everywhere. People would become ready to live in accordance with imperial law, not through the use of force but through their own inclination.[40]

Although Gattinara drew on Dante for his universalism, he relied on other sources as well. He used Habsburg, and perhaps French, historiography for his praise of Charlemagne. He employed the teachings of fourteenth-century legists, such as Bartolus of Sassoferato, for positioning the Roman emperor as the overlord of the world.[41] From these sources, he composed a synthetic ideology of imperial universalism that amalgamated Dantean eschatological peace theory, Maximilianean dynasticism and juristic traditions of Roman law. In a further memorandum supplied two years later, Gattinara added several practical suggestions. He specified that Charles should begin to implement the universalistic design for peace by intervening in Italian affairs, taking direct control over the Italian peninsula and using the peninsula as a stepping stone towards a crusade against the Ottoman Turkish Empire and, eventually, rule over the world.

With the exception of Maximilianean dynasticism, Gattinara's imperial ideology was identical with the assets of the imperial ideology that Cortés adduced for his exculpation[42] and which German legal advisers like Lazarus Spengler used against growing demands for autonomy of the imperial estates.[43] Charles's zealous response to the 'Lutheran heresy' revealed the strength of his exposure to these assets of imperial universalism in the early years of his reign. But he turned against Gattinara and kept his ideology of empire focused on the tri-continental *ecumene*. The emerging New World was of little significance in Charles self-portrait as universal ruler. Instead, the New World featured as 'islands and firm lands' in his titles, attached to his Spanish royal titles, but not as a token of world rule.[44] To Charles as the Spanish ruler, the New World mattered merely to the extent that the Native American population could be converted to Catholicism. Likewise, he did not allow the Spice Islands in the South Pacific to obtain priority in his political agenda, as they were contested between Portugal and the Spanish kingdoms; he would merely consider the islands as a bargain in a future marriage deal with Portugal.[45] In the early years of his reign, Gattinara's ideologies of universal empire pulled Charles away from the Spanish overseas dependencies and pushed him towards strategic designs for a crusade against the Ottoman Turkish Empire. It positioned the maintenance or restoration of the Catholic faith and the expansion of the Christian religion in the tri-continental *ecumene* as a condition for peace. Charles's dilemma was that he saw himself as a ruler who had to excel in the achievements of a warrior before being able to act as the bringer of peace.

This dilemma was at the core of the criticism that promoters of the ethics of Renaissance humanism directed at the politics of their time. Renaissance humanists bluntly denied the logic according to which peace needed wars to be accomplished. First and foremost among them was Erasmus of Rotterdam. Charles's chancellor for the Netherlands, Jean de Sauvages, instructed Erasmus in 1516 to reflect on the conditions for the improvement of peace among the several European polities. In a pamphlet written in response to Sauvage's instruction, Erasmus, who did not ban the crusading plans from his mind, rejected the idea that human nature promoted bellicose behaviour. Instead, he categorised war as the result of purposeful action against peace, deeply deplored the war-proneness of his own time and demanded that rulers should take into consideration the amount of human suffering and political instability that resulted from wars. In Erasmus's view, these negative consequences seriously reduced the legitimacy of warfare even when just arguments for a war were at hand. He urged the three young rulers who had just taken their offices to 'forget the evils of the past' and make a fresh effort to accomplish peace.[46] He demanded that they conclude a perpetual union against any powerful tyrant because nature provided the examples for unions against war and for peace. Common sense and humanity, Erasmus insisted, were directing human action towards peace. Hence, in his theory, peace resulted not from subjection to the world emperor but from the establishment of a permanent alliance against war among the rulers of Christendom.[47]

The emperor followed Gattinara and other advisers, such as his father confessors, who were staunch supporters of the demand that the Catholic faith should be defended by all available means, including the use of martial arms.[48] Erasmus did advise Charles on matters of dynastic policy, reminding him of the fate of his uncle Juan and warning that the vicissitudes of life and death can make marriage arrangements incalculable.[49] But there was only one occasion on which Charles accepted Erasmus's attitude towards peace, even though Erasmus did not opt against support for crusading plans. This was a multilateral treaty into which Charles entered together with Henry VIII, Francis I and a number of other rulers in 1518. The treaty that the Burgundian chancellery had proposed was signed in London on 2 October 1518, solemnly proclaimed in St Paul's Cathedral and sworn by the representatives of Henry VIII, Francis I, Charles and Pope Leo X. The signatory parties invited others to accede.[50] Eventually, Maximilian joined for the empire, and with him the rulers and governments of Denmark, Scotland, Portugal, Hungary (and Bohemia), Navarre, Savoy, Lorraine, Venice, Urbino, Gueldres, Ferrara, Mantua, Monferrato, Salerno, with Margaret and Ferdinand for the lands under their control as well as the Hanseatic League and the Swiss Confederacy.[51] The treaty stipulated a union of Christian rulers for the purpose of banning wars of aggression and accomplishing peace in the world. It proclaimed a 'good, sincere, true, sound, perfect, faithful and firm amity, union, league, provision of information, confederation and peace among the signatory parties, to be valid on land, the open seas as well as sweet water basins, seaports, and places wherever, for perpetual duration into the future'.[52] The peace agreed upon was to be nothing short of a comprehensive, universal and everlasting condition, and the signatory parties waived their right to resort to war and even accepted the sanction that aggressors acting in breach of the treaty were to be punished by the use of martial arms. At the same time, the treaty prohibited interventions into the domestic affairs of each signatory party through such measures as the support of rebels, other persons guilty of crimes against the Crown and the granting of safe haven to fugitives.[53] The preamble of the treaty contained a reference to the then ongoing Turkish conquests in the eastern Mediterranean Sea and the Balkans, and demanded joint military action in the form of a crusade. In this respect, the treaty echoed Pope Leo X's warnings of a Turkish threat at the end of 1517 and his bull of 6 March 1518. In his bull Leo X proclaimed a five-year truce among rulers of Christendom with the aim of facilitating a crusade against the Ottoman Turkish Empire.[54] To implement the bull Leo X sent out legates to France, the Spanish kingdoms, England and the German-speaking areas.[55] As the second son of Lorenzo de' Medici and a military commander under his predecessor Pope Julius II, Leo X was well versed in military matters. Thus he envisaged the crusade not merely in the spiritual respects through granting letters of indulgence but, like Maximilian, conceived it as a veritable conquest of the Ottoman Turkish Empire.[56] Yet, in Erasmus's pamphlet and in the treaty the crusade appeared as a distant goal unrelated to strategic planning. A wide gulf separated Erasmus's pamphlet and the treaty from Pope Leo X's plan and Emperor Maximilian's efforts to compose a strategic design for the conquest of the Ottoman Turkish Empire, recruit an armed force under imperial leadership and send it on its way to the eastern Mediterranean Sea.

Despite its martial components, the treaty represented a daring step towards multilateralism and could be regarded as a framework of international law that overarched existing bilateral peace treaties and other agreements. It implemented Erasmian thought by constituting peace in the form of an agreement among rulers and the polities under their control. There was not only no Dantean plea for the establishment of some form of universal rule as a precondition for the peace, but the treaty explicitly enforced mutual guarantees of non-intervention among all signatory parties. The signatories retained what might be called sovereign decision-making power, including the implementation of sanctions against infringements of the treaty. Although no explicit procedural rules were set for decisions upon and the implementation of sanctions, it was understood that the English king, in whose capital the treaty had been concluded, would act as an arbiter in the event of crises. But that does not mean that the treaty was the brainchild of Henry VIII or his leading minister, Cardinal Wolsey, Archbishop of York.

CHARLES'S PROMISES: THE ELECTION CAPITULARIES

Rulers' promises were part of the installation ceremonial of the Middle Ages. The oldest specimens date back to the ninth century. It was a common habit to establish a balance between what was considered to be 'popular' consent to the newly elected ruler and the formal statement of core principles that the newly elected rulers intended to follow during their reign.[57] In the course of the high and late Middle Ages, a formulary evolved that consisted of the pledge to bring good government. The pledge included the promise to respect established rights and liberties, observe justice and safeguard peace and unity among the ruled. The counter-pledge of loyalty by the ruled was conditional upon the assurance of good government from the side of the ruler. The installation ceremony was thus a ritual through which the balance of rights and obligations became visually and aurally manifest. In Charles's case the ritual followed the medieval pattern even though the promises were, for the first time in the case of an imperial election, laid down in a carefully drafted and printed text for general distribution. Thus the promises remained an accessible document beyond the installation ceremony. They could be communicated to people who were not present at the ceremony and thereby obtained the status of a programme of government. They could be commented upon and checked as long as Charles remained in office.

In terms of contents, Charles's promises mainly followed the medieval traditions. He obliged himself to respect the basic laws of the empire, specifically the Golden Bull of 1356 and the perpetual peace agreed upon in 1495. Among other things, he promised to 'implant and establish peace, law and unity' in the empire and to form a government of 'pious, respectable, brave, competent and honest office-holders of the German nation'. He also gave assurance that the holders of imperial offices would not interfere in the established privileges of the electors. He declared that he was willing to fight against evil alliances and revolts or the exercise of any kind of unlawful force. He announced that he would neither form any alliances with rulers inside or outside the empire nor begin a war without having consulted with the electors fairly and a long time in advance. He pledged that he would only recruit persons for high office who had prominent names, a good reputation, were aristocrats or otherwise persons of decent origin and born 'Germans'. He admitted only Latin and German as official languages for the imperial administration. And he bound himself not to try to transform the empire into a hereditary monarchy but to guarantee the right of the free election of his successor.[58]

With these promises Charles responded to the proto-nationalism that had been the ferment of his campaign. He allowed the empire to be classed as an institution that was run by and for Germans. Indeed, the empire was widely perceived in the narrower sense of a territorially defined polity in 1519. Without being able to know details of the imperial installation ceremony, even Cortés shared this perception. When he advertised the riches of the Aztec Empire that he claimed to have conquered in Charles's service, he did not forget to insist that these riches were more lavish than what, in Cortés's judgement, Charles could expect from his holdings in the German-speaking area.[59] Charles respected not merely the spatial boundaries but also the constitutional framework of what was described as an elective monarchy. He did so against his own *faible* for dynastic politics, specifically his efforts to use ruling offices for the advancement of the power and prestige of his own kin group. His own political goals conflicted with the promises he was making.

The promises as a publicly accessible legal document reminded Charles of what he had pledged. An early occasion was the Worms imperial diet of Worms of 1521 when Charles struggled with the estates over the competences of the imperial government. The compromise that was accomplished, namely that the imperial government would be a caretaker institution during periods of the emperor's absence from the empire, was perhaps fair but it was not exactly equivalent to his pledge to entrust the government of the empire to capable and honest officials. Instead, he insisted that he should be entitled to rule himself when present in the empire. Further occasions of conflict occurred when Charles decided to take a strong stand against the 'Lutheran heresy' in 1536 and, most dramatically, when he tried to designate his heir in accordance with his dynastic plans in the 1550s.

The promises should thus be read as a legal document drawn up for a specific purpose, not as a kind of basic law. It was one-sided in stating merely the emperor's duties. But this did not mean that the emperor had neither rights nor power-conveying privileges. Within the entire installation ritual the promises were supplemented by ceremonies that gave expression to these rights and privileges. Thus the unction was the most conspicuous rite, signifying the mystical transfer of divine legitimacy and power to the emperor, whereas the imposition of the crown or crowns and the handing over of temporal and spiritual regalia made manifest the demand that the emperor's just orders were to be obeyed. The empire was not a club of German-speaking aristocrats who merely chose one of their own as their representative.[60] Although he did not receive the unction, coronation and investiture with temporal and spiritual regalia in conjunction with his election, Charles had good reason to expect that the imperial office might add not only to his duties but also to his power and honour. But it was hazardous for him to take for granted that his words of command, the displays of his political power and the deployment of martial arms would alone suffice to enforce obedience.

FOUR

Scenes of the Struggle for Power: Dynastic Politics and the Crusade (1521–30)

POWER POLITICS

M uch of politics consists of struggles over the distribution of power. But what is power? As Charles was not the person to worry about philosophical niceties we cannot expect from him an explicit answer to this question. Nevertheless, we can try to determine which of the several definitions of power that were current at his time he preferred.

Defining power

Sixteenth-century intellectuals and administrators who reflected on politics agreed that power was to be assessed in rough approximations rather than measured with precision. Francesco Guicciardini was foremost among the intellectuals concerned with the assessment of power and, as an administrator of papal lands, he gained insight into the practical business of exercising power. Guicciardini stood under the influence of proto-nationalism when he wrote his *History of Italy* in the 1530s. At the beginning of this book he compared the political condition of the Italian peninsula in the second half of the fifteenth century with that of his own time and concluded that in the sixteenth century, Italian polities were suffering from a loss of autonomy and self-governing capability following the invasion by Charles VIII. Guicciardini's proto-nationalist inclination led him to deplore the current state of Italian political affairs. Searching for the factors of the apparent decline, he detected a difference in the power-balancing ability of rulers, holders of offices and influential private persons. He admired the diplomatic skills of Lorenzo de' Medici, who appeared to him to have been able to keep a balance between the powers of the several rulers in the Italian peninsula. In Guicciardini's perception, Lorenzo's achievement was praiseworthy because up until his death in 1492, he did not himself hold a high government office in his native city of Florence. Thus Lorenzo seemed to have been able to exercise power without resort to the enforcement capabilities of an office.[1] In Guicciardini's view, then, power was mainly a personal gift, and individuals endowed with it could choose to use it for public benefit or not to do so. Guicciardini blamed the disaster that encroached upon the Italian peninsula after Lorenzo's death on the vanity of the government of the Republic of Venice. He attacked the Venetian government for its lack of power-balancing capability and reproached Charles VIII as an inept ruler, not gifted with the wisdom of exercising power fairly. From these observations, Guicciardini drew the conclusion that power as a personal gift and wisdom in the exercise of power were crucial for determining the long-term political conditions of a system of polities.

Several years later the Lutheran Italian émigré Alberico Gentili, professor of law at the University of Oxford, used the language of physics and suggested a different definition of power in a system of polities to which he referred as a 'union':

The maintenance of union among the atoms is dependent upon their equal distribution; and on the fact that one molecule is not surpassed in any respect by another. This it is which was the constant care of Lorenzo de' Medici, that wise man, friend of peace and father of peace, namely, that the balance of power should be maintained among the rulers of Italy. This he believed would give peace to Italy as indeed it did so as long as he lived and preserved that state of affairs. Both the peace and the balance of power ended with him, great scion of the Medici and mighty bulwark of his native city and the rest of Italy. Is not this even to-day our concern that one man may not have supreme power and that all Europe may not submit to the rule of a single man?[2]

91

Gentili's account is based on Guicciardini's. Lorenzo appears as the master of balancing power in Italy. The balance breaks down with his death. But Gentili, the jurist, had more a principled interest in Lorenzo's politics than Guicciardini, the chronicler. Where Guicciardini ascribed the maintenance of balance among rulers to Lorenzo's personal capability that could not be transferred to others, Gentili was certain that the balance of power, which he compared to the distribution of molecules in an atom, could in principle be maintained by anyone in any given area. To Gentili, then, the institutional capacities of balancing power could and, of right, ought to have a constraining impact on the decisions of rulers. Gentili thus defined power as the appurtenance of an office that individual incumbents could temporarily occupy. The power of the office was transmitted from one incumbent to the successor. It was ready for use by any incumbent without becoming any incumbent's personal gift. In Gentili's rendering power was *per se* neither good nor bad; its exercise was merely more or less useful within the framework of the office in which it was exercised. This framework was constituted in legal terms, so that law-abiding office-holders were expected to use the power of their office for the benefit of all. Sixteenth-century intellectuals thus defined power in terms of either personal gifts or institutional capacities.

Among the administrators close to Charles, his chancellor Gattinara was most articulate in explicating political concepts. In a memorandum written on 30 July 1521 Gattinara displayed great concern for the emperor's opportunity to acquire what he termed 'respect'. He urged Charles to be aware of the necessity of gaining 'respect' through enterprises that everyone could accept as 'worthy of so great an emperor' as Charles was.[3] He emphasised the importance of accumulating 'respect' for the purpose of becoming able to threaten the emperor's enemies and to increase the number of his friends.[4] Gattinara predicted that Charles's accumulated 'respect' would allow him to balance the power of others, friends and enemies alike. He recommended success in war as the best means of gathering more 'respect'. What Gattinara called 'respect' was no different from what Guicciardini referred to as power, namely the personal gift of imposing the power-holder's will upon others.

In contrast, members of Charles's Spanish entourage, notably Archbishop Juan Pardo de Tavera and Lopez Rubios, his legal adviser, took a legalistic stand. They took seriously Diego Velázquez's accusation that Cortés had conquered the Aztec Empire in an act of insurgency against the Spanish Crowns, and put him on trial. Abuse of office was a heavy crime in their view, specifically because the power to act in office was delegated by the ruler and was exercised in the ruler's name.[5]

But Charles followed Gattinara and Guicciardini. In a thought piece which he drafted in a moment of despair at the turn of the year 1525, he put on record his anxiety that time was running out for him and that he had never used his office to gain 'respect'. He admitted that no serious obstacle had so far prevented him from achieving something truly great and deplored that he was becoming reproachable for not having acted with more determination. He accepted the view that there was no longer any reason to deter him from doing something great soon. He was optimistic that he would succeed, as the divinity had placed him in control of many realms and would allow him to accumulate enough power to eventually accomplish peace and balance.[6] However, like his mentor, Charles regarded war as an essential instrument for the enlargement of his power. While he followed Gattinara in restating the conviction that war was necessary to control Italy, he expanded Gattinara's design by insisting that peace in Italy was the precondition for 'universal peace' everywhere in Christendom and that 'universal peace' in Christendom was the prime condition for the conduct of a successful crusade against the Ottoman Turkish Empire.[7]

At the end of 1528, when preparations for the military expedition to Italy were finally beginning, Charles addressed his Spanish advisers among whom dissatisfaction about the emperor's departure prevailed. According to a report about the address, he informed the advisers that he had decided to start the war because the divinity had so far always awarded victory, because he wanted to restore unity to Christendom and because only he could bring peace to Italy. Reportedly Charles concluded his address saying:

Exactly like the prelates, who have the duty of herding their congregations, we rulers have to visit our subjects and present them with good government. These are the motives for the expedition which will charge much from myself and my funds. But good and virtuous work is not undertaken for the purpose of some utility. I have told you all that, not to solicit your opinion on whether or not I should go but only on how I should organise the expedition and in whose company I should go.[8]

The report let Charles display a degree of determination that bordered on arrogance. It is doubtful whether the report provides a verbatim record of the address because the wording reflects more the imagination of a subaltern office-holder than what Charles may have said. But the report appeared in Santa Cruz's *History*, which can be classed as an official account of Charles's reign.[9] It is unlikely that Charles's commissioned historiographer invented the contents and the wording against the emperor's interest and what the Spanish audience could accept as an appropriate rendering of the event.[10] Moreover, the text confirms Charles's earlier views that he was personally in possession of power as a divine gift and that he ought to use his power for the benefit of the populations under his control. He saw it as his task to restore unity and to promote good government. He was convinced that these benefits could flow on to the ruled as if they were emanations from his personal power. The only noteworthy difference between the contents of the address and Charles's earlier statements is the lack of reference in the 1528 text to the crusade among the stated motives for the Italian expedition.

The triumvirate of rulers and the quest for peace

In practice, the struggle for power took place within the triumvirate of Charles, Francis I and Henry VIII, to whom the pope acceded at times. Charles's relations with Henry VIII were mostly amicable, although they came under pressure ever so often. Several popes with whom Charles was bound to cooperate in his capacity as the imperial defender of the Catholic Church were nevertheless more

inclined to support Francis I than Charles, usually because they were
fearful of imperial interventions in Italian political matters. On
occasions Charles and Francis clashed over the conflict between
their personal wishes and desires and what they perceived as their
official duties. During periods when they believed they could follow
their personal wishes and desires, their relations were amicable. But
during other periods their relations were hostile and shaped by
mutual mistrust, insinuations of evil intentions, accuses of breach of
faith and treaty obligations, and all that despite the close kinship ties
that were arranged between them. Henry usually kept some distance
from Francis although the platform of connections between them
was solid enough to permit alliances under conditions that they
believed were favourable (Plate 6).

Thus the personalities of the triumvirate of secular rulers shaped
politics in Europe during the first half of the sixteenth century. The
three rulers shared the perception of power as a personal gift and
believed that their own role in the struggle for power was crucial.
Charles met Francis and Henry for person-to-person talks and all
three of them met once in a grand pageant between Guines and
Ardres, not far from Calais, in 1520. Each of them maintained
permanent embassies to the others' courts and they observed each
other closely and carefully. They had common goals, namely the
restoration of the unity of Christendom and the conduct of a
crusade against the Ottoman Turkish Empire. Throughout the long
period of their incumbency, none of them dared to break away
publicly from their often-declared consensus. Thus, when Francis
played with the idea of establishing an alliance with the Ottoman
Turkish sultan, Charles, Henry and the pope united and threatened
to ostracise Francis. As a result, Francis's alliance plans did not
develop beyond preliminary consultations. Vice versa, when Henry
broke away from the Catholic Church in order to be able to dissolve
his marriage, he provoked a *rapprochement* between Charles and
the pope to which Francis could easily accede. In the end, Henry
remained outside the Catholic Church but did not join the ranks of
the 'Lutheran heresy'. Hence there was the sense of a balance of
power within the triumvirate of secular rulers. Each of the three

rulers could claim that one was in a position to weaken or strengthen the position of the other two by acting in favour of one and against the other.

Nevertheless, Charles became a troublemaker on occasion. In accordance with Erasmus's proposal, Wolsey assumed that the pact of 1518 obliged its signatories to 'forget the evils of the past', that is, agree on a general amnesty and refrain from attempts to settle ancient disputes and old bills. Wolsey thus continued to try to maintain equidistant relations with Charles and Francis in terms of friendly neutrality that could allow him to operate as an arbiter in cases of need. Accordingly, Charles endorsed the view that the pact of 1518 had in fact superseded all previous legal arrangements and that the *status quo* which the treaty was guaranteeing included the mutual assurance of rights and titles that had existed at the time of the treaty's proclamation.[11] For Charles, this meant that contests over the control of Navarre, Naples, Sicily and Milan had ended. This was, of course, not a position that Francis could accept. Nevertheless, Charles went a step further. Once at the helm of the empire he followed his grandfather's lead and, in 1520, began to claim the exclusive competence for the preparation of a crusade.[12] In addition, Charles even felt justified in ignoring his obligations in the treaty of Noyon concerning his marriage with Louise, daughter of Francis I, and the withdrawal of Aragonese forces from Navarre. Judging that Henry VIII would be neither willing nor able to mobilise his forces against France, Francis I decided to act in May 1520. He asked the deposed King of Navarre, Henri d'Albret, to lead an army into Navarre and simultaneously requested Robert de la Marck, Lord of Bouillon and Sedan and in that capacity holder of an imperial estate, to invade Luxemburg, which was under Margaret's control. Francis wanted to force Charles to execute his obligations from the treaty of Noyon against the stipulations of the non-aggression pact of 1518.

An imperial force under the command of Henry, Count of Nassau and Franz von Sickingen soon repelled la Marck's ill-organised troops, who were left without French support, and pursued the aggressor into France. But French troops marched into Navarre, penetrated into areas south of the Pyrenees and raised the French flag on Spanish soil. Charles's realms had been invaded, while Francis played the ruler of a seemingly peaceful state on whose territory an imperial army had encroached. Although diplomats were familiar with the fact that Francis had provoked both assaults,[13] Francis appealed to Wolsey for implementing sanctions against the emperor by the stipulations of the treaty of 1518. The cardinal responded eagerly and convened a meeting of the two contending parties under his chairmanship. The meeting was to be held in the town of Calais, then the only place on the Continent over which the English king still held sway. Stopping over in the Netherlands on his way back to the Iberian peninsula from the imperial election campaign, Charles dispatched his chancellor Gattinara, while Francis sent his chancellor Duprat. The delegations met in Calais from August to December 1521. Their discussions took place under awkward conditions and ended in a complete failure. On his way to Calais, Gattinara sent a memorandum to Charles urging the emperor not to agree on a premature peace with France.[14] In the course of the discussions Gattinara used deliberately humiliating language to provoke French wrath. The French side responded in a similarly aggressive tone, condemning Charles for lack of willingness to carry out treaty obligations, marriage pledges and dowry payments.[15] Unimpressed by the verbal insults flying back and forth, Wolsey continued to labour in the hope of rescuing the treaty of 1518 and accomplishing a peaceful settlement. But Charles had difficulties in controlling his emotions. In November 1521 he seems to have exploded in Margaret's presence, shouting in a flash of anger:

I can see what's going on. The cardinal wants to do the same thing to me that he has also advised our emissaries to do to the French, namely he wants me to do something unreasonable, something that I could not possibly admit for the sake of my honour and advantage. Obviously he wants to manipulate me to everything in accordance with his wishes and to their advantage, almost as if I were their prisoner. But he is approaching the wrong man; for if the one side does not want me, the other side asks me favours. I do not have a scarcity of brides, and there is no reason to sell them so cheaply.[16]

Margaret was shocked at the outburst of Charles's temper and immediately reported the event to her *confidant* in London. She told him to act swiftly so that irreparable friction between the emperor and Henry VIII could be prevented.[17] In her view, Charles's message was clear: he was neither going to suffer a disgrace as emperor nor was he going to give up crucial assets as Spanish ruler. He classed his sisters as his most important diplomatic trump cards, followed Gattinara's advice and risked the collapse of the Calais negotiations.

While Margaret was concerned about the future of peaceful relations in western Europe, Pope Leo X was impressed by Charles's stubbornness. Despite his being the *spiritus rector* of the treaty of 1518, Leo X was far more concerned with his position as a secular ruler in the Italian peninsula than with the organisation of a crusade. Realising that the French garrison in Milan could easily destroy his hopes of expanding papal rule in the northern part of the Italian peninsula, he struck a deal with the emperor. The pope would help to drive the French garrison out of Milan, return the duchy to imperial authority, and the emperor would agree to surrender Siena, Ferrara, Parma and Piacenza to papal control, once the French troops had left Milan. The pope then gathered a large fighting force on papal territory outside Milan, waiting for Lescun, the French commander of the city, to attack. The chance came when some Italian freebooters gathered outside the city. Lescun lost his nerves and marched into the papal states. Construing the invasion as a breach of the treaty of 1518, the pope ordered all his troops to strike at Milan. The city fell early in December 1521.

Wolsey was no less eager to remain on good terms with Charles.[18] To make sure that relations between the two rulers did not deteriorate as a consequence of the war with France, Wolsey hurried to conclude the treaty on Charles's marriage with Mary at Bruges on 25 August 1521. This was done while the Calais meeting was going on. The treaty also set the conditions of a future joint war that

Charles and Henry agreed to conduct against France.[19] During his visit to England, another agreement was signed on 2 July 1522, confirming the previous marriage arrangement and repeating the joint pledge for a war against France.[20]

Yet preparations for the war took time. Charles returned to his Spanish realms and found that his royal coffers were empty and that the Cortes was reluctant to provide additional funds. In June 1523 Henry issued the claim that the French royal crown belonged to him after his expected victory in the war against France. But the move was premature. A further treaty needed to be signed on 2 July 1523, stipulating that Charles was to invade Guyenne and that Henry was to take Boulogne before 16 August 1523. Yet, luckily for the French side, English armaments were insufficient. The clumsy process of military preparations confirmed Wolsey's greatest concern that Henry might not be able to impose sanctions against France according to the treaty of 1518 because of lack of means to implement them.

Nevertheless, time was finally running out for Francis. Duke Charles of Bourbon, one of the most powerful vassals of the French king, revolted against Francis and entered into a coalition with the emperor, Henry VIII and Ferdinand. The duke agreed to serve the emperor in return for the promise of imperial investiture with Milan. According to the deal, Charles was to lead an army into Narbonne and Henry was to descend upon Normandy before the end of August 1523. However, when the English army finally crossed the Channel in 1524 it got stuck outside Boulogne, was unable to take the city and could not do further harm to Francis. Charles's army fared no better. In the same year it invaded Provence without accomplishing any victory.

By March 1522 Wolsey and the imperial ambassador in London had reached an understanding that peace was unlikely to prevail.[21] But Charles disagreed and tried to restore the treaty instead. A reorientation of papal policy boosted the resumption of the search for a general peace. Pope Leo X had died during the conquest of Milan and his successor Adrian VI was Charles's former teacher Adrian of Utrecht. Adrian showed more concern for the crusade than for Italian affairs, particularly as Ottoman Turkish armies took Rhodes in 1522 and continued to advance into the eastern Mediterranean and the Balkans. After the victory of imperial troops over a French contingent at Bicocca in 1522, Adrian VI urged Charles to make peace with Francis I. He took the view that an anti-Turkish alliance was useless as long as it remained confined to the pope, Charles and Henry VIII. Consequently, he advocated the establishment of a general peace for all Christendom on the basis of the treaty of 1518.[22] Charles got the message. By the stipulations of the treaty of 1518 he had illegally intervened in French domestic affairs, even supporting a rebellion against the French king. Passing over in silence this breach of the treaty, he now proclaimed the urgency of a comprehensive European crusade against the Ottoman Turkish Empire and demanded that the pope should fix a timetable for the conclusion of a general peace among all rulers of Christendom.[23]

Because the aged pope was ill and did not respond to the demand, Charles acted himself. In a curious memorandum to his ambassador to the Holy See dated 14 May 1524, he drafted his own proposals for the conclusion of a general peace and the preparation of a crusade under imperial leadership. The proposal consisted of seven suggestions in a sequence. Except for the first, each suggestion stood under the condition that the previously specified suggestion might turn out to be infeasible. The first suggestion was that conflicts among rulers in Christendom should be settled by judges in accordance with law and equity; each ruler should choose two judges and the pope should swear in one of the judges in the case where no compromise might be reached; parties should bind themselves under heavy fines to accept the papal decision. Charles made his second suggestion under the condition that the first suggestion should prove unacceptable. In this case, all existing treaties should be abolished in favour of a new general treaty; Charles offered the duchy of Milan as a fief to Francis I, if he agreed, but would not surrender Genoa and the Milanese territories that belonged to the Church. If no agreement could be established on the second suggestion, Charles offered to invest Francis I over the entire duchy within the boundaries that existed at the time when the

French had been driven out of Milan. Should the third suggestion turn out to be infeasible Charles proposed exchanging Milan for the duchy of Burgundy and continuing negotiations about the other territories contested between Francis and Charles, namely Tournai, Flanders, Artois and Naples. If Francis rejected the fourth suggestion, there was the possibility that the queen of France would soon die and Francis would then be ready for a new marriage; Charles envisaged his sister Eleanor as a suitable consort and promised to give the duchy of Milan as a dowry. If Francis refused to marry Eleanor or if the present queen lived on, the pope was to arrange marriages between the Dauphin and Princess Mary of Portugal, Charles's niece; the king of Scotland and Mary, Henry VIII's daughter; and the Duke of Milan with Renée, Louis XII's daughter; lastly, Charles declared his willingness to marry Charlotte, Francis I's daughter. If this suggestion failed, all activity was to fall back on the pope, who would then have to ask the king of France to recall all troops from the Italian peninsula.[24]

The logic of the memorandum is straightforward. In the first place, Charles positioned himself as umpire among the rulers of Christendom, the organiser and leader of a crusade. He restated core elements of the treaty of 1518, namely arbitration and amnesty, and then supplemented this suggestion by withdrawing to more limited conventional means of power politics. He suggested allocating control over territories and people and using marriage arrangements as foundations for political relations among ruling dynasties. The pope came in only as the last resort. The political background against which Charles's proposal has to be read is evident. The new pope Clement VII, successor to Adrian VI, was a member of the Medici family and a cousin of Leo X. Clement VII was as much concerned about Italian affairs as Leo X had been, and Charles was right in anticipating that the new pope was ready to accommodate himself with Francis. But the emperor's initiative led nowhere, as all of the seven suggestions remained unfulfilled. Instead of accomplishing the withdrawal of French troops from the Italian peninsula, Charles had to withdraw his troops from Provence when Francis crossed the Alps with a new army to restore French control over Milan. Indeed, the city fell on 26 October 1524. In December of the same year, Clement VII concluded an alliance with Francis I and the Republic of Venice. At the end of 1524, Charles had to accept the fact that Wolsey's treaty was finally dead.

The triumvirate of rulers at war

The situation was not made easier by simultaneously mounting troubles in Scandinavia and the German-speaking areas. Christian II's autocratic rule sparked widespread dissatisfaction, mainly in Denmark and Sweden, and peaked in an open rebellion in 1523. The King had to flee with his family and took up residence at Margaret's court in the Netherlands. While Queen Isabel died in exile in 1526, a protracted controversy about the king's restoration to power continued throughout the 1520s and ended with the defeat of loyalist forces and Christian's house arrest in 1532. Christian's retreat buried Habsburg plans for a dynastic union with the Scandinavian kingdoms. In the German-speaking areas, coordinated revolts of dissatisfied farmers and urban artisans began in 1524; they protested against what they considered to be unfair local governments. The revolt turned violent in Alsace, Thuringia, southern Germany and the Alpine lands under the control of the Habsburgs and affiliated rulers. Some lesser aristocrats joined the rebels, became their military leaders and gained military victories in skirmishes. Eventually, the revolt collapsed under the pressure of organised forces led by members of the high aristocracy and urban elites who were afraid of losing their established privileges. The revolt disclosed a potentially serious lack of stability in the core lands under Ferdinand's rule. It took place in areas from which traditionally imperial armies were recruiting the warriors for the battles Charles was eager to fight. Although Luther eventually took a strong stand against the rebels, whom he denounced as 'murderous peasants', many authorities feared that the revolt might boost the spread of the 'Lutheran heresy'.[25]

Yet military success returned quickly and unexpectedly, and Charles gained 'respect' or power as a warring emperor. Outside the city of Pavia, the French army led by Francis I and imperial troops under the command of Charles de Lannoy engaged in a battle on 24 February 1525. When de Lannoy's soldiers took Francis prisoner, the French side surrendered. The day of the battle became memorable as Charles's twenty-fifth birthday. When the emperor received the news on 10 March 1525,[26] his advisers and the diplomats observing the scene agreed that the divinity had granted the victory. Reportedly, Charles responded with humility and led observers to expect that the divinity would grant him further victories in the future. Implicitly recalling the treaty of 1518, Henry's ambassador at Charles's Spanish court reported to Wolsey on 15 March 1525 that he had congratulated the emperor on the victory because it opened new prospects for the universal peace in Christendom and for the reform of the Church. In the ambassador's view the victory would strengthen the imperial party in European politics because it was even more profitable for the emperor's friends than for the emperor himself (Plate 8).[27]

Charles did not display any clemency towards Francis I. Exactly one month after the day of the battle he issued his demands to Louise of Savoy, Francis I's mother and regent during the time of his captivity. The demands were harsh: Francis was to surrender Burgundy to Charles, revoke his overlordship over Tournai, Flanders and Artois, renounce his claims to Provence, the duchy of Milan and Naples and hand over the duchies of Normandy, Guyenne and Gascony to Henry VIII, before he could be released.[28] To the end of demonstrating the change of power relations between the emperor and the French king, propaganda pamphlets were issued in print in the German-speaking area. The pamphlets contained accounts of the battle and a list of prisoners of war featuring Francis I as number one.[29] Respect for the winner characterised Francis's initial response: he pledged to be the emperor's servant for ever if treated with generosity.[30]

Yet Charles's propaganda helped little to implement his demands. Francis was taken to Madrid where he arrived on 19 June 1525 and was kept in the confinement of the court. Having recovered from the initial shock, Francis shrewdly replied that the demands were equal to the dismemberment of his kingdom and that he was unable to execute them as long as he was Charles's prisoner. In the autumn of 1525 he protested against the length of his imprisonment and had a notary confirm that all the treaties or other pledges that had been forced upon him during his imprisonment were null and void and violated his personal honour and duties towards the kingdom.[31] Charles ignored Francis most of the time and refused to include him in the negotiations with Louise. He did, however, look after his prisoner when news arrived that Francis had fallen ill.[32] The negotiations were difficult and protracted. They were conducted at Lyon where Charles's ambassador acted as imperial plenipotentiary, and at Toledo where Francis's sister Margaret represented the French side. Through his representatives, Francis offered to waive his rights over Tournai, Flanders and Artois, to give up his claim over the Italian peninsula and to pay a ransom of three million *soleils d'or*. Charles responded that he was not interested in money but wanted to be restored to his ancient rights. To him this meant, first and foremost, control over Burgundy. By mid-December 1525 Francis was ready to accept this demand on condition that he be released and could himself administer the transfer. On this basis, agreement was eventually reached that Charles release Francis to implement all imperial demands and that Francis guarantee to execute his obligations within six weeks of returning to France. Francis also agreed to marry Charles's sister Eleanor and to give his two sons as hostages into the emperor's custody. A peace treaty was signed at Madrid on 14 January 1526. Against the advice of Gattinara, who feared that the treaty was worthless, Charles and his advisers took the view that they could not keep the French king in custody for much longer and that the French–Habsburg marriage deal was promising. Hence they decided to take the risk.[33] Francis was escorted to the French border and, when bidding farewell, promised to return to the Spanish kingdoms as a prisoner should he be unable to implement the treaty.

In the meantime Charles's relations with Henry entered a period of difficulty if not strain. Problems arose once again over marriage issues. Acting upon counsel by his Spanish advisers, Charles decided to get married before Henry's daughter Mary came of age. Charles intended to produce an heir to his many lands before departing for the Italian peninsula. The battle of Pavia suggested that there might be some truth in Gattinara's word that the Italian peninsula was the stepping stone to more far-reaching goals, and Charles had never seen his Italian realms. But he could not leave his Spanish kingdoms again without a legitimate and reliable regent. In his view, only kin members could perform his task. Consequently, if Charles wanted to wrest control over the Italian peninsula from the French and the pope, he had to end his bachelor status as soon as possible. Although the marriage with Mary was to be concluded no later than three more years according to the Bruges treaty of 1521, he dispatched a request to Henry VIII on 7 June 1525 demanding that Mary, then nine years old, be sent immediately.[34] As Henry decided that the issue was not pressing, Mary remained in England for the time being, even though Charles was now in a hurry. On 11 June 1525 Henry had received word that Charles had always wanted to marry Mary, did not wish to weaken his friendship with Henry but was now inclined to propose to Isabel, sister of King John III of Portugal and a cousin through his aunt Mary. The Portuguese king had just married Charles's sister Catherine. Charles now expressed his hope that Henry would agree to the project.[35] During the summer, negotiations advanced to the degree that obliged Charles to inform Henry directly of his decision to abrogate the Bruges treaty. In a letter dated 11 August 1525 Charles went to great lengths in trying to explain why he was about to marry Isabel. He argued that his subjects were asking him to give priority to the Portuguese over the English princess, that he intended to execute his duty of subduing the 'Lutheran heresy' and that he was forced to confront the armies of the Ottoman Turkish sultan. During these risky times, Charles explained, he did not dare to leave his Spanish lands without an heir and, consequently, he had to marry as soon as possible.[36] But Henry was outraged and thought of revenge. His chancellery accused Charles of breach of treaties in twenty cases. In the perception of Henry's chancellery, Charles was guilty of refusing to repay his debts, failing to support Henry militarily during the recent war against Francis, breaking marriage agreements, supporting the Scots, Henry's enemies, and of single-handedly controlling the French king as a prisoner although the campaign had been fought as an English–imperial coalition war.[37] Wolsey quickly restored normal relations with Francis through a treaty signed at his residence at Moore Palace on 30 August 1525. And Henry's outburst of anger soon ended, allowing his old friendship with Charles to resurface. On 21 September 1525 Henry instructed his ambassadors to Charles to report that he had agreed to the cancellation of the marriage project involving his daughter Mary, provided Charles paid an indemnity and did not conclude a separate peace treaty with Francis.[38] Charles did neither. The Madrid treaty, he said, was a bilateral agreement between himself and Francis and did not touch upon relations with England, as imperial, not English, forces had captured Francis. And, to his regret, there was no money in imperial and Spanish coffers to repay the dowry for Mary (Plate 11).

But Charles was going too far. Even the pope hesitated to approve of the Portuguese marriage. Being approached to give his dispensation for the marriage of Charles and Isabel, Clement VII appeared so astonished that he set up a brief dispensation letter that did not specify the bride's name, ostensibly, so Charles's ambassador in Rome believed, in order not to alienate Henry VIII.[39] But the pope soon had to change his mind and wrote a second dispensation letter containing Isabel's name.[40] Nevertheless, Henry began to call into question the wisdom of his friendship with the emperor and considered other options. The immediate victim was his wife Catherine, Charles's aunt; the temporary beneficiary was Francis I.

Upon returning to his kingdom and after consultation with his mother, Francis refused to proceed with the ratification of the Madrid treaty. Charles played into Francis's hands by allowing the publication of the treaty in the Netherlands during the period that had been agreed upon for the ratification. Francis could thus use the argument that the premature release of the contents made it politically impossible for him to enforce the treaty. The argument was threadbare and could not defend him against the accusation that he had merely sworn the treaty to regain his freedom without being genuinely willing to enforce it after his return. From 1526 at the latest to the end of his life Francis had to live with the stigma of being an unreliable treaty partner and remained seriously restricted in his choice of alliance partners. Yet, for the time being, Francis made political headway as he could exploit Henry's and other rulers' fear that Charles was becoming too powerful. French diplomats acted ruthlessly and quickly. They pulled together what was in practice an anti-Habsburg alliance, even though Charles was invited to join. Thus Francis, the pope, the republics of Florence and Venice and the duchy of Milan concluded the alliance at Cognac on 22 May 1526 for the purpose of restoring French suzerainty over the Italian peninsula. Henry considered joining it but, for the time being, shied away from openly breaking with the emperor. On his own side Francis took an even more daring step, declaring that he would not waive his rights over Tournai, Flanders, Artois and Burgundy and even postponing his marriage with Eleanor. Ferdinand offered to help his brother and suggested leading an army across the Alps into the Italian peninsula. But Charles, wary of Ferdinand's plans to strengthen his Italian influence, remained cool and told Ferdinand to remain in his Austrian lands as a guard against the sultan.

Hence Charles and his advisers had to write off the Madrid treaty. In anger Charles demanded that Francis meet him for a duel. Even though Francis's two sons remained in imperial custody, they were of little value as long as the emperor pursued his policy of maximalist demands. Indeed, Charles soon had to adopt a softer voice. His commanders lost control over parts of the fighting force that had beaten Francis in 1525 and had remained under arms to enforce imperial rule in the peninsula. Some of the troops were poorly paid and mutinied. They converted into a marauding warrior band that decided to move to Rome and take by force whatever booty they could obtain there. No counterforce was strong enough to stop them, no political pressure strong enough to restore order and discipline among them, and no offer of ransom high enough to obstruct the advance. The warrior band besieged, sacked and plundered the city for six weeks in 1527. Six thousand people lost

107

their lives in one single day. Altogether the death toll may have been more than 200,000 people. Rome suffered from an irreparable destruction of property and buildings. Eventually the warrior band even took the pope prisoner and kept him in confinement for about six months.[41] As the commander-in-chief of the imperial forces Charles had to take responsibility. Gattinara advised the emperor to apologise to all rulers of Christendom and to take rapid action to free the pope. The latter was easier said than done. Charles had no other fighting force in the peninsula. To make things worse, the rebel Charles of Bourbon was shot in 1527, so that the last remaining check against Francis's domestic power in France was removed and the succession to the duchy of Milan had to be decided once more. Upon receiving the then unconfirmed news of the duke's death, Ferdinand sent another letter to his brother repeating his offer to invade the peninsula and restore order. Furthermore, Ferdinand now demanded his own investiture as duke of Milan. With barely concealed displeasure Charles rejected Ferdinand's offer again, saying that Ferdinand was needed in the Habsburg hereditary lands and should keep himself ready for battle against the Ottoman Turkish army. The League of Cognac appeared to triumph while the pope was in the hands of a warrior band that had once fought for the emperor.

Against this background Henry VIII felt strong enough to risk a momentous decision. He had initially protested his father's demand to take over his deceased brother's bride. While Henry and Catherine subsequently accommodated each other, the most serious remaining problem was that, as the years were passing by, Henry could no longer expect a (male) heir from his wife. When he fixed the marriage agreement between his daughter Mary and Charles in 1522, this expectation was already cast in legal terms: in the marriage treaty Charles agreed to waive his succession rights if Mary should succeed her father as queen of England. When Charles unilaterally withdrew from the deal with Henry's explicit approval in 1525, Mary was of little use in guaranteeing the continuity of Henry's line, as long as no equal-ranking marriage partner came in sight. It was then consistent for Henry to look out for another wife, expecting to receive a male heir from her. When Sir Thomas Boleyn, Viscount Rochford, earl of Wiltshire and Ormond, joyful courtier and Henry's companion, agreed to mate his daughter Anne with the king, the conditions for a divorce were set. On 13 July 1527 Charles's ambassador in England reported the disconcerting news that Henry intended to dissolve his marriage with Catherine.[42] Charles rushed to support his aunt and demanded the repayment of the dowry. But, as Charles had to face his Italian problems, he decided to limit his activity to formal protests.

Charles stayed remarkably calm during these times of intense trouble. To the great bewilderment of his Spanish advisers he spent much time in the company of his wife and displayed more concern with family matters than with political affairs. On 21 May 1527 Isabel gave birth to a boy who received the name Philip. In the meantime Charles's illegitimate daughter Margaret, born in 1522, grew up in the Netherlands to become another trump card for a marriage deal.

Francis was ready to help Henry out. Wolsey and French diplomats hammered out the plan for a joint war against the emperor. On 22 January 1528, English and French emissaries faced Charles at Burgos to formally abrogate all legal obligations, end all friendly relations and declare war. Francis returned Charles's proposal of 1526, demanded a duel and suggested that Charles should determine a safe location. Charles responded coolly that Francis was his prisoner and had no right to issue any demands.[43] But he took a conciliatory attitude towards Henry. On 20 January 1528 he dispatched a note to Henry saying that he regarded the English king as a mediator between himself and Francis. He apologised for not having fulfilled the stipulations of the treaty of 1518 with the argument that it was not his fault that the crusade against the Ottoman Turkish Empire had not materialised. He did not forget to add that the pope had been freed in the meantime and that he recognised, and had never refused to recognise, his obligation to repay his debts to Henry.[44]

Charles's plea accomplished its goal. Henry was wary of the war if only for the reason that its main theatre was Charles's Italian dependencies for which Henry had little concern. As the war was unpopular in England, Aunt Margaret managed to establish a truce in July 1528. Yet Francis continued to be determined to remove the emperor from the Italian peninsula. To that end French forces even besieged Naples. Unfortunately for Francis, not all of his Italian allies were reliable. Perhaps as early as in 1527 and with Gattinara's mediation, Andrea Doria, the doge of Genoa, began negotiations with the emperor seeking to ally his considerable naval forces with the imperial land army. On 1 July 1528 Doria signed a two-year treaty by which he entered imperial service. Charles could thus use the powerful Genoese fleet to rescue his beleaguered forces in Naples and, more importantly, obtained access to the affluent Genoese bankers. Doria's fleet ended the French blockade of Naples and opened the port of Genoa to supply reinforcements for the imperial army in the peninsula. French troops were eventually beaten at Landriano on 21 June 1529. The pope deserted the League of Cognac, lured by imperial promises for the strengthening of his political influence. Indeed, in 1529, the pope and the emperor signed a treaty preparing the marriage of Charles's illegitimate daughter Margaret with Clement VII's nephew Alessandro de' Medici, whom Charles restored as ruler over Florence. The marriage was finally concluded in 1536 but Alessandro was murdered in the following year. The pope also agreed to take charge of the English divorce issue – thereby allowing Charles to interact with Henry as if Catherine continued to be queen of England – and even bestowed the dignity of cardinal upon Gattinara, Charles's chancellor and chief adviser.

Eventually, Francis's entourage arrived at the conclusion that it was not worth continuing the war. Mother Louise and Aunt Margaret, her sister-in-law, used their friendly relations and good offices to negotiate a peace. The negotiations were smooth and produced a fair deal. Francis acknowledged the treaty of Madrid of 1526, except for the provision concerning Burgundy, and paid two million *soleils d'or* as a ransom for his two sons. Charles implicitly renounced the use of force concerning Burgundy and pledged to pursue the path of peaceful arbitration. Charles became invested as ruler of Tournai, Flanders and Artois in his own right. Francis retained the integrity of his kingdom but withdrew from the Italian peninsula and gave up his claim over the duchy of Milan. The treaty was signed at Cambrai on 30 October 1529[45] and has since then been known as the Ladies' Peace. Francis treated Charles's emissaries as good friends, and Henry buried his grudge. The old triumvirate of young rulers was back in operation.

Ottoman Turkish troops advancing northwards through the Balkans

Meanwhile, Charles got ready to depart for the Italian peninsula. According to Gattinara, the final decision to do so had already been made at the turn of 1529 but preparations were speeded up only as tensions with France eased. Charles appointed his wife as regent for the Spanish kingdoms and wrote a last will that was later destroyed. Accompanied by Gattinara he embarked at Barcelona and reached Monaco on 6 August 1529. He arrived at Bologna while Turkish troops laid siege to Vienna. He tried to calm down Ferdinand, promising to continue to Vienna soon.[46] Yet, in fact, Charles stayed at Bologna for almost six months to restore peace in the Italian peninsula.

The struggle for power between Charles, Francis and Henry had taken place against the rapid advance of Ottoman Turkish troops in the eastern Mediterranean Sea, through the Balkans and towards the Habsburg hereditary lands. When Charles first arrived in the Spanish kingdoms in 1517, the Mameluke polity in Egypt fell under the sultan's control. When Charles tried to end the 'Lutheran heresy' in 1521, Belgrade fell and the northern Balkans were open to Turkish conquest. While Charles was journeying to return to the Spanish kingdoms in 1522, Turkish troops moved into Rhodes after a long siege. In response, a wave of anti-Muslim propaganda swept across the Christian Occident. Lutherans were more articulate in proclaiming Muslims as the 'perpetual enemies of Christendom', which was a name for the devil. They addressed their hopes for the destruction of the Ottoman Turkish Empire to the emperor, pledging their support for a crusade that Charles was to lead.[47] Charles

111

repeatedly promised help for beleaguered towns and islands. But he had no troops to spare and thus could not interfere directly in the contested areas. Moreover, his insistence that the future crusade against the Ottoman Turkish Empire could only take place under the emperor's personal leadership alienated some of his potential partners, most importantly the king of France and the Republic of Venice.

An important factor stimulating Turkish northward military expansion was the lack of willingness of the triumvirate of rulers, their respective partners and allies to coordinate an effective defence. As a result, the defence had to be organised by the rulers in the areas coming under immediate Turkish attack. At the time of the formation of the League of Cognac, the king of Hungary and Bohemia had to shoulder the main burden of opposing the Turkish armies. But King Louis II, who had succeeded to the Hungarian and Bohemian crowns in 1516, had only limited means at his disposal, and his generalship was poor. The Turkish army, led by Sultan Suleiman the Magnificent in person, was well equipped with cavalry, infantry and heavy artillery, and the sultan was determined to use his military power. Without realising the mortal danger he was in, Louis II personally led an inferior force against the advancing Turkish armies, fought them at Mohács on 28 August 1526 but lost the battle and drowned while fleeing from the battlefield. With the exception of its north-western fringes, the Hungarian kingdom became a Turkish province and the succession to the Hungarian and Bohemian crowns a diplomatic issue. Queen Mary, Charles's sister, withdrew to Vienna as a widow and asked her brother Ferdinand, Ladislaus's son-in-law, to take the Hungarian and Bohemian crowns. But before the Habsburg succession could be secured, Hungarian aristocrats elected John Zapolya, one of their own, as king. Zapolya took control of a kingdom that no longer existed, while Ferdinand was elected as the new king of Bohemia. Ferdinand decided to claim the Hungarian crown for himself as well, with the consequence that Ferdinand and Zapolya became rivals over the titular kingdom. They had to substantiate their claims by demonstrating superior capability to succeed militarily against the Turkish armies. While Zapolya's forces were weaker than those of his contender, Ferdinand, the German-speaking Spanish aristocrat, was an outsider among Hungarians, not much different from their Turkish rulers.

Ferdinand was thus hard pressed to fight a war on several fronts. He felt obliged to support his brother's claims in the Italian peninsula; Charles's position as emperor elect and the king of the Romans needed consolidation after the farmers' and artisans' revolt in the German-speaking areas; in Hungary Zapolya was unwilling to give in, and the Turkish northward advance continued. Aunt Margaret kept sending threatening messages that revenues from the Netherlands were running short and did not allow her to send further subsidies. The future of the Habsburg dynasty thus looked bleak. In 1529 Turkish troops stood before Vienna, ready for the siege of the unofficial imperial capital. Ferdinand and even members of the Spanish courts urged Charles to proceed to Vienna immediately. Margaret concurred, reminding Charles of the necessity to rescue the city. But Charles remained unimpressed. He responded coolly that the pacification of the Italian peninsula had priority for him, as Turkish troops might invade the peninsula as well.[48] Eventually, late in 1529, the Turkish army lifted its siege of Vienna at its own discretion and retreated into Hungary. Charles heard the good news while he was journeying in the northern part of the Italian peninsula. He praised divine wisdom for the turn of events, which was another way of saying that he had been right in not proceeding to Vienna. However, Charles had to pay a high price for his *hubris*. In leaving to Ferdinand the task of defending Vienna against the Turkish army, he conveyed the message that the defence of the Roman Empire had no priority for him as emperor. Charles's decision to leave to Ferdinand the defence of Vienna also disappointed many radical Lutherans, whereby Charles became less attractive as the focus of loyalty. At the end of the 1520s the defence of the Roman Empire and the war against advancing Turkish armies were thus reduced from the core task of the emperor to the business of whoever could claim to rule over Hungary and its adjacent areas. As long as Charles lived, Ferdinand was placed in charge of defending the eastern frontiers of the Roman Empire against the troops of the Turkish sultan. The crusade gradually vanished from the political agenda and with it the quest for universal rule.

THE BALANCE OF POWER

Charles was not the only person to sense the strategy conflict between universal rule and the balance of power. For his universalism he drew on the legacy of Dantean political theory, to which he was introduced by his chancellor Gattinara. According to Dante, the universal ruler alone could provide justice.[49] Justice, Dante assumed, following Aristotle, was a condition of things from which all obliqueness is absent.[50] This meant that the rule of justice guarantees equal rights and can be symbolised by the figure of *Iustitia* holding the scales. In the case of greed one scale becomes heavier and goes down. This is not only bad in itself but also entails the further negative consequence that the other scale goes up and lifts the victim of greediness to a morally superior and politically more powerful position. Dante's conclusion from Aristotle's definition then was that justice required someone to hold the scales and that the universal ruler was most qualified to perform this task of enforcing a general moral code to the end of avoiding greed. In addition, Dante positioned justice as the core condition for the maintenance of peace.

However, early in the sixteenth century, Dantean universalism was no longer the only theoretical context in which the scales model of the balance of power was applied. In a passage of his *History of Italy*, to which reference has already been made, Francesco Guicciardini drew the application of the scales model from the high level of the world at large down to the small world of the particular relations between the city of Florence, neighbouring urban communities and the papal states. In Guicciardini's description, Lorenzo de' Medici acts as the balancer, not the universal ruler: the emperor is a remote figure and the pope merely one of the rulers in the Italian peninsula.[51] Because the scales measure the weight of a pair and can only move in one dimension, its use as a model for the balance of power among polities in the Italian peninsula was only possible on condition that the relations among these polities were perceived as bilateral. Guicciardini thus constructed a system of bilateral relations among polities and placed Lorenzo in a kind of superior position that enabled him to overlook the whole. According to Guicciardini, Lorenzo could manage to maintain the balance of power because he was competent to use his own power as a personal gift. Peace among the Italian polities was the outcome of Lorenzo's superior capability but not the result of the application of a general moral code that the universal ruler enforced to the end of avoiding greed.

Moreover, Guicciardini had a rival in Machiavelli. The Florentine theorist and administrator disagreed with Guicciardini about the principles of balance-of-power politics. He denied that peace and stability in the Italian peninsula up to the end of the fifteenth century had been due to Lorenzo's personal achievement. Far from believing that the Republic of Venice had acted immorally at the time of the invasion of Charles VIII in 1494, he accused it of misjudgement. In his view, the Venetians had simply chosen the wrong ally because the forces of the French king were stronger than the Venetian military might and therefore could not be kept under control once they had entered the peninsula. Hence, Machiavelli's conclusion was that the Venetian attempt to balance power had led to disaster. He equated balance of power with neutrality, which he denounced as evil. Instead of trying to preserve the balance, Machiavelli taught, rulers should unequivocally opt for one side and choose the strongest party as their ally.[52] In his memoranda to the young emperor Gattinara ignored Machiavelli and tried to combine Guicciardinian particularism with Dantean universalism by claiming that control of affairs in the Italian peninsula was the stepping-stone towards universal rule in Dante's sense. If Charles followed his chancellor's advice, he risked conflict with his brother Ferdinand, Aunt Margaret and his fellows in the triumvirate of rulers.

Yet Guicciardinian particularism had its attraction: it grew out of a concept of human action that was gaining currency at the turn of the sixteenth century. This concept of action can best be illustrated by the combat techniques of Maximilian's lansquenet fighting force.

Pictorial sources from the early sixteenth century show battle scenes as dual combats into which military formations become dissolved soon after the initial shock (Plates 7 and 8).[53] The scenes represent warriors acting with their bodies in an upright position, thrusting their pikes as far to the front as possible, and standing with their legs wide apart. The turning point of the body is rather low, around the hip. The lansquenets so depicted may make movements in many directions without changing their position. In real combat this bodily bearing allowed lansquenets to keep a firm equilibrium even when they moved the upper parts of their bodies at high speed. It made possible the combination of the quest for a stable position and the demand for rapid movements. Lansquenets thus considered stability as the foundation for self-assertive and self-reliant action and placed the maintenance of equilibrium at a high level in their priority of goals. The lansquenets were Maximilian's preferred fighting force, and Charles inherited them. On occasions Maximilian reproached his troops for their disobedience and neglect of articles of war that prescribed discipline and subordination. But Maximilian did not restrict their capability of moving. Instead he urged them to train themselves in order to increase their physical strength and become prepared for dual combat.[54] Lansquenet modes of fighting became the standard technique of warfare in the first half of the sixteenth century, specifically in Charles's Italian campaigns. Not only German and French but also Italian authors praised Charles's warriors for their discipline and fighting power, even though the Sack of Rome put on record how dangerous this fighting force could become.[55] Guicciardini, the lansquenets and even Machiavelli shared this sense of human action. All of them based their arguments and actions on the assumption that the personal power and the particular goals of individuals as rulers or warriors mattered more than the moral constraints that a remote universal ruler might be able to enforce in a distant future. Among early sixteenth-century intellectuals and military men, balancing power thus appeared to demand purposeful human action rather than reliance on divine benevolence.

THE QUEST FOR CONTROL: CHARLES'S REFLECTIONS ON HIS
POLITICAL GOALS AND THE FORMULATION OF HIS IMPERIAL TITLE

The struggle for power within the triumvirate of Charles, Francis I
and Henry VIII made it necessary for the emperor to decide on
priorities. Throughout much of the 1520s we see him acting mainly
as the territorial ruler of the Spanish kingdoms and their
dependencies in the Mediterranean Sea. He displayed great concern
for dynastic matters; for the maintenance or restoration of the
control over lands that he took to be part of his heritage; and for the
preservation of friendly relations with Portugal. Yet during this
period he betrayed little or no interest in the Spanish American
dependencies; he confined his concern about the Ottoman Turkish
advance largely to propagandistic responses in situations of
immediate threat or manifest defeat on the side of Christian rulers
and their armies; following the Worms imperial diet of 1521 he
restrained his anti-Lutheran rhetoric and refrained from personal
involvement in the political affairs of the empire. Although he
remained verbally committed to the pursuit of a general peace
among the rulers of Christendom he envisaged this state of political
affairs merely at the end of a long series of disputes that he intended
to settle on the way thither. He claimed that everyone had to follow
him on the path towards the future general peace but, in the
immediate present, acted merely to balance rival interests to the
advancement of the interests of his own dynasty.

Two texts from the end of 1528 and the beginning of 1530 reveal
the widening gap between the universalistic and irenic goals of
imperial policy and the particularistic means that Charles chose to
implement them in territorial polities here and there. The first text,
to which reference was made above, consists of the statement that
Charles reportedly addressed to his Spanish advisers on the reasons
for his departure from the Spanish kingdoms in 1528. The second
text is a lengthy letter that Charles wrote to his brother Ferdinand
on 11 January 1530 in reply to several of Ferdinand's messages that
are no longer extant. In 1528 Charles seems to have purposefully
chosen the arrogant tone of an *ex cathedra* pronouncement against

which reasoning was unwarranted. He was aware of the lack of support for his decision to depart from his Spanish realms and would no longer consider further objections. Yet he mentioned some objections that he had previously encountered. The first was that the continuing war with France and England could jeopardise the Italian expedition. In response to this Charles boasted that he would move to the Italian peninsula with a force so large that no one would dare to stand up against him. The second objection was that frustration about the Sack of Rome and the disgruntlement of the pope would not allow the emperor to accomplish political goals. Charles dismissed this objection with the following arguments. First he maintained that the pope was much more worried about French troops in their current position south of the Alps than about matters of the past; then he insisted that the pope knew well that the emperor had no personal responsibility for the evil that his troops had perpetrated. The third objection was that wars required funds that were not currently available. Charles refused to accept this point. He replied that fighting had been going on for eight years and that financial resources had always been available to conduct and win the war. Instead of yielding to seeming financial constraints, he was about to accomplish something heroic and would allow no one and nothing to obstruct his path.

After having made an effort to destroy the arguments of his opponents Charles moved on to disclose his goals. Obtaining the imperial and the other crowns was not his prime objective, he explained. Nor was he attempting to take revenge on his Italian enemies and to suppress their polities. At no time, he exclaimed, had he ever fought a war over someone else's property. Instead, he had only campaigned to safeguard or restore what was rightly his. He finally described what he categorised as his sole and true purpose, and that was to bring about a general council to end the 'Lutheran heresy' and to reform the Catholic Church. Beyond this major goal he was merely striving to provide peace and good government to his Italian subjects.[56]

The text is interesting even though it is unlikely that it represents a verbatim report. It is conspicuous for the lack of references to universalistic concerns such as the general peace in Christendom and the crusade. Despite its arrogant wording, it is apologetic in tone. The emperor felt compelled to state and refute objections, to present counter-arguments and to declare his own goals. He entrusted these motives secretly to his Spanish audience, whom he ordered not to disclose what he had told them. Although a contemporary printed version of the address proves that the text was soon communicated to the outside world, the question remains why the emperor may have wished to keep secret that he intended to subdue the 'Lutheran heresy'. The answer may be contained in the letter with Charles's second statement of principles, written after his arrival at Bologna. Despite its excessive repetitiveness Charles's letter is a well-structured piece of persuasion that he claimed to have written with his own hand, although Gattinara may have masterminded the contents. The style is in conformity with the usual mode of correspondence between the two brothers. But this piece is characterised by its apologetic tone. While, in the address to his Spanish advisers, Charles strove to explain why he had to go, in his letter to Ferdinand he tried to explain why he could not have gone at the time he was expected to go. He placed himself at the interface of several dilemmas and drew a gloomy picture of a volatile world in which war was in sight and he himself, Ferdinand and a few others appeared as sensible and good-willed people engaged in a deadly struggle against incompetent and evil folk. To describe the dilemmas he divided the letter into three sections: in the first he discussed the difficulties he had to overcome in order to be able to depart from his Spanish realms; in the second, he explained the difficulties that he was facing during his stay at Bologna; and in the third he presented the difficulties of making up his mind what to do next.

In the first section Charles characterised himself as a person driven by his imperial task to promote peace. He insisted that he had to go wherever peace was to be accomplished most urgently and that he left his Spanish kingdoms in an emergency forced upon him rather than following a well-considered decision. He gave paramount importance to the goal of obtaining the imperial crown and added that his imperial coronation was the essential precondition for allowing Ferdinand to become elected as king of the Romans in succession to Charles. As long as Charles continued to be merely emperor elect, the framework of imperial public law did not allow the election of a new king of the Romans as the heir apparent to the emperor; so Charles argued. He acknowledged the growing significance of the 'big heresies in Germany', that is, the 'Lutheran heresy', and disclosed his fear that the Lutherans might thwart Ferdinand's election as king of the Romans. But he did not forget to mention the kingdom of Naples as a further trouble spot where his presence appeared to be mandatory for the establishment of peace and good government. He then repeated the argument that he was fearful of an impending Turkish attack on the Italian peninsula and hoped to deflect Turkish troops through his presence. Charles thus portrayed himself as the holder of a power that he felt obliged to use for the benefit of population, under his control. But in the face of many competing problems he felt the difficulty of deciding which of the problems he should tackle first.

In the second section of his letter to Ferdinand, Charles explained why he left for the Italian peninsula later, and was staying there longer, than he had initially intended. He mentioned the clumsiness of military preparations that were slow because of the lack of Spanish domestic support for the expedition; financial constraints resulting from the delay of payments from Portugal; the continuing war with the king of France, who accepted the Ladies' Peace only after Charles had departed from his Spanish realms; and the disappointing news of the Turkish advance that forced him to agree upon some purportedly unfavourable stipulations in the Ladies' Peace. Once on his way Charles encountered protracted disputes in the Italian peninsula. He complained that Francis I was an unreliable treaty partner and that it was an open question how long the Ladies' Peace would last. Finally, Charles adduced Henry's divorce case as a reason that kept him tied to Italian matters. He would not exclude the possibility that Henry 'might do something outrageous', which would trigger another war, and that, in this event, Francis would side with the English king. Under these conditions Charles would be forced to secure his Italian positions, perhaps with the help of Andrea Doria and the Genoese fleet.

In the third section of his letter Charles addressed the question of how to proceed. He insisted that the imperial coronation had to be performed first, that is, before he could leave the peninsula. But it remained to be decided what to do next. Charles offered three options: first, he could be crowned emperor as soon as possible, even outside Rome, and proceed to the German-speaking areas at the earliest opportunity; second, he might travel from Bologna to Rome to receive the imperial crown there and then continue to the German-speaking lands; third, he could move further south from Rome to visit Naples and arrive in areas north of the Alps only later in the year. Because Charles felt that his visit to Naples was urgent, he argued that his stay in the German-speaking lands would be short if he chose one of the first two options. Consequently, if Ferdinand wanted the emperor to stay for some time in the areas north of the Alps, he would have to allow Charles to go to Naples first.[57] Ferdinand's reply was unequivocal: the emperor should proceed to the German-speaking lands at the earliest time. Aunt Margaret supported Ferdinand's view that the imperial coronation was the most important goal to be accomplished during Charles's Italian campaign. Charles took these opinions seriously and left for the German-speaking areas soon after he received the crowns.[58]

The apologetic tone marks the most important commonality between Charles's two statements of principle that he wrote in 1528 and 1530. Yet two striking differences in argument seem to carry more significance. The first difference is that, in 1528, Charles was made to portray himself to his Spanish advisers as a ruler who was in full control of the decision-making process. By contrast, he described himself to Ferdinand as a ruler driven by awkward circumstances, seemingly beyond his influence, and asked for advice in 1530. According to this self-portrait Charles was trying to do his best but awkward circumstances and evil-minded people would not let him succeed. The second difference is that he made explicit various goals for his actions. When still in his Spanish realms he claimed to have to act for the purpose of suppressing the

'Lutheran heresy' in the first place, whereas all other considerations were classed as irrelevant. Explicitly Charles then denied that he was primarily motivated to travel to the Italian peninsula in order to accept his imperial coronation. By contrast, the 'Lutheran heresy' merely features as a background factor in the later text, with a potentially negative influence on the election of Ferdinand as king of the Romans. Because Charles's imperial coronation emerged as the essential condition for Ferdinand's election, it assumed the status of an essential goal to be accomplished during the Italian expedition. While Charles's most important goal was the restoration of the unity of Christendom in 1528, his most important goal in 1530 was to regulate the succession in the empire to the advantage of the Habsburg dynasty. In 1530 Charles did not take the 'Lutheran heresy' seriously in its own right but merely as a check against Habsburg dynastic power. The difference in argument can hardly be explained in terms of the lapse of time between the two statements; for it is unlikely that Charles did not have dynastic concerns in his mind when he addressed his Spanish advisers. Hence Charles phrased the explanations of his goals in accordance with what he believed his audience wanted to hear. Perhaps this was why he obliged his Spanish audience to keep his message secret.

However, the particularistic discourse about dynastic power of 1530 did not necessarily invalidate the resort to the unity of Christendom in the universalistic discourse of 1528. In the Spanish kingdoms, resort to the dynastic concerns of the Habsburg family would have provided little argumentative advantage against the prevailing reluctance to let the emperor go on his expedition. That Charles admitted the suppression of the 'Lutheran heresy' as his prime goal in 1528 made sense against the backdrop of the quest for general peace that he himself, his chancellor Gattinara and some of his Spanish advisers had propagated for several years. Hence the crucial differences in Charles's argument were not necessarily the result of hypocrisy or purposeful lying. Instead, they can be derived from Charles's awareness that mutually exclusive demands existed among the many population groups he was trying to 'pacify'.

This reading can be confirmed by a memorandum that Gattinara drew up on the imperial titles for Charles at the turn of 1530, that is, before the imperial coronation eventually took place.[59] All styles were to identify Charles as 'By divine clemency King of the Romans and Emperor Elect, *semper augustus*.'[60] This part of the title reflected the fact that Charles had been elected and crowned king of the Romans in 1519 and 1520 but could not bear the title of emperor of the Romans by divine grace before his coronation. Gattinara then proceeded to propose the use of four different styles by the chancelleries for Aragon, Castile, the German-speaking areas as well as Burgundy, Flanders and the French-speaking areas. The styles for Aragon and Castile featured Charles together with his mother Juana as joint rulers in the following form (the originals are in Latin for Aragon and in Castilian for Castile): 'Charles, by divine clemency King of the Romans and Emperor Elect, *semper augustus*, and Juana, his mother, and the same Charles, her firstborn son, by the same grace, kings, etc.' and: 'Charles, by divine grace King of the Romans and future Emperor, *semper augustus*, Juana, his mother, and the same Charles, by the same grace, Kings of Castile, etc.' The clumsy formulations show the importance given to Juana's position as joint ruler. But Gattinara was not only willing to keep the Spanish kingdoms separate but also granted Juana the position of a joint ruler over Aragon as well as Castile, even though Charles had succeeded in Aragon alone and in his own right.

For the German-speaking lands, Gattinara proposed the following phrase (the original is in Latin): 'Charles, by divine clemency King of the Romans, future Emperor, *semper augustus*, King of the Spaniards, Two Sicilies, Jerusalem, the Baleares, Canaries, the Indian islands and islands and firm lands in the Ocean Sea, Archduke of Austria, Duke of Burgundy, etc.' Finally, the style for Burgundy and the adjacent lands was to take the following form (the original is in French): 'Charles, by divine clemency King of the Romans, Emperor Elect, *semper augustus*, King of the Spaniards, of the Two Sicilies, Jerusalem, Sardinia, Mallorca, Corsica, the Canaries, the Indian islands and the firm lands of the Ocean Sea, Archduke of Austria, Duke of Burgundy, etc.'

Gattinara seems to have taken for granted that the constitutional niceties of the Spanish kingdoms were of no significance outside the Iberian peninsula and thus awarded to Charles the then non-existent title of 'King of the Spaniards', in which reference was made to population groups rather than to territories. With regard to other areas Gattinara gave preference to more detail in the styles for the German and the Burgundian chancelleries. The German chancellery was to specify the Spanish overseas dependencies, including islands in the Mediterranean Sea and the island worlds that Columbus and Magellan had visited. In these cases, emphasis lay on territories rather than population groups. It is also noteworthy that Gattinara placed the same chancellery in control over Charles's German- and Italian-speaking subjects and thereby made reference to the territorial extension of the Roman Empire over areas north as well as south of the Alps. The style created for the Burgundian chancellery followed that for the German one, except that the islands of Sardinia, Corsica and Mallorca received specific mention only in the style for the Burgundian chancellery.

There is a dramatic lack of concern for oceanic islands and solid lands in Gattinara's title programme. They featured as mere dependencies to the Spanish kingdoms, on the same footing as the islands in the western Mediterranean Sea. They ranked far behind Jerusalem, which appeared as a subsidiary to the kingdom of the Two Sicilies in the tradition going back to Emperor Frederick II in the thirteenth century. Neither Charles's overseas dependencies nor his extravagant claim to rule over Jerusalem were associated with the empire. The population groups and territories over which Charles was made to rule appeared in arrays of names to which the empire was prefixed as an additional item. The programme anticipated that Charles was to receive the imperial crown as one precious jewel but not the symbol of the whole. The peoples and lands whose ruler Charles was styled as remained diverse. Population groups articulated demands to their ruler that were widely different from each other and often mutually exclusive. Balancing these demands against each other was an art in itself. Using these multifarious peoples and lands as the platform for more

124

far-reaching strategies towards the accomplishment of unity in Christendom and the provision of a general peace was an impossible task.

By 1530 Charles seemed to have obtained insight into the complexity of his duties as he used the imagery of a ruler torn back and forth between conflicting obligations. His way out of the dilemma was to address different messages to different audiences while trying to satisfy a minimum of demands. His conception of power as a personal gift lured him into contest with his peers in England and France whom he tried to impress with rights and titles rather than with military might. When he had to use armed forces in battle he took a cautious approach, to say the least, and laid the burden of the defence of Vienna and Hungary against Ottoman Turkish armies on his brother's shoulders. In this world of seeming uncertainties the potential for stability rested no longer in the supreme power of the universal ruler but in the maintenance of the balance between the powers of various rulers.

FIVE

Defence of the Realms: European Wars, Spanish and New World Affairs (1530–48)

THE WARRING EMPEROR

War can be an appropriate means to increase a ruler's honour. At least, this is what Charles expected, in return for the ruler's capability to provide the necessary funds, propagate a morally defensible war aim and return victorious from the battlefield.[1] Indeed, imperial and Spanish armies operated on many battlefields, and, in 1528, Charles could still claim that he had never lost a battle. But did the emperor's honour increase? What, after all, was honour? And how could it be measured? Within a long tradition that lasted from the late Middle Ages to the early eighteenth century, these questions were of relevance for many people, not merely rulers.

Defining honour

First and foremost, honour was important in business. An artisan or a merchant, being publicly disgraced, faced serious difficulty in attracting customers. Honour, like power, could be regarded as a personal gift that determined social status, economic capabilities and political influence. It could also be a legal term. Law suits are on record in which individuals sued government institutions for unjustified or excessive public disgrace, that is, the government-enforced reduction of a person's honour.[2] At the level of rulership honour mattered as a factor of legitimacy in domestic respects and as an ideological ferment of alliance- and war-making capability in the relations among rulers.

There are a considerable number of references to honour in policy statements by Charles or in his name. They begin with his reflections at the turn of 1525, when the emperor provided a record of his anxiety that he had not yet accomplished anything adding to his honour.[3] Moreover, the report on his address to his Spanish advisers in 1528 let Charles say that he had only fought wars defensively for the restoration of his seemingly rightful property.[4] The report suggests that Charles considered it disgraceful to allow the alienation of rights and titles to rule that he could claim to have inherited from his ancestors. It also implies that Charles considered it mandatory to acquire additional honour through his own presence on the battlefield or at places where important decisions were to be made. He restated this view in the testament of 1543 when he explained to his son Philip that he needed to be physically present in the empire to be able to add to his honour.[5]

The defensiveness of Charles's declared war aims connects well with his lack of interest in the Spanish overseas dependencies. Charles cared little about the influx of mineral resources that were robbed from American gold and silver mines. Even though they contributed substantively to Spanish revenues and thus allowed him to conduct military campaigns in Europe and in the Mediterranean Sea, he never gave a more prominent place in his official titles to the Spanish American dependencies than the one that Gattinara had proposed in 1530. Charles thus retained the geographical terminology of the 'islands and firm lands' of Columbus's voyages. More importantly, he refused to implement Cortés's advice that he should regard the Spanish American dependencies as more significant than the German-speaking realms. Charles did not display more lasting concerns about the South Pacific where Magellan's expedition had sought to promote Spanish interests. In 1523 he gave a promise to the Castilian Cortes that he would never accept an agreement that waived Spanish rights in the South Pacific, and he repeated the pledge in 1525. But the Spanish penetration into these waterways provoked Portuguese objections that were based on the Tordesillas treaty. This treaty regulated access to the island worlds that Columbus had visited and not to the waters off the Asian coast. Hence new negotiations became inevitable in the aftermath of the Magellan expedition. Both sides agreed to organise a joint expedition but did not succeed in sending it out. By 1527 Charles was ready to accept a deal according to which the Spanish side withdrew from the Spice Islands in return for a Portuguese compensation of 350,000 guilders. Charles was eager to invest the money into the Italian campaign that was under preparation. The treaty of Saragossa of 1529 confirmed the agreement through the establishment of another line that divided the Portuguese and Spanish zones of influence in the Pacific east of the group of islands now known as the Philippines.[6] Despite his previous pledges to the contrary he persuaded the Castilian Cortes to accept the deal by including the option of repurchasing the islands through the repayment of the compensation. For about twenty years Castilian merchants repeatedly submitted proposals for the repurchase. Charles ignored them and eventually, in 1548, prohibited further submissions on this matter.[7] The Spanish overseas expansion thus added to the Spanish coffers but not to the emperor's honour.

Throughout the 1530s and 1540s Charles consistently referred to honour in his campaigns against Francis I. For example, in 1535, when the emperor and the French king were engaged in a public controversy over dynastic projects, Charles described himself as an honourable ruler acting with restraint towards the king of France, while he denounced his counterpart as a liar and an unreliable partner with the habit of breaking treaties. He repeated that he was not developing offensive strategies against anyone but was merely driven by his desire to keep together his heritage.[8] Charles's Spanish advisers agreed in 1536. There was talk then about a possible French invasion of the Iberian peninsula, and Charles was given to understand that the successful defence of his Spanish realms would add to his honour.[9] But the advisers also argued that it was more urgent and simultaneously more honourable for the king to restore peace with Francis. If Francis were to invade the Iberian peninsula after the conclusion of the peace, everyone would condemn the action as disgraceful and side with Charles.[10]

The imperial coronation

Not merely warfare, but also ceremonies played their role as factors of honour, and it is in this context that the imperial coronation obtained its paramount importance for Charles. Receiving the imperial regalia not only added to the emperor's power but also promoted their holder to the highest level of honour. However, it was difficult to stage the imperial coronation outside the Italian realms, and the Italian peninsula was a difficult terrain when Charles arrived there in 1529. Ferdinand, who resented the expedition anyway, urged him to proceed to the German-speaking areas as soon as possible. Charles gave in to Ferdinand's plea. On 21 January 1530 he issued an invitation for an imperial diet to be convened at Augsburg in June of the same year. As Charles was expected to be present at the opening ceremony, time was running out for him. But political bickering about the distribution of power kept the emperor in the peninsula. After the battle of Pavia in 1525 Charles had been invested with the duchy of Milan, much to Gattinara's dismay. The chancellor took the view that locals should rule the Italian principalities and was thus concerned that Charles's investiture over Milan might trigger anti-Habsburg sentiment. He urged Charles to restore Francis II Sforza as duke, who had held this office since 1521. Eventually, Charles gave in to Gattinara's pleas and invested Francis as duke in 1529. Another trouble spot was Florence. Clement VII, a member of the Medici family, was eager to advance his dynastic interests and to add to his power as a territorial ruler. His first and foremost goal was the restitution of the Medici family as rulers over Florence, from where they had been driven out in 1527. Clement VII could request support on dynastic grounds because Charles's daughter Margaret was pledged to the pope's nephew Alessandro de' Medici. The pope insisted that he would proceed with the coronation only if Charles helped restore the Medici to power in Florence. Moreover, in the eternal city, the bad memories of the Sack of Rome lingered on, and the calamity continued to be associated with the emperor's name. Charles agreed to place Florence under siege until its citizens accepted Alessandro's return. Next to Florence, Venice posed problems. The republic was a trading state with firm interests in the eastern Mediterranean Sea and western Asia and was thus focused on maintaining good relations with the Ottoman Turkish Empire. They continued to do so while Turkish armed forces advanced westwards to the Mediterranean Sea and northwards through the Balkans. Venice was thus useless as Charles's partner in a crusade and a potential ally for Francis I in diplomatic negotiations with the sultan. To neutralise Venice's pro-French inclinations its most formidable rival Genoa switched from a pro-French to a pro-imperial position in 1528. Charles welcomed the move because it reduced the French grip on the northern part of the peninsula. Further to the south, Charles had done little to consolidate his position in the kingdom of the Two Sicilies. The pope continued to hold suzerainty rights over Sicily. Charles believed that government in the kingdom was in disarray because his subjects there often had to make tough choices between being loyal to their immediate lord and following their ultimate suzerain. To accomplish his coronation Charles was bound to be on good terms with the pope about Sicilian policies. But Charles needed the pope not only for the coronation. Other urgent matters required his cooperation. There was Henry VIII's divorce and a variety of papal privileges that Charles hoped to obtain. Thus, plenty of issues were to be resolved in the negotiations between Charles and Clement VII during their stay at Bologna, before the imperial coronation ceremony could be performed.

Surprisingly little record is extant about these negotiations, which continued from autumn 1529 to spring 1530. A note that Charles may have written himself specifies merely two issues, namely Henry's divorce and the papal edicts. Other sources reveal that the place and the procedure of the coronation also featured in the debates, as did the papal request for imperial assistance in the Florentine conundrums. Clement was willing to proceed with the coronation directly at Bologna. But he was unwilling to act strongly against Henry VIII. For lack of time and resources Charles had to accept the conditions that the pope was setting. The date for the coronation was fixed for 24 February 1530, Charles's birthday, while Florence continued to be under siege. He ignored Gattinara's plea that he should receive the crown in Rome, as Lutherans might call into question the legitimacy of an imperial coronation outside the Eternal City.[11] Charles also gave up his plan to visit Naples and to establish 'good government' in the kingdom of the Two Sicilies.

An instructive document on the coronation ceremony is extant in the form of a print that shows the pope with the emperor in a procession on horseback after the coronation (Plate 9). The artist was Nicolaus Hogenberg, a Flemish woodcutter and copperplate engraver who worked for Margaret's court. The picture shows the two rulers on horseback under a baldachin carried by four men, in front of a crowd of warriors with halberds. Clement VII wears the papal tiara and Charles the imperial crown. The pope rides on the emperor's right side. Although the emperor appears in the front of the picture, the pope's horse takes a slight lead of little more than a nose length ahead of the emperor's horse. The pope thus turns left and looks back at the emperor. The pope's head is shown slightly higher than the emperor's and the tall tiara confers upon the pope an imposing stature that dominates the central part of the picture. Behind the pope Charles appears smaller and in a more delicate shape. Hogenberg, who belonged to Charles's party, placed the pope at a higher level than the emperor, thereby following the convention of medieval coronation pictures. These pictures commonly ranked the crowning bishop as the central figure and master of the ceremony above the ruler being crowned. As the picture cannot be classed as a piece of papal propaganda it must be accepted as an illustration of the public opinion prevailing at the time that the pope continued to play a central role in the making of an emperor. Charles seems to have approved of the view even if he may not have liked it.

What mattered to Charles was not the ceremony but its result, namely that now he was crowned emperor by divine grace. Hastily he made preparations for departure even before Florence fell and the Medici returned to the city on 12 August 1530. In March 1530 he was on his way from Bologna via Mantua, Rovereto and Trento to Innsbruck. Gattinara continued to accompany the emperor, although with waning energy. In bringing the emperor to the Italian peninsula, setting the stage for the coronation and boosting Charles's honour as the bringer of peace, he had accomplished his most important tasks. Gattinara died at Innsbruck on 5 June 1530. Not much later, on 1 December 1530, Aunt Margaret's life of dynastic obligations ended. Charles lost his two most influential and loyal senior advisers. He did not appoint a successor to Gattinara but called upon his sister Mary, widowed queen of Hungary, to succeed Margaret as regent for the Netherlands. She proved to be Charles's best choice, his most reliable lieutenant right down to her death in 1558.

Clashes with Lutherans and Muslims

At the Augsburg imperial diet Charles hoped to be able to subdue the 'Lutheran heresy' through his honour and the power of his personal presence and, if this strategy should fail, through the forces that he kept under arms south of the Alps. Moreover, the other urgent matter to be accomplished at the diet was Ferdinand's election as king of the Romans and heir apparent to Charles in the empire. On 20 June 1530 Charles opened the diet with an ardent plea for the unity of Christendom, but soon encountered massive resistance from the side of the Lutherans. Ignoring Charles's display of personal power, Lutheran estates used the diet as the platform to reveal their own 'Confession' of belief and thereby converted the diet into a forum for discussion about the fundamentals of religious doctrine.[12] Charles was not prepared for a debate about theological matters. At the end of his wits, he played with the idea of mobilising his Italian armed forces.[13] But before he could take serious action Charles decided to move on to the Netherlands. Early in 1531, the Electoral College gave in to Charles's pressure and elected Ferdinand as king of the Romans. Nevertheless, the election itself was far from smooth and found full acceptance only in 1534 when agreement was reached that the electors were free to choose anyone as king of the Romans during the lifetime of the emperor. Moreover, Ferdinand's election added to the growing resentment among Catholics and Lutherans against the emperor. The duke of Bavaria (a Catholic), the landgrave of Hesse (a Lutheran) and the duke of Saxony (a Lutheran) formed an alliance calling into question the legitimacy of Ferdinand's election. It accomplished little and Charles ignored it. But it set a precedent for further alliances between Catholic and Lutheran imperial estates against the emperor.

From Brussels Charles dispatched a decree establishing Ferdinand's rights and duties as king of the Romans. Charles gave to his brother wide-ranging control over the internal affairs of the imperial estates, such as jurisdiction, the rights of granting privileges and giving out imperial fiefs. But Ferdinand had to consult with and seek approval from his brother on all matters relevant to the empire as a whole, specifically the formation of alliances. Charles had no intention of completely renouncing control over the empire. He allowed a bureaucracy to develop over which Ferdinand held sway. But he insisted that Ferdinand's decrees were to be issued 'through us, Ferdinand, Roman King, in lieu of the Emperor'.[14]

Having had to realise that the 'Lutheran heresy' could not be suppressed by a manifestation of the emperor's honour and power, Charles cut short his stay in the German-speaking areas and the Netherlands. As early as 1532 he was back in Bologna attempting to arrange matters with the pope that had been left unsettled during the previous meeting. The pope joined Charles for another series of discussions which, Charles insisted, established the foundation for peace in the Italian peninsula. But Isabel, his regent for the Spanish kingdoms during his absence, pressed him to return as early as possible. Charles postponed his visit to Naples and proceeded directly to Barcelona.

In fact Charles did not really succeed in imposing a settlement in the Italian peninsula. In spring 1533 Francis I had convinced himself that Charles was sufficiently remote from the empire and the Italian peninsula to allow an initiative towards the revision of the Ladies' Peace. On 12 May 1533 Francis proposed a meeting with the pope. Receiving intelligence about the French proposal, Charles responded with concern about the stability of his arrangements of Italian affairs but found no means of preventing the meeting.[15] Indeed the meeting took place, paved the way for a *rapprochement* between the pope and the French king and led to the marriage of Henry, Francis's son and heir apparent, with the pope's niece Catherine de' Medici in 1533. Moreover, it soon transpired that Francis intended to exploit the confessional controversy in the German-speaking areas for his own advantage. In a statement addressed to Charles, perhaps in the summer of 1534, Francis demanded the investiture of one of his children with the duchy of Milan in return for his agreement to the marriage of his remaining son with one of the emperor's daughters. Francis claimed the duchy with the argument that Charles had alienated ancient French rights in 1529 when restoring Francis II Sforza as duke. In a further statement, addressed to the imperial estates on 25 February 1535, Francis added the argument that the emperor had failed to deal appropriately with the Ottoman Turkish Empire and was thus incapable of defending the Roman Empire and performing his duties as a crusading leader. Francis went on to proclaim himself as the true defender of Christendom and declared his determination to lead an armed force against the sultan. He announced that he had turned down Turkish proposals for peace negotiations and that Henry VIII had agreed to join the campaign. Francis thus mobilised Lutheran anti-Muslim radicalism to portray himself as the veritable defender of Christendom and the most suitable crusading leader. In Francis's propaganda, Charles appeared as a feeble warmonger.[16]

Charles did not respond directly to this attack against the core foundations of his quest for leadership in Christendom but dispatched Adrian of Croy, count of Roeulx, as a special envoy to the empire with the task of immunising the imperial estates against the effects of Francis's propaganda. He instructed Adrian to denounce the French king as a ruler without honour who was telling lies and breaking treaties. He also asked Adrian to underline that he, Charles, was and remained the foremost defender of Christendom against the Ottoman Turkish Empire, and that he had sacrificed his own dynastic rights, that is, part of his honour, to promote peace and unity among Christian rulers. This was an implicit reference to the Ladies' Peace and the restoration of Francis II Sforza as duke of Milan. At the same time, Charles urged Lutherans to settle their disputes with the pope and join the united front against the sultan's armed forces.[17]

The propaganda war put on record that the Lutherans were gaining political power in the contest between Charles and Francis I for leadership in Christendom. Francis strove to alienate them from the emperor so as to weaken Charles's power base in the empire. Charles counteracted with a plea for loyalty and unity under his leadership. Charles could only hope to succeed if he soon received the chance of demonstrating his leadership through manifest action.

Charles was lucky. In August 1534 Muley Hassan, Hafsid ruler of Tunis, appeared in the Italian peninsula while the French–Habsburg propaganda war was going on, and appealed for help because he had been ousted from his city.[18] Charles seized the opportunity and decided to lead a campaign to conquer Tunis. The details of the campaign will be described in the following chapter but it is important to note here that Charles gained an unexpected victory at Tunis in the summer of 1535 and could thereby aggrandise his honour as a successful defender of Christendom. He decided to use his boosted honour for what he may have intended as the definitive strike against Francis. His Italian army invaded Provence in 1536 to teach Francis a lesson. But while Charles returned to Spain in triumph, the advance of his armed forces stopped and considerations about another peace arrangement began. Charles eventually accepted the proposal of his Spanish advisers to negotiate a ten-year truce under the mediation of the new pope Paul III, who had succeeded Clement VII in 1534. The negotiations took place at Nice in 1538 and led to new marriage projects. Charles gave his widowed illegitimate daughter Margaret to the pope's grandson Ottavio Farnese, Duke of Parma; agreed to marry Ferdinand's second daughter to Francis's son, and accepted the surrender of the duchy of Milan to the latter couple after the conclusion of the marriage. The duchy was vacant once again after Francis II Sforza had died suddenly on 24 October 1535. Charles forced his brother to accept the deal in order to boost the emperor's position as the leader of Christendom.[19]

Through its restoration of French control over Milan with the explicit support of the pope, the truce of Nice revised an essential part of the Ladies' Peace of 1529. It recognised Charles's aggression against France as a complete failure and pushed the emperor back into the triumvirate of rulers. He accepted Francis's invitation to travel to France for a family reunion with the two rulers and Charles's sister Eleanor, the queen of France. The meeting took place at Aigues-Mortes in Provence and helped restore cordial relations between the two rulers. At the end of 1538 Charles returned to his Spanish realms in a happy mood. But his stay was short. His wife Isabel died suddenly in 1539 after having given birth to her seventh child. As a widower Charles displayed declining interest in his Spanish kingdoms and in the same year, 1539, followed another invitation by Francis I to pass through France on his way to the Netherlands. The provinces were in uproar after protest in the city of Ghent threatened to spill over into neighbouring Flanders. Francis promised to be a good host despite ill health. Indeed, Charles enjoyed the journey and praised Francis for his hospitality. Relations between the two rulers remained cordial during the forthcoming four years, as Francis did not support the rebels in Ghent. Returning from the empire (where he presided over the imperial diet at Ratisbon) to his Spanish realms in 1541, Charles remained restless and decided to further advance his honour as the defender of Christendom by launching an expedition against Muslims operating in the Mediterranean Sea. Another armada was dispatched to the North African coast, this time composed of a Spanish force, because Muslim sailors were accused of jeopardising Spanish trade in the Mediterranean Sea from their base at Algiers. Charles joined the expedition hoping to return with the alleged pirates dead or imprisoned. But poor preparations and bad weather thwarted the attack. Charles was lucky to have a few ships saved that could take him back to his Spanish realms. The honour he had gained at Tunis was lost.

The trouble with Henry

In the meantime Henry VIII was a remote but active participant in the triumvirate. In 1531 he showed determination to separate from his wife Catherine and began to wash his dirty linen in public. He used his ambassadors to place old stories once more on the agenda of European diplomacy. His unfortunate elder brother obtained a key role in legal opinions that Henry requested from his advisers. Henry expected jurists to provide evidence for the claim that Arthur's marriage with Catherine had not been consummated due to the bridegroom's ill health. Consequently, the marriage deal between Ferdinand of Aragon and Henry VII had remained unfulfilled.[20] Hence Henry VII had not been justified in asking his son to take over the bride for the purpose of keeping the dowry in England and, as a result, the younger Henry did not have an obligation to pay back the dowry for Catherine in the event of his divorce.[21] Furthermore, Charles had not yet repaid the dowry after dissolving his betrothal with the younger Mary. Henry VIII was struggling on two fronts: the pope was reluctant to accept the divorce on theological grounds, and Charles was unwilling to agree without receiving Catherine's dowry back in his coffers. But his protests were far from threatening, for there was Henry's daughter Mary. If the pope eventually dissolved Henry's marriage, Mary was likely to be declared illegitimate and thus excluded from succession to the throne. From Charles's point of view, Henry's behaviour towards Catherine was already scandalous; but denying Mary her right of succession was anathema to the emperor because Mary continued to feature prominently in his plans for placing the Habsburg dynasty in control over England. Nevertheless, Henry was unwilling to wait longer for his male heir; he decided to act against all impediments and introduced Anne Boleyn as his new consort. Charles's ambassador in London wrote angry reports about the king's activities and ridiculed Anne as a concubine. When Anne was delivered of a daughter in 1533 the ambassador could hardly conceal his joy and reported to Charles that all the king's sorcerers, priests and medical men had been wrong in predicting the birth of a son.[22] But Charles remained calm and displayed surprisingly little interest in Henry's offspring. The pope took a similarly detached attitude. Failing to find recognition for his new heiress, Henry began to take risks. He allowed the distribution of Lutheran pamphlets in England,[23] banned Catherine and Mary from the court and forced them to live in unfavourable seclusion, hoping that the two women would return to the Spanish kingdoms. But Catherine was determined to remain loyal and decided to stay on. She accepted the *fait accompli* but continued to demand respect as queen of England until she died in 1536. Charles gave her moral support but did not try to intervene in her favour.[24] Pope Paul III eventually excommunicated Henry in 1539, after Henry had ordered the execution of Anne Boleyn.

Throughout the 1530s Charles's relations with Henry were strained but never reached the level of open enmity. Charles explicitly acknowledged his obligation to repay the dowry after dissolving his betrothal with the younger Mary, and Henry presented a record of his acts of good will in the past. Fortunately, Henry's third wife gave birth to the long-desired male heir named Edward in 1537, and the king was in good spirits. Nevertheless, he reminded Charles that he had made possible his friend's unanimous election as emperor by withdrawing from the race. Henry was thus also engaged in a quest for honour. For the purpose of establishing the equality of his and Charles's dynasties he produced a record purporting that Brennus – reportedly the Celtic conqueror of Rome in 387 BC – and Emperor Constantine were of English origin. He used these reports as a platform for the claim that the kings of England and the Roman emperors had common ancestors and that, in consequence, the Tudors were no less prestigious than the Habsburgs. Yet despite such quibbles, Henry supported Charles's bid for leadership in the struggle against the Ottoman Turkish Empire and kept his own relations with Francis below the level of a military alliance. Much to Francis's dismay, Charles and Henry were again considering the prospects of a marriage alliance in 1538, this time uniting Henry's daughter Mary with Charles's son Philip.[25] While Charles was annoyed at Henry's indirect support for the Lutherans, Henry neither joined their camp nor supported them with subsidies or political sympathies. Only on the occasion of Henry's marriage to his fourth wife, Anne of Cleves, in 1540 did Charles respond with concern because Duke William of Cleves, her brother, was one of the emperor's major foes and a supporter of the

'Lutheran heresy'. But the affair was short-lived, as Henry divorced Anne and sent her back to Cleves in the same year.

War against France resumed

In 1543 Charles and Henry were ready for a new offensive alliance against Francis I. Francis was annoyed with Charles because the emperor acted against the stipulations of the truce of Nice and invested his son Philip as duke of Milan in 1540. Francis responded by cooperating with the Ottoman Turkish Empire to accomplish the conquest of Nice, and gave subsidies to the Dutch rebel Martin van Rossem, who campaigned against Charles together with Charles of Cleves. Charles left his Spanish realms for another visit to the empire. He entrusted his Spanish kingdoms to the regency of his eldest son Philip, whom he advised to get married soon,[26] and began to look out for an opportunity to obtain new honour. Even though he had failed against the sultan's lieutenants, the Lutherans were still there to be dealt with. Philip complied and married Mary of Portugal. Charles and Henry signed a treaty preparing for the conquest of France. Charles took on the task of proceeding towards Paris from the Netherlands while Henry was to cross the Channel and approach the city from the north. Charles moved against the duke of Cleves and defeated him in 1543. But in order to strike against Francis I, Charles needed support not only from the Netherlands but also from the imperial estates. At the imperial diet of Spires in 1544, Charles requested approval of imperial wars against France and the Ottoman Turkish Empire and tried to include the pope in his alliance against France. But the pope was reluctant to join. Paul III sent his nuncio to the empire and commissioned him to request that the estates should intermediate between Charles and Francis. Charles responded in anger, saying that the pope was unfair in placing the emperor as the defender of Christendom on the same footing as the king of France, whom Charles accused of collaborating with the sultan.[27]

Despite all odds, the Spires imperial diet granted Charles funds for the recruitment of a force of some 25,000 men. The declaration of war against Francis mirrored the procedure that Francis had chosen in 1528. Following the tradition of the medieval feud, Charles cancelled all relations with France and announced his open enmity of words and deeds.[28] While Henry crossed the English Channel, Charles led his hastily assembled and poorly equipped troops into France until they reached the city of Metz and laid it under siege. But Henry's military actions were delayed because of difficulties in the preparation process, so that Francis could afford to deal with the two alliance partners one after the other. He took a defensive strategy against Charles's army while the siege of Metz continued. Lack of supplies and bad weather forced Charles to break off and end the campaign.[29] Negotiations began at Crépy and a peace treaty was signed there on 18 September 1544. The peace restored the conditions of the truce of Nice, except for Milan, which remained under Philip's rule, and stipulated new marriage arrangements. As at Nice they involved Ferdinand's sons, one of whom was to be married to Francis's daughter. Charles left it to Francis to choose between Ferdinand's first- and second-born sons. This was a surprising move because Charles had previously agreed that Ferdinand's eldest son Maximilian should marry Charles's daughter Mary.

At Crépy, both negotiating parties were in a conciliatory mood and engaged in demonstrations of goodwill. Henry VIII was informed about but not included in the treaty of Crépy. A further treaty, signed at Meudon on 19 September 1544, was kept secret as it stipulated the close cooperation between the emperor and the French against the 'Lutheran heresy' in the empire. Henry articulated his grudge about Charles's seemingly hasty conclusion of a peace, when the English campaign had not even begun. But more serious was the protest by Henry, Francis's eldest son and heir apparent. Because Milan remained under Philip's rule, Henry openly articulated his objections against the treaty of Crépy and declared it not binding for himself.[30] Henry VIII began his campaign in 1545 by focusing on Boulogne, which he laid under siege. Again Francis responded with restraint and dispatched negotiators. When the French commander of the city capitulated, Boulogne was lent to the English as security until a final settlement could be reached. This

1 Peter Paul Rubens, portrait of Charles V, 1635. (*Vienna, Akademie der bildenden Künste*)

2 *Christ Intervenes for Philip the Fair*, 1506. (*Paris, Louvre*)

3 Gold and enamel jewel showing
Charles V as king of Castile, Leon,
Granada, Aragon and Sicily. (*Vienna,
Kunsthistorisches Museum*)

4 The Habsburg
peacock,
Augsburg 1550,
with the coats-of-
arms representing
the possessions of
the Habsburg
dynasty.
(*Innsbruck,
Schloss Ambras*)

5 Hans Weiditz, broadsheet showing Charles as candidate for the imperial election, 1519. (*Vienna, Graphische Sammlung Albertina*)

6 *Field of the Cloth of Gold, 1520. (Copy of the original painting at Hampton Court Palace)*

Puluer cannitzen eysen

7 A lansquenet warrior. (*Vienna, Österreichische Nationalbibliothek, Cod.10824*)

8 Hans Holbein, the Younger, 'Lansquenet Battle'. (*Basle, Öffentliche Kunstsammlung*)

9 Nicolas Hogenberg, *Procession of Clement VII and Charles V after the imperial coronation at Bologna*, 1530. (*Vienna, Graphische Sammlung Albertina*)

CLEMENS VII PONT MAX IMP CAES CAROLVS V P F AVG

10 *Allegory of Europe*. (From Sebastian Münster, *Cosmographia*, first edn Basle, 1544)

11 Titian, *Isabel of Portugal*, wife of Charles V, 1543. (*Archiv für Kunst und Geschichte, Berlin*)

12 *Apotheosis of Charles V, c. 1593/94. (Museum Nordico, Linz, Inv-Nr 11009)*

13 Jörg Breu, the Elder, *Charles on horseback, entering the city of Augsburg,* 1530. (*Brunswick, Herzog-Anton-Ulrich-Museum*)

14 Titian, *Charles at Mühlberg,* 1548. (*Archiv fur Kunst und Geschichte Berlin*)

15 Titian, *Pope Paul III.* (*Archiv für Kunst und Geschichte Berlin*)

16 Triumphal arch for Philip II, Ghent 1549. (*Printed in* Arcus Triumphalis a S.P.Q.Gand *(Antwerp, 1549) Ghent, Universiteitsbibliotheek*)

settlement came into existence in 1546 when both sides signed a treaty at Fontainebleau on 1 August 1546 to end the war. Henry VIII argued with Charles and complained that he had not been included in the treaty of Crépy but soon accepted the state of affairs.

After years of military campaigns, the honour of the triumvirate of rulers was at a low ebb. Charles gained nothing from the Sack of Tunis, Henry had not succeeded in expanding his realm, and Francis barely managed to keep his kingdom together. Maintaining the *status quo* did not increase the rulers' honour but appeared a poor achievement after almost twenty years of diplomatic controversy and warfare. Charles received harsh criticism in the empire, which Lutherans compared to a stable with sheep under the control of their butcher.[31] Francis was ill and intended to end his life in peace. The decision to accept the *status quo* was an easy one for the English king because a new marriage arrangement was at hand that seemed to solve many long-term problems. Philip's first wife died suddenly in 1545, so that Charles could find him a new wife. The solution to almost half a century of bickering over an English–Habsburg marriage was eventually found, as Philip agreed to marry Henry's daughter Mary. The project could settle all dowry bills and opened the prospect of a Habsburg succession in England.

For a short time the old triumvirate of rulers was restored. But the once-promising rulers were now ill and ageing rapidly. Henry VIII's sixth wife watched over his final months until he died on 28 January 1547. Francis's life came to a close on 31 March 1547. With two of his rival friends gone, Charles remained as a lonely figure with the self-imposed task of dealing with the 'Lutheran heresy'.

THE QUEST FOR RULERSHIP: BUREAUCRACIES, ADVISERS AND A
TRAVELLING EMPEROR

Itinerant rulership was a common feature in the Roman Empire of the medieval Occident. Instead of obliging the subjects to proceed to a residential capital to do business with their ruler, the emperors toured their realms and visited their subjects at more or less regular intervals. Outside the empire, however, capitals emerged in the kingdoms and other polities. The dualism of decentralised itinerancy versus centralised residential capitals thus permeated the political processes and administrative structures of the late medieval and early modern Occident. Centralisation eased and even precipitated the establishment of offices with a tendency to bureaucratisation. As early as the thirteenth century, the English government under King Henry III was a nascent bureaucratic institution with specialist administrators in charge of fiscal, military and judicial affairs and expensive mechanisms for the control of its administrative staff. France and Burgundy took a similar path from the fourteenth century. High-ranking government officials were often jurists trained in Roman law at universities such as Bologna or Padua.

The trend towards bureaucratisation affected the empire as well, but only in the course of the fifteenth century, when Vienna developed into the residential capital of the Habsburg family. The trend had positive as well as negative implications for Charles's position at the helm of the empire and his many other realms. The most important asset of bureaucratisation was that it eased government *in absentia*; its most significant demerit was that it downgraded the degree of power and honour available to the ruler as his or her personal gift. Charles and his family of rulers could thus more easily claim positions of rulership in many different places than their medieval predecessors, but the effect of their activities as rulers declined. Charles was no longer an itinerant ruler in the tradition of his medieval predecessors. Instead, he journeyed back and forth between several administrative centres, such as Madrid, Rome and Brussels, as well as imperial cities such as Nuremberg, Ratisbon, Ulm and Augsburg in what today is southern Germany. His visits to Vienna were rare and brief.

Charles travelled because he felt compelled to do so. At least up to his wife's death he often postponed his departures from the Iberian peninsula; he tended to excuse himself for having to depart, once he had decided to go; he even counted his journeys and kept records of them.[32] What appears to be a pedantic attitude was in fact a common habit in the earlier sixteenth century. Even the author and scribe of an urban chronicle, the Ulm shoemaker Sebastian Fischer, meticulously recorded the number of Charles's visits to the city.[33] Travelling was thus no longer the normal obligation of rulers that it had been for medieval occidental emperors, but developed into a burden that rulers and their hosts shouldered only when necessary. Journeys continued to appear as dangerous enterprises, even though Charles was never exposed to actual threats while on the move. Yet the emperor carefully selected his routes and was worried about his safety.[34] Before taking up residence in an imperial city in southern Germany he enquired carefully about his hosts and made efforts to find accommodation in the house of a reliable Catholic inhabitant, even when the choice was limited.[35]

The nascent bureaucracies had to be in charge of specifiable population groups in well-demarcated territories. Thus bureaucratisation meant territorialisation. Territories were relatively easy to demarcate in Charles's Spanish realms, Burgundy, and the kingdoms of England and France. In these parts of Europe, territorial polities were in the making from the later Middle Ages, as were some of the Italian principalities. Yet bureaucratisation and territorialisation carried with them a dilemma for the empire. If the empire was a universal polity it could not be demarcated by spatial boundaries; and if the empire was to be bureaucratised it could no longer be universal. Charles had little scope to decide. The trend towards bureaucratisation did not stop at the empire's borders but penetrated into the imperial institutions, specifically at the level of the estates. Bureaucratisation followed the stern logic of military, fiscal and political factors over which Charles had little control.

Bureaucratising war

With respect to military organisation, the continuing long-term numerical increase in fighting forces sparked the amplification of bureaucracies. Up until the end of the thirteenth century, the standard occidental fighting force could be measured in hundreds or thousands. Thus the armies of 13,000 or so men that King Edward I of England commanded during his Scottish and Welsh campaigns were considered remarkable for their size. But when Charles led approximately 30,000 infantrymen and some 400 cavalrymen into France in 1544, contemporary commentators on the war classed the rank and file as insufficient for the accomplishment of the declared goal, namely the conquest of France.[36] The sixteenth century was an excessively war-prone period in European history, with no shortage of young men ready to risk their lives for the expectation of profits from the risky business of war. Cortés exploited their daring during his campaigns against the Aztec Empire no less than Charles in his campaigns against Tunis and Algiers. But large numbers of daring people equipped with arms were a challenge for military organisers. The Sack of Rome merely established an unnecessary and cruel record of what was self-evident, that imperfectly disciplined warrior bands could make decisions at their own discretion and act against their commanders or ignore their commands. Rulers and commanders responded by issuing a flurry of legal texts termed 'articles of war'[37] through which they tried to regulate combatant behaviour and establish discipline. But they needed bureaucracies to enforce their 'articles of war'.

These bureaucracies were expensive and a nuisance when warriors were disbanded at the end of a campaign. Disbanding warriors was a widespread practice in the sixteenth century, when armies were recruited for the purpose of a particular campaign of several weeks or months. While the state of war could continue through many years, few campaigns lasted more than a year. Yet Charles gave repeated orders not to disband armies at the end of a campaign and continued to do so even after the disaster of the Sack of Rome. He decided on this in the expectation that the men under arms could more easily be mobilised in an emergency and, more importantly, that they could serve as an instrument of political power even while they remained in garrison. Yet these decisions meant that Charles had to take into account the costs of a discipline-enforcing bureaucracy. He knew the problem but allocated the duty of controlling warriors to his commanders. But the commanders could hardly accomplish the task because they had insufficient funds either to pay for the warriors while they remained inactive, or to staff a policing bureaucracy. These nascent standing armies could only accomplish their tasks if the rulers in control of them provided the necessary funds. Moreover, technologically sophisticated weapons, such as cannon and portable firearms, were expensive and had to be stocked and provided by rulers. The provision of funds was the core problem of military organisation, as Charles was painfully aware. His many realms did not generate sufficient revenue to keep the required numbers of men under arms for the period of time that he believed to be necessary. He repeatedly complained that his plans were thwarted by lack of funds.[38] Financial shortages conditioned delays of campaigns, their premature ending, insufficient recruitment and poor equipment.

Bureaucratising the revenue collection

The demand for bureaucratising military organisation implied the bureaucratisation of the collection of revenue. In the thirteenth century merchants already understood the necessity of regular bookkeeping to ascertain the balance between debit and credit. However, even in the early sixteenth century bookkeeping did not form part of the regular business of rulers' administrations. Rulers habitually demanded revenue after rather than before making political and military decisions. The habit led to the overuse of regular revenue and, in consequence, to excessive demands for credit in the terms of loans charged by bankers or other entrepreneurs. Because the obligation to repay loans with interest was in excess of current account income, rulers were often unable to honour their debts and ruined or even indirectly expropriated their business partners. The habit had gravely negative economic consequences, and Charles's realms were no exception. In the empire, imperial diets had to approve of revenue demanded by the emperor and the estates had the duty to collect the revenue. For example, the 'Common Penny' was agreed upon as a tax by the imperial diet of Worms of 1495 to support a crusade against the Ottoman Turkish Empire.[39] But the tax was insufficient and the collection procedure clumsy. Hence the 'Common Penny' neither filled the imperial coffers nor advanced the preparations for the crusade. Therefore, additional funds had to be appropriated for specific needs, such as the defence of Vienna in 1529 or for Charles's war of 1544. The emperor thus developed a thoroughly sceptical attitude towards the financial resources of the empire and, instead, resorted to funds provided by the Netherlands, the Spanish kingdoms and private financiers. The Netherlands had a heavy tax burden to bear, although Margaret had already warned of the dangers of overtaxation in the 1520s. Her successor, Charles's sister Mary, had to face serious resistance that grew into open rebellion in 1540. The Spanish kingdoms relied for their revenue mainly on the gold and silver that was robbed from American mines. In 1522, Charles established the Consejo de la Hacienda as an agency for the control of fiscal matters. But the Hacienda proved incapable of assessing the incoming revenue and thus could not provide reliable asset calculations. In fact, Charles's Spanish administrators persistently overspent their resources and low-ranking officials often concealed the dramatically low real income figures from their superiors in the Hacienda. On occasion Charles received information that the available assets did not suffice to support his ambitious military plans. But the eventual way out of the dilemma was often to borrow from private bankers, mainly the Fugger family at Augsburg. He used them for short-term and for long-term loans. As interest rates for both types of loans had to be paid simultaneously, the interest burden could amount to 40 per cent per annum. Still Charles insisted that his honour was more important than his debt obligations. The results of his policy were undeclared public bankruptcies in the form of acute currency shortages. In these circumstances, debts could only be repaid through further loans. Creditors provided Charles with further money for the sole reason that, if they failed to give support, they would have to write off all their loans. In aggregate sums, Charles received loans of 6,406,843 guilders from 1519–31; 10,595,785 guilders from 1532–41; 11,324,555 guilders from 1542–51, and 11,043,837 guilders from 1552–6. The annual average increased from 533,903 guilders in the first period to 2,208,767 guilders during the last period.[40] Most of the growing debt burden was to be repaid from Spanish revenues, in turn drawn on the overseas mines.

But the debit was far in excess of the inflow of gold and silver from America.

Charles noticed the problem without attempting to find a solution to it. Because he ranked his honour higher than the fiscal stability of his administrations, he took no steps beyond deploring his financial constraints. Indeed, remedies would have been difficult. They would have required an efficient, effective and bureaucratic fiscal administration under the exclusive control of the emperor, king or otherwise highest-ranking territorial ruler. But none of the sixteenth-century European territorial rulers had the legitimacy and political power to enforce such a bureaucracy. Charles suffered more than any other ruler from his deficit of legitimacy and power. Not only did his own perception of power as a personal gift restrict his appreciation of the potential benefit of bureaucratising rule; what was more important was the felt necessity to travel from court to court 'to bring good government' to the subjects, enforce peace and secure titles to rule. Medieval itinerant rulers were accompanied by entourages of aristocrats and usually several clerical scribes. Their entourages were neither insignificant in size nor cheap to maintain, but they were a far cry from the demands of the sixteenth-century rulers. Charles could not afford to travel with entire bureaucracies. Instead, Gattinara joined him as a chancellor in 1529; in later years it was Nicolas Perrenot, sieur de Granvelle, chief minister in Charles's Spanish cabinet from 1530–50, and until 1539, sometimes Francisco de los Cobos as Charles's chief fiscal administrator. He thus organised his administration so as to mirror the territories under his control and left them largely uncoordinated. An administration in charge of one territory or a group of territories hardly knew what was going on elsewhere in Charles's realms. As Charles toured from court to court, the disintegration among the territorialising bureaucracies grew.

Territorialising bureaucracies

The practical problems of maintaining control over expanding bureaucracies can still be judged from the massive corpus of more than 100,000 government and private papers that bear Charles's name. Obviously, Charles was unable to take notice of all the contents of the letters, charters and treaties that bear his name. The several administrations were autonomous and could issue acts in the name of Charles as ruler, even if Charles was not physically present. Charles appeared in these acts as an abstract and remote product of court scribes rather than as a personal ruler. At most places in his many and diverse realms he was omnipresent on paper and unavailable as a person. Bureaucratic administration thus stood against Charles's quest for personal power and honour. While Charles appears to have accepted the practice of bureaucractic government, he was keen on keeping some control over the correspondence coming in from and going out to his closest relatives, namely Aunt Margaret, his brother Ferdinand, his wife Isabel, his sisters Mary and Eleanor, his son Philip, his daughter Mary and her husband Maximilian. The leading members of the Habsburg dynasty cooperated intensely throughout Charles's tenure. In his political testament of 1548 Charles advised his son to trust his nearest relatives and gave his own relations with Ferdinand, Mary and Eleanor as examples.[41] But the Spanish overseas dependencies remained exempt from Habsburg rule. Thus viceroys appointed by the Spanish government always ruled the kingdom of the Two Sicilies, as was the case with the governors of the dependencies on the other side of the Atlantic.

Beyond this inner circle of relatives Charles was most concerned with the triumvirate of rulers. First and foremost, the three rulers were tied together through bonds of kinship. By virtue of these ties Charles could perceive England and France as polities over which he intended to hold some future sway; he expected Francis I and Henry VIII to be his partners in the gradual process of the establishment of a dynastic union of Christian rulers under the emperor's leadership. Whenever Charles was angry with them, it was because, in his perception, they did not act in conformity with his expectations. But these periods of disappointment never led to irrevocable breaches of relations. The triumvirate continued to operate beyond temporary crises because the strategic bonds of kinship were tight enough to endure controversies over tactical matters and political issues. A Venetian diplomat who described the relations within the triumvirate as one of cordial hatred overstated their antagonism. Instead, kin relations and person-to-person visits underpinned the sense of cooperation within the triumvirate and helped restore amicable relations.[42]

The popes were the only rulers with whom Charles maintained personal ties outside his kin groups and the triumvirate. Because popes were normally elected at an advanced age, their tenure was usually short. Thus six popes held the Holy See while Charles was Spanish ruler. Charles established the principle of trying to maintain beneficial relations with all of them, including Clement VII, the victim of the Sack of Rome of 1527. Charles engaged in lengthy discussions with Clement VII in 1529/30 and again in 1532, and tried to sustain amicable personal relations by concluding marriages. From 1534 he proceeded along similar lines with Clement VII's successor, Paul III. Charles never travelled to meet other rulers outside the empire in his Spanish and Italian realms.

The third rank of Charles's entourage features close personal advisers and father confessors. The personal advisers were mainly of Burgundian origin or spent parts of their careers there. Charles's teacher William of Croy, sieur de Chièvres, an aristocrat from the Franche-Comté, served as Charles's chief chamberlain (chief minister) from 1515 to his death in 1521. Jean de Sauvages, a jurist born in Flanders, held the office of chancellor for Burgundy until his death in 1518. Because he was Chièvres's staunch enemy he seems to have had little direct influence on the young duke. Mercurino d'Arborio Gattinara gained experience as an administrator in Burgundy before Margaret picked him as chancellor in succession to Sauvages. The jurist Nicolas Perrenot de Granvelle came from the Franche-Comté, was of bourgeois origin and was ennobled while serving Gattinara. In 1521 he accompanied Gattinara to the Calais conference chaired by Cardinal Wolsey. He advanced to the position of Charles's chief personal adviser after Gattinara's death in 1530. His son, Antoine Perrenot de Granvelle, was trained as a court administrator in Charles's entourage before being elected bishop of Arras as a fief in 1538. He succeeded his father in 1550 and accompanied Charles during the final years. The office of the chief chamberlain declined in significance after Chièvres's death. Charles picked Henry, Count of Nassau, as successor to Chièvres but used him mainly as his emissary.

The court of the Burgundian dukes consisted mainly of aristocrats whose roles in serving the ruler were not dependent on the honours that they received from the duke or retained as family heritage. Their independence from the duke's budget exempted them from bureaucratic pressures and reduced dependence on the ruler's will. Burgundian ducal administration was thus more relational than rational, time-consuming and not always under the control of the duke. The chancellor and the chief chamberlain governed the Burgundian court, whereby the chief chamberlain had held the more influential and prestigious office under Charles the Bold and his daughter Mary. Maximilian and Margaret allowed the office to decline to the advantage of that of the chancellor. Charles terminated the tradition of both offices, as he did not appoint successors to Gattinara for Burgundy or to Henry of Nassau.

As Charles was determined to increase the effectiveness of his court administration, particularly in fiscal respects, he needed to rely on specialist office-holders who were dependent on the ruler rather than on their own fiefs and privileges. Indeed, Charles took steps to bar aristocrats from access to his entourage, gave more powers to the Indian Council that he inherited from Ferdinand of Aragon, allowed Gattinara to establish special administrative offices for Aragon and Castile in 1521, and created a State Council in 1524. Gattinara seems to have had the goal of developing the State Council as the central institution of government to which other agencies had to report as subsidiaries. Although he remained Charles's chief adviser, he failed to accomplish his goal. Instead, the State Council remained an advisory board without decision-making competence of its own. In 1526 Charles recruited five new members to the council. All of them were of Spanish origin, so that the period of overwhelming Burgundian influence in Charles's Spanish government came to an end. The next step came in 1529, when Charles appointed Francisco de los Cobos to the office of secretary of the State Council and placed him in charge of fiscal matters. Cobos was also a member of the Indian Council and, in that capacity, controlled the melting of the gold and silver coming in from America. After Gattinara's death, two chancelleries came into existence. Granvelle took charge of Burgundian, imperial and European affairs and used French in the section under his control, whereas Spanish and overseas affairs were entrusted to Cobos, who used Spanish as the language of communication.

The creation of the State Council and the other offices meant that professional administrators took over the effective government of Charles's realms. Administrative offices were no longer granted as fiefs or 'honours' to people of high rank. Instead, office-holders were recruited on the basis of merit. The ruler's court was no longer dominated by autonomous aristocrats allied with the ruler through bonds of kinship or political ties, but consisted essentially of personnel who depended on the ruler's coffers for their existence. As Burgundians, father and son Granvelle were the only major administrators who continued in their positions while Charles's court mutated from a gathering of aristocrats to a nascent bureaucratic institution.

The restructuring of Charles's court reveals the close interconnection between bureaucratisation and territorialisation. Although the Habsburgs continued to be a translocal and transnational ruling dynasty as long as Charles reigned, most of the administrators and personal advisers in Habsburg service were recruited locally. The administration of the Spanish kingdoms emerged as a territorial bureaucracy in which the few non-Spanish office-holders endured with a foreign status. Charles documented the importance of merit in his judgement about the administrators in his entourage when he wrote his secret instruction to Philip on the occasion of his departure for the empire in 1543. In the instruction Charles reviewed the achievements of his senior office-holders in the State Council and praised their competence and loyalty. He requested that Philip should trust Cobos and Granvelle, even though he displayed awareness of their motivation to enrich themselves and leave a valuable heritage to their sons.[43]

151

Bureaucratisation advanced in the empire with similar consequences, even though its complement territorialisation was more difficult to accomplish. Charles won the imperial election on a 'proto-nationalist' ticket but cared little about the administrative needs of the empire. The nucleus of a central administration for the Habsburg hereditary lands was developing in Vienna from Maximilian's time. The Aulic Council came into existence in 1527 as the supreme imperial authority, consisting of high-ranking church officials and trained jurists. Many members of the Aulic Council continued in office beyond Maximilian's death, but only two of them followed Charles to the Iberian peninsula. For the rest of Charles's reign, the council was understaffed and lacked political leverage against its rival, the imperial chancellery. Officially, the archbishop of Mainz, one of the electors, headed the institution as the arch-chancellour for the empire. From 1486 the archbishop was entitled to administer the imperial chancellery by himself or through his representative.

The chancellery was more than a scribal office for imperial charters. It was a policy-making agency for the empire as a whole, and the archbishop of Mainz held core prerogatives in the empire. Charles confirmed these prerogatives on his election in 1519. But two years later, the archbishop transferred his rights as arch-chancellor to Gattinara during periods of his absence. Because Charles was in the Spanish kingdoms during the 1520s, Gattinara was effectively in control of imperial administration. After Gattinara's death the archbishops of Mainz did not use their right of appointing their representative for the imperial chancellery, but left it to Charles to rule through imperial vice-chancellors whom he recruited. Charles's early appointees were bourgeois theologians and jurists who had already been in Maximilian's service. The jurist Nicolaus Ziegler held the office until 1527, when he was replaced by Balthasar Merklin, theologian. Ziegler was elected bishop of Hildesheim in the same year and served in both offices until his death in 1531. While Ziegler stayed in the German-speaking areas, Merklin accompanied Charles to the Spanish kingdoms. Merklin's successor was Matthias Held, a jurist who accompanied Charles during his journeys from 1532–6. Held developed a strongly anti-Lutheran sentiment and made many enemies before Charles fired him in 1541. Held's successor was Jean Naves de Messancy, an aristocrat trained in jurisprudence. Naves assisted Charles in the campaign against the Lutherans until his death in 1547. Georg Sigmund Seld, another jurist, followed Naves as Charles's senior administrator for the empire, but Granvelle opposed his promotion to the office of vice-chancellor. Seld obtained this office only in 1551, after Granvelle had died, and held it to the end of Charles's reign.

The influence of the vice-chancellors was limited to the periods when they were actually present in the empire as Charles's emissaries or when they joined him in his travelling entourage. During the periods of their absence from the empire, the imperial government took over the daily administrative work, over which Ferdinand presided from 1521. Upon Ferdinand's eventual election as king of the Romans in 1531, Charles gave up control over daily administrative matters of the empire and reserved for himself the right to decide on issues that he took to be of prime importance for his own 'honour'.[44] In an attempt to counterbalance Ferdinand's influence Charles sought to appoint vice-chancellors who had connections with the Netherlands. According to the proto-nationalist stipulations of his election promises, he had to appoint German-speaking office-holders for the empire. Seeking German-speaking administrators from the Netherlands was one way of acting in accordance with his promises and, simultaneously, appointing office-holders with closer relations to Charles than to Ferdinand. Hence, when Charles appointed vice-chancellors who had not already served in Maximilian's time, he appointed Held and Naves, both of whom were born in Luxemburg, and Seld, who was born in Augsburg but had studied law at Ingolstadt under Viglius van Zwichem from the Netherlands. Van Zwichem later became a member of the Spanish State Council.

Even though Charles recruited staff from the Netherlands to exercise some influence over imperial affairs, he could not overcome Ferdinand's towering position as man on the spot in the empire. Much as this process of terriorialisation of imperial administration occurred against Charles's will, there was little he could do against it. Under Ferdinand's sway the Vienna administration of the Habsburg hereditary lands took charge of the imperial bueauacracies. In requesting that Ferdinand should mainly draw on his own funds to conduct the wars against the Ottoman Turkish forces advancing northwards through the Balkans, Charles withdrew not only from the front line of the actual combat but also from the bureaucracies that made the wars possible. In other words, by allocating to Ferdinand the task of defending the eastern flanks of the empire, Charles unwillingly contributed to the process of territorialising Ferdinand's administration of the empire.

There were merely three ways left for Charles to manifest himself as the kin elder of the Habsburg family of rulers, the head of the Roman Empire and the ruler over a vast array of further territories. First, he could lead military campaigns and journey from court to court to oversee ongoing administrative work and 'bring good government'. Second, he could remain settled and keep up regular correspondence with the leading members of the Habsburg dynasty and the major courts in the vicinity. Third, he could dispatch his ambassadors to represent him at these courts and appoint regents at home while he was travelling. Rather than making an effort to integrate the diverse realms under his control, Charles thus could only proffer separatism. In the course of his reign Europe evolved as a world of states-in-the-making. Tossed back and forth between the Scylla of universalistic ideologies of rule and the Charybdis of territorial administrative practices, Charles hopped from bureaucracy to bureaucracy across widening gaps between his many realms.

CONCERNS FOR THE RULE OF LAW

In the early phase of their campaigns in America, the Spanish *conquistadores* drew on the crusading ideology, which they employed as the platform for the justification of the ongoing genocide of Native Americans. A population census that the colonial administration established in the 1560s[45] revealed that, at this time, there were islands in the Caribbean where not a single Native

American was alive. In other areas the number of Native Americans decreased to 20 per cent of the total population of European immigrants and Africans who were deported as slaves across the Atlantic from 1517. Some Dominican friars following Columbus as missionary priests took a strong stand against the cruelties involved in the conquest and made incessant efforts to report on the crimes that the *conquistadores* were inflicting upon Native Americans. Yet Charles did not display any moral concerns about the genocide; nor did the Indian Council take decisive steps against it until the 1540s, when it was too late. It was Cardinal Garcia Loaysa, president of the council, who responded to the arguments of the Dominican friars and set out to promulgate new legislation conceived as an instrument for the protection of Native Americans. The results of the move were the *Leyes Nuevas* (New Laws), which were promulgated in 1542. Charles enforced them in his capacity as Roman emperor.[46] Loaysa tried to prohibit the enslavement of Native Americans and to restrict further conquests. But the laws had little immediate impact because Charles revoked them in 1545.

It was questionable whether Charles had any title to legislate in the Spanish overseas dependencies in his capacity as Roman emperor. In 1536 the Dominican Francisco de Vitoria, theologian at the University of Salamanca, delivered a series of lectures on the legal status of the 'newly found Indian islands'. In the lectures he confirmed the view that Cardinal Cajetan and Erasmus of Rotterdam had taken earlier in the sixteenth century and denied universal rule to the Roman emperors.[47] Moreover, he elaborated on the late medieval just war theories and tried to apply them in his answer to the question of whether the Spanish overseas conquest was just. In agreement with Thomas Aquinas, Vitoria admitted no ground other than the restitution of previously inflicted injustice as a condition for just wars. By this standard the Spanish conquests were unjust because no Native American had previously done anything wrong to any subject of the Spanish rulers. In Vitoria's view no one had a right to subject Native Americans to harsh treatment.

Vitoria thus posited natural law as divine law as the guideline for moral action in international relations. To him natural law was the set of norms and rules that ought to be accepted as universally valid by divine will in times of war when all other rules and obligations were abrogated. In Vitoria's view, natural law overarched the legislative and decision-making competence of the governments of territorial polities and the Roman Empire, and was part of the inalterable divinely created world and thus in no need of human activity in the form of legislation. Charles took up this position only in 1548, when he made an explicit reference to the natural law tradition. In an instruction promulgated during the Augsburg imperial diet of 1548 he prohibited arbitrary treatment of Native Americans at the hands of the *conquistadores*. Nevertheless, he ordered Native Americans to live in reservations that were to be separated from the colonies of European immigrants and the settlements of African slaves. He instructed specially appointed priests to continue the mission among Native Americans and allowed the priests to tolerate Native American rules and norms to the extent that they did not militate against Catholic religious doctrine.[48]

Yet the conquests went on and with them the cruelties against Native Americans. In his grand disputation before the Indian Council at Valladolid in 1550 and 1551, Bishop Bartolomé de Las Casas took a stand against Juan Ginés de Sepúlveda, theologian and Charles's court historiographer. Sepúlveda continued to adhere to the early sixteenth-century position that Native Americans were slaves by nature. Against this formidable rival Las Casas defended his position that Native Americans ought to be protected. Las Casas argued that the Spanish conquest was unjust to the extent that it entailed enslavement and genocide but denied ever having said that it was fully unjust.[49] His opponent defended the Spanish conquest on the grounds that the *conquistadores* had done nothing wrong.[50] The council sympathised with Las Casas without intending to condemn Sepúlveda. While Charles was far away, struggling against Lutherans in the empire, the council left the issue pending, and the conquest went on. Only in 1573, when nothing was left to conquer, did Philip II declare conquests illegal.

SIX

Triumph and Showdown: The War against the Ottoman Turkish Empire and the Struggle against the Lutherans (1530–48)

TURKS AND LUTHERANS, ENEMIES OF THE EMPEROR

A Turkish army before Vienna

Faith, discipline and justice are cardinal virtues of rulers, according to the ethical theory which Charles professed at the end of his reign.[1] They were essentially the virtues that the philosophers of the Middle Stoa had propagated in Roman antiquity. Charles arranged these virtues into a peculiar sequence. Faith (*fides*) came first, thus taking priority; discipline (*continentia*) took the second rank ahead of justice (*iustitia*), which he placed at the end. He believed that faith led the ruler to sincerity and steadfastness and thus regarded faith as the essential condition of the ruler's honour. Discipline was a condition for power. The logic was as follows: if rulers were committed to act with discipline they could demand the same from their subjects. If the subjects could be induced to act with discipline they would become more ready to execute the commands of their ruler. Eventually, rulers could, in this way, gain power over their subjects. Justice at last could convey virtue upon the rulers' subjects. In summary, faith could produce honour that could give the power to rulers of bringing good government to their subjects. At the Worms imperial diet of 1521, Charles had placed on record his determination not to allow disturbances of faith. The ranking scheme of rulers' values accompanied the emperor throughout his reign, as he remained deeply devoted to the Catholic Church.

Charles was firm in pursuit of the strategic goal of suppressing the 'Lutheran heresy', even though his tactics changed from time to time. He was equally strongly opposed to the Ottoman Turkish Empire and would not give up his quest for leadership in the war against it, even though he allowed the war to be postponed again and again. Nevertheless, in the course of the 1520s, politics had forced the emperor to accept that his struggle against the 'Lutheran heresy' was interconnected with the war. Charles had to realise that he had to pacify the Lutherans within the Roman Empire before he could strike against the Ottoman Turkish Empire. Yet the first advance of Turkish armies against Vienna in 1529 encouraged Charles to redefine the enemy. In his early years he followed his grandfather's attitude. He categorised the envisaged campaigns as a crusade with the offensive goal of destroying the Ottoman Turkish Empire and equated the sultan with the devil. But from the second half of the 1530s he referred to the military measures against Turkish armies more often as a war for the purpose of defending Christendom. In Charles's new perception the sultan mutated from the alleged incarnation of the devil to a player in European and Mediterranean politics, to whom Charles ascribed the power and potential to intervene in imperial politics and the relations within the triumvirate of rulers. Throughout the 1530s Charles remained preoccupied with the war against the Ottoman Turkish Empire, whereas the suppression of the 'Lutheran heresy' had priority in the 1540s.

There were two fronts on which imperial and Habsburg armed forces were engaged in combat against Turkish armies or their auxiliaries. One was Hungary, the other North Africa. In Hungary imperial and Habsburg forces stood under Ferdinand's command and were on the defensive. After ending their siege of Vienna, Turkish troops retreated into Hungary where they dug themselves in. The sultan established his government in control over most of the medieval kingdom, except for its northern and western fringes. It was in these areas that Ferdinand and Zapolya continued to compete for the Hungarian crown, because the Hungarian aristocrats supporting Zapolya rejected Ferdinand as an alien ruler who was not much different from the sultan. Therefore it was difficult for the Habsburg contender to rely on Hungarian forces for the war against the Ottoman Turkish armies. Charles's Spanish advisers supported Ferdinand's view that the war against the Turkish armies was a combined struggle for the defence of Habsburg dynastic interests and the eastern and south-eastern borders of the empire.[2] While advancing northwards through the Balkans, Turkish armies not only posed a military threat against the empire; more importantly, their manifest actions enforced recognition of the fact that the Roman Empire was not a universal but a territorial polity, and one with shrinking boundaries at that. In short, Ottoman Turkish armies operating in the Balkans forced the emperor and his lieutenants to defend rather than to expand the empire.

However, the imperial forces were not to be underestimated. Even though Charles often left Ferdinand alone with the task of defending the empire's eastern flanks, its territorial extension remained formidable for any potential aggressor, particularly the core areas around Vienna, Prague, the southern German cities and some northern German principalities. From 1529, Suleiman the Magnificent (Charles's counterpart during most of the first half of the sixteenth century) and his field commanders became aware of the strategic and logistical problems of pushing their frontier further northwards and westwards beyond Hungary. Instead they switched to a containment strategy. But Charles refused to take notice of the change of Turkish strategy. While he was travelling in the empire during the years 1530, 1531 and 1532, his correspondence repeatedly revealed his worries about impending Turkish attacks on the empire and its Italian dependencies.[3] In his correspondence Charles urged the mobilisation of further imperial troops and insisted that the Lutherans had to give up their protest in order to allow an effective defence of the empire. The Lutherans did not have to be pressured into joining a crusade, for they were no less opposed to the Ottoman Turkish Empire than was Charles. Luther himself was a radical exponent of Protestant anti-Muslim sentiment and classed Muslims as incarnations of the devil.[4] Yet in practice, Charles's plea that the unity of the empire should have priority over the crusade allowed him to effectively postpone the crusade, to place matters of defence against Turkish armies into Ferdinand's hands and to load the defence burden on to the inhabitants of the Habsburg hereditary lands. Indeed, a Turkish army led by Suleiman set out again for a further northward advance in 1532, while Charles was travelling in the empire. It stopped at the Hungarian fortress of Güns (modern Köszeg), which it laid under siege in August 1532. An imperial army of about 100,000 men was marched to Hungary, while Suleiman ended the siege early in September and retreated southwards. Imperial troops fought skirmishes against rearguard Turkish cavalry, who were beaten and forced to retreat. More than 150 years were to pass until another Turkish army returned to Vienna.

When Charles came to Vienna on 23 September 1532 to tour the city for a few days the issue was settled, as Charles was unwilling to pursue the Turkish army through Hungary. From the end of 1532 at the latest Suleiman as well as Charles opted for the common strategy of maintaining the *status quo* on land. Imperial forces left Turkish troops unmolested and refused to cooperate with Zapolya's resistance forces. Turkish forces avoided direct confrontation with imperial troops in big battles. The strategy of maintaining the *status quo* in continental Europe was awkward for Charles. From the beginning of his imperial reign he had pledged to lead a crusade against the Ottoman Turkish Empire, in order to fulfil his duties as the defender of Christendom and to aggrandise his honour as a successful warrior. Yet if he continued to avoid battle with Turkish armies, he risked reducing his honour or even ending straightforwardly in disgrace. In his own perception, then, Charles faced the danger that his legitimacy as emperor might decline unless he could win a battle against Turkish armies or at least against an armed force that he could categorise as Turkish. But his judgement that the empire would not provide sufficient support for a crusade led him to reduce his radical anti-Muslim plans to a limited campaign that could have military success even without enforcement of imperial troops. This campaign was to take place in the Mediterranean Sea. At sea, Charles strove to revise the *status quo*. The Turkish forces operating in the southern and western Mediterranean Sea were not formidable. An imperial fleet under Andrea Doria won a skirmish against them at Patras while Suleiman was operating in Hungary. Although the Turkish navy advanced its control over the eastern Mediterranean Sea it did not appear consistently in the south and the west. Here the sultan confined himself to the exercise of some form of suzerainty over various principalities in North Africa, most notably Tunis and Algiers.

Honour regained: the Tunis expedition

In turning his attention away from Istanbul and towards the North African coasts, Charles followed advice given to him by Italian intellectuals, and he also drew on the strategy that his grandfather Ferdinand of Aragon had already pursued.[5] He focused on the security of trading routes in the western Mediterranean Sea and argued that it was in the interest of the Iberian peninsula to occupy some strongholds on the African coast in order to increase the safety of trade between Aragon and its Italian dependencies. His initial target was Algiers. When the Turkish loyalist Chaireddin Barbarossa, leader of a sizeable fleet operating in the Mediterranean Sea in support of the Turkish navy, took Algiers in 1529, Charles ordered Andrea Doria to sack the Muslim fortress of Cherchel west of Algiers. Doria succeeded. After returning from the empire to the Iberian peninsula via Bologna in 1533 Charles renewed the plans for a strike against Muslim sailors operating in the western and southern Mediterranean Sea. From the Spanish point of view their activities appeared as acts of piracy, jeopardising the trade between the kingdom of the Two Sicilies and the Spanish mainland. Charles repeatedly expressed his concerns about the safety of the seaways in the western Mediterranean Sea. But his goals were not merely defensive in this part of the world. Instead, he looked out for a weak spot allowing him to break up the Ottoman Turkish alliance system in North Africa.

In August 1534 Chaireddin Barbarossa defeated Muley Hassan, Hafsid ruler of Tunis, and forced him into exile. Muley Hassan appeared in the Italian peninsula and appealed for help.[6] Initially, Charles tried to establish friendly relations with Chaireddin. He sent an emissary offering to cede control over all of North Africa as an imperial fief if Chaireddin converted to Christianity. But Chaireddin had the emissary executed. Charles then seized the opportunity and decided to lead a campaign against Chaireddin with the intention of conquering Tunis and restoring Muley Hassan. Despite protests from his closest advisers, among them Cardinal Juan de Tavera, archbishop of Toledo, Charles insisted on leading the campaign in person, hoping to increase his honour.[7] He also overrode the reservations of his field commanders, who regarded the expedition as too risky, and quickly assembled an armada of reportedly 402 vessels to ship Spanish and Italian forces of allegedly 51,000 men to Tunis to sack the city, together with other fortresses of Chaireddin's. Indeed, the armada set sail in July 1535 and, despite the fears of sceptics, accomplished its tasks. Its cannon destroyed the maritime fortress of La Goletta outside Tunis, which allowed Charles to approach Tunis by land and sea. His warriors proved strong enough to survive the extreme summer heat in the desert outside the city, even under attack by Chaireddin's forces. Tunis fell on 21 July 1535 after a rising of the large community of its Christian inhabitants. Charles allowed Chaireddin to escape and establish himself in Algiers, while Spanish troops were plundering Tunis. Muley Hassan returned to Tunis and, even though Muley was again driven out of the place in 1543, the city remained under Spanish control until 1573. Charles attributed his victory to divine grace and returned safely to Sicily.[8] The victory boosted his honour and, perhaps even more, his power as crusader and defender of Christendom. Although Tunis was of no strategic importance for the Ottoman Turkish Empire, the Turkish navy scaled down its westward advance (Plate 10).

A tour of triumph

With the victory in his pocket Charles could eventually visit his southern Italian dependencies. He received a warm, even exuberant, welcome as a victorious and peace-bringing ruler and successful crusader. At Messina he began a tour of triumph that took him to Naples, Siena, Florence and Rome, and continued during the remaining part of the year. Each city excelled the previous one in its praise of the emperor through lavish pageantry. Citizens built triumphal arches and organised triumphal processions. At Messina, the painter Polidoro da Caravaggio designed the procession and the ephemeral architecture for the imperial triumph.[9] On one chariot there were six Moors lying in chains at the feet of an altar laden with trophies. A further chariot showed the four cardinal virtues while two angels carried two hemispheres representing heaven. The emperor stood on a revolving globe above the hemispheres. He had a crown on his head and a statue of victory in his hand. When the procession reached the cathedral, the chariot with the prisoners stopped and twenty-four angels flew down from heaven, sown thickly with stars, to pick up the trophies and take them back with them, while singing songs of praise for the emperor. These visions of a crusading emperor were repeated on the following day at holy mass. A model of the city of Constantinople hovered in the church aisle, crowned with the Turkish coat of arms. After the lecture the surprised congregation witnessed how an eagle swooped through the air, attacking the model of the city, destroying the Turkish coat of arms and replacing it with a cross.[10]

Apparently, the citizens of Messina were the first to greet Charles with the praise that his realms were so large that the sun never set on them. At Naples Charles was received as victor of a crusade, with Tunis taking the place of Istanbul, and Charles appeared as the world emperor. Charles's motto PLVS ULTRA appeared to have gained a new meaning, now expressing the southward expansion of the empire to Africa in emulation of the Roman heroes and emperors of antiquity.[11] In songs of praise and panegyric pictures Charles appeared as the reincarnation of heroes like Scipio Africanus, Julius Caesar and even the great Alexander of Macedon, while the crusaders of the Middle Ages were passed over in silence. In Rome the ancient triumphal arches of Constantine and Septimius Severus received new decorations displaying the places of Charles's victory.[12] A plethora of reports about the expedition was printed and distributed all over the empire in German and Italian,[13] presenting the emperor's victory in the most glorious of terms. The reports classed the victory as Charles's personal accomplishment and left out the news that Tunis had fallen mainly in consequence of the domestic revolt of its inhabitants against Chaireddin. The reports thus represented careful propaganda work designed to increase the emperor's honour.

The propaganda was well planned from the beginning of the campaign. Charles invited the Brussels painter Jan Vermeer to join the expedition and produce cartoons for future pictorial representations of the main events of the campaign. Eventually a series of ten large tapestries celebrated the victory. Vermeer painted the scenes in accordance with the antique traditions of imperial victory and the model provided by Duke Charles the Bold.[14] Nevertheless, Charles himself was perhaps the best propagandist of his victory, for he described the campaign at great length in his correspondence, mainly with his sister Mary. In his own reports he emphasised his qualities as a military commander who was receiving divine support by right.[15]

After the Tunis expedition, Charles's image of the ruler over Europe and Africa continued throughout the sixteenth century. Sebastian Fischer, master shoemaker and chronicler of the city's affairs, witnessed Charles's visit to Ulm in 1548 and described the formal entry into the city:

> The emperor rode to the church in the company of his Spanish lords, and two of them rode in front of him with silver-plated columns that they carried on their shoulders. I asked what the meaning of the two columns was or what their name was, and I was told that they were called *plus ultra* (that means: still further). The two columns, which were carried in front of him, refer to the columns which Emperor Hercules had erected at the end of the land of Spain where the sea is most narrow. And Hercules placed the other column (opposite to Spain) on the other side of the sea, where the other third of the world is, namely Africa, that is,

Barbary, Egypt, Ethiopia and Libya. He placed the other columns there as a reminder that no one could go any further or extend his power any further. Therefore, our emperor uses the two columns with the headline *plus ultra* (that means, still further), and extends his arm into the direction of the columns.[16]

Fischer's clumsy explanation of the emperor's motto is interesting because he did not hesitate to put on record his ignorance of its meaning. When Fischer was writing, the motto had been in use for about thirty years, had appeared in many prints and pictures, including the published versions of the decrees of imperial diets. Nevertheless, Fischer was unfamiliar with the symbolism used on the occasion of Charles's formal entry into Ulm. Moreover, his explanation made no reference to America. The pageant reflected Charles's position as an Old World ruler.

Things changed in the late sixteenth century. In the 1590s an apotheosis was painted showing Charles as the world ruler and winner of battles with divine help, in full armour, with a youthful bearded face, his mouth closed, and with his left foot stepping on an *orbiculum*, a miniature globe (Plate 12).[17] He wears a laurel wreath, symbol of eternity according to Pope Gregory I,[18] towers over carefully arrayed groups of rulers and points with his left hand towards a landscape that is identified as AFRICA DEVICTA (the completely defeated Africa). In its background the picture features two columns with the inscription PLVS VLTRA / VICTORI ORBIS ET VRBIS (still further; to the victor over the world and the city). Like the Messina pageant, the picture combines Charles's motto with the claim that his rule extended over the entire globe. Curiously, the anonymous painter revised the orientation of the picture. In placing the African continent on the emperor's left and Europe on his right, the painter positioned the south on Charles's left and the north on his right. Within this arrangement the columns at his back are positioned towards the east, that is, towards Istanbul and not towards the Atlantic, where they used to point in emblems decorating books of imperial edicts during Charles's reign.[19]

Charles ended his Italian tour with a visit to Pope Paul III and the College of Cardinals in Rome, whom he addressed in a formal meeting at Easter 1536. In the address he displayed his determination to use his recently aggrandised honour to prepare for what he propagated as the impending definitive strike against his rival, Francis I. Reportedly Charles delivered the address without notes. With apparently substantive rhetorical skill he tried to prepare the cardinals for a war with Francis I. He denounced the French king as a traitor and accused him of breaches of faith. He criticised Francis for lack of support for the Tunis expedition, which he construed as a crusade against the Ottoman Turkish Empire. He requested church backing for an attempt to liberate the Italian peninsula from allegedly disastrous French influence and concluded with the suggestion of a duel between himself and Francis.[20] The address must have been carefully prepared because printed Italian and German versions appeared shortly after its delivery. The printed version was styled according to the tradition of a fictitious dialogue between Pasquilio, a character representing a notoriously critical Roman citizen, and a cardinal. Pasquilio reported on what the emperor had said in the address, praised him for the victory at Tunis and urged the cardinal to support forthcoming military actions against the French king.[21]

While the fictitious cardinal accepted Pasquilio's plea, Charles found it difficult to rally the real-world cardinals behind him. The Catholic Church opted for a neutral position and sought to balance imperial against French power. Moreover, the cardinals were unimpressed by Charles's claim that he had struck decisively against Ottoman Turkish power. In their eyes Charles continued to face the task of leading a veritable crusade against the sultan and conquering Istanbul not merely in a pageant but in reality. Charles left Rome with empty hands to oversee another fruitless war against Francis I. The effect of his triumphs evaporated as his troops got stuck in Provence. When Charles returned to the Spanish kingdoms, Francis declared that he was willing to accept the emperor as a leader of an attack against Istanbul only on condition that he become invested with control over the duchy of Milan.[22]

166

Honour lost again: the Algiers expedition

Eventually, Charles gave in. In 1538 he agreed to Francis's demand and accepted the chance to become empowered as the field marshal of an armed force composed of troops from occidental Christendom. In the same year Venetian ambassadors at Charles's court twice reported to their government that Charles was ready to begin the campaign, and they estimated that it would take place in 1539.[23] Charles remained under pressure to intensify his war preparations and strike at the centre of the Ottoman Turkish Empire. However, instead of directly advancing to the eastern Mediterranean Sea, he tried to solidify his position as the field marshal of a crusade. To that end he journeyed through France to the empire to proffer his friendship to Francis I and make a further effort to suppress the 'Lutheran heresy'. At the Ratisbon imperial diet that met from February to June 1541 the negotiations between the emperor and the imperial estates were difficult. The estates were willing to support action against Turkish troops only on condition that the emperor respected Lutheran religious doctrine and gave safety guarantees to the Lutheran estates. Eventually, Charles accepted a compromise according to which the estates approved a campaign against Ottoman Turkish forces in Hungary with 10,000 infantrymen and 2,000 cavalry under Ferdinand's command and left the emperor on his own with his more far-reaching plans. Charles left the empire again with empty hands and was forced to rely on the Netherlands, Spanish and Italian forces and funds.

Ferdinand moved against the Turkish forces operating in Hungary but could not prevent the fall of Buda on 26 August 1541. In the meantime Charles travelled across the Alps to meet Pope Paul III. He promised to lead a direct attack against the centre of the Ottoman Turkish Empire in person and did so against Mary's urgent advice. She told her brother to stay away from such a dangerous expedition that was too costly for her and the emperor's budget.[24] In her view a strike against the sultan made sense only if a victory was likely, but she was not convinced of this. With this warning in his mind Charles returned to the Iberian peninsula where he received the news that the Turkish army had withdrawn from Buda. Without further delay he ordered the Spanish fleet to advance against Algiers, to sack the city and take Chaireddin Barbarossa prisoner. To placate his sister he projected that the sack of Algiers would put pressure on the Turkish army to retreat from the whole of Hungary.[25]

With the emperor on board, the Spanish fleet set sail in October 1541 against the advice of naval commanders, who predicted that weather conditions were unfavourable for the campaign. But Charles would not listen to them. The armada reached Algiers in good shape and managed to land the troops. Yet on 25 October 1541 about 150 ships sank in strong winds. Charles acted against the advice of his commanders once more and called off the campaign before the siege of Algiers could begin. By sheer luck, the number of ships in a decent condition of repair sufficed to carry the emperor and his remaining troops back home. Charles blamed the disaster on bad weather. Whatever the reason may have been, the result of the failed expedition was that Charles's honour reached its lowest level since the months before the battle of Pavia in 1525.[26]

The elder Granvelle encapsulated the mood of despair in a memorandum of 28 November 1541,[27] naming the emperor's most ardent enemies as the 'Lutheran heresy', the Ottoman Turkish armies and the king of France. He took the view that the imperial estates would only approve of defensive military measures under Ferdinand's command and that the emperor could not receive more than had been offered him by the Ratisbon imperial diet earlier that year. This assessment led Granvelle to warn Charles that it was neither in his interest to leave the Spanish kingdoms in support of Ferdinand's campaigns nor feasible for him to lead an undermanned, ill-financed and poorly equipped army against Istanbul. And it was uncertain whether, and if so where, the king of France would choose to resume his attacks. In this depressing situation Charles could only wait to see how his opponents chose to act. Indeed, the Lutherans and other imperial estates remained committed to supporting Ferdinand.[28] Chaireddin Barbarossa used Algiers as a base to conduct a series of attacks on Malta, Sicily and even Spanish ports like Seville. Francis remained calm for the moment, but was determined to strike again in the future.

French–Turkish diplomacy

Charles's and Francis's strategies against the Ottoman Turkish Empire differed fundamentally although they shared concern for the defence of Christendom. Whereas Charles conceived of responses towards the sultan's activities primarily in military terms, Francis preferred diplomacy. From 1528 Francis dispatched emissaries to Istanbul[29] with instructions to conclude alliances. He tried to play the Lutherans off against Charles in imperial matters or controversies over Charles's hereditary rights, and sought to use the sultan as a balancing force against what appeared to him as the emperor's quest for universal rule. Francis's diplomatic efforts received support from the government of the Republic of Venice, which was interested in maintaining beneficial relations with Muslims in the eastern Mediterranean Sea and western Asia. In 1540 the republic concluded a peace with the sultan that neutralised the Venetian fleet in combat against the Turkish navy.[30] In the summer of 1541 Charles and Francis were engaged in a dispute about the principles of policy towards the Ottoman Turkish Empire. The dispute escalated into a diplomatic row when Charles's men captured Rincon, the French emissary to the sultan, and two of his company when they were travelling on the River Po to return to Istanbul via Venice. Rincon and his company were murdered, most likely at the behest of the commander of Milan, which was then under Philip's control. Charles insisted that the commander had not known of the treachery that his men had committed, but his defence was clumsy. Rincon had been the emperor's subject before entering French service and had journeyed repeatedly to Istanbul since 1528. As late as March 1541 Charles expressed regret about the failure of imperial troops to catch Rincon and to drown or hang him.[31]

Even though Francis had already been angered by Philip's investiture as duke of Milan in 1540, he refrained from immediate revenge through military action. Instead, he confined himself to withdrawing his ambassador from Charles's court, and had the archbishop of Valencia arrested while the latter archbishop was travelling in France. The archbishop was George of Austria, one of Maximilian's illegitimate sons. Subsequently, Francis intensified his cooperation with the sultan. He allowed the Turkish navy to seek safe haven in Toulon in the winter of 1543/44, and the Turkish navy supported the operations of the French army under the duke of Enghien in the Italian peninsula in 1544. The sultan reduced the size of his fleet in the western Mediterranean Sea only in 1545, when the Turkish Empire came under attack from Persian forces operating on its eastern border. Charles could only respond to the malaise by calling Francis a traitor. He did so for the purpose of reducing the potential for alliances between Lutheran estates in the empire and the French king.

Lack of political support, financial constraints as well as his rivalry with Francis thus compelled Charles to postpone and eventually to bury his plans to prop up his honour at the expense of the Ottoman Turkish sultan. His crucial decision of 1529 to leave the defence of Vienna to his brother Ferdinand transformed the relationship between the two Habsburg rulers in the long term. Whereas Ferdinand received long-term recognition and support from the estates as the foremost defender of the empire, Charles's triumphs were short-lived and without lasting consequences. Charles was rocked back and forth between the pressure to preserve the *status quo* in his relations with the triumvirate of rulers and with the sultan on the one side and, on the other, the quest for leadership of occidental Christendom. In his memorandum of 1541 Granvelle offered comfort and advice: 'the main point is how your majesty can proceed with regard to your own person in a situation where so many issues have to be solved at the same time but at different places. It seems necessary to consider each issue one by one in accordance with its own prospects and urgencies rather than focusing only on one matter and neglect the others.'[32] This was what Charles was in fact doing during most of his reign without, however, solving any of the issues he perceived as relevant to himself. Now there were not many issues left to be solved. In spring 1543, after little more than a year of consideration, Charles decided to strike against the Lutherans.

Turning against the Lutherans

There was no doubt that the Lutherans posed a problem that Charles could no longer ignore in the 1530s. From the mid-1520s Charles had been worried that the Lutherans might become capable of protracting or obstructing his decisions as emperor and of giving his enemies leverage to intervene in the affairs of the empire. He tried to use his personal power to subdue the 'Lutheran heresy', even though it did not take priority in his political agenda. Charles took for granted that the Lutheran church organisation would cease to exist once the heretic thoughts and evil practices were eradicated. This was the logic of his response to Luther at the Worms imperial diet of 1521 and of the ensuing imperial edict banning Luther's works. For about twenty years Charles failed to recognise that the Lutherans were putting more at stake than church doctrine. In fact, Lutheranism affected three interwoven issues touching on the very foundations upon which imperial rule rested: first, the question of what constituted the 'Lutheran heresy' and who or what institution was legitimised to pass judgements on the purportedly 'heretic' character of the movement. This was the issue of due process to be followed in conflicts over doctrinal matters. It challenged the legitimacy of the positions of the emperor and the pope as supreme judges. Second, there was the question whether rulers and their subjects should have the freedom to choose their own religious doctrine. This issue referred to the organisation of the Church and put on the political agenda the problem of whether the Church had the right to enforce theological doctrine even against imperial estates. Third, there was the question of the unity of the Roman Empire, that is, whether or not the empire could exist as a Christian empire if the confessional divisions continued and how the Catholic emperor could act as the representative of those imperial subjects who had opted for the 'Lutheran heresy'. This issue concerned the imperial constitution and was of primary importance for the stability of the empire.

With regard to the first question, the pope was unacceptable as the ultimate judge because he was at the centre of the controversy.

Hence there were three principal answers to the question about the process of the resolution of the controversy on doctrinal matters. It was arguable that the emperor should have the right to pass final judgement. It was also conceivable that a church council for the empire should settle the controversy. And it was thinkable that a general church council should end the controversy. Charles opted for the first answer during the Worms imperial diet of 1521 but failed to impose his will on the contending parties. This strategy was considered viable throughout the 1520s and 1530s. In 1530, for example, his Spanish advisers recommended conducting friendly negotiations with the Lutherans with the aim of bringing them back into the united Catholic Church, but recommended using force if they failed to accept the emperor's plea.[33] At the same time, however, his father confessors, most importantly Garcia Loaysa, took a strong stand against the Lutherans and requested that Charles use his power to end their 'heresy'.[34] Both groups expected that the emperor had the willingness and the capability to end the controversy by using his own power. The second answer had already been ruled out in 1524 with the argument that the 'Lutheran heresy' posed a threat to the entire Catholic Church and that consequently, a church council only for the empire was not a solution. But Charles put this strategy back on the agenda in the 1540s, when other strategies seemed to lead nowhere. The third answer was popular from the late 1520s, not only in the emperor's entourage but also at the courts of Francis I and Henry VIII. But it had formidable opponents in the popes. From Leo X to Paul III, the popes mobilised insurmountable resistance to a general council. They were afraid of the restoration of the fifteenth-century conciliar movement that had severely reduced papal control over church administrative affairs. As the Lutheran movement grew out of dissatisfaction with and objections to the doings of popes and the papal position in the church, it was reasonable for the popes to anticipate that the Lutherans would use the requested general council as a platform for their criticisms.

None of the three strategies was easily and straightforwardly applicable. The emperor remained approachable only as long as he took a neutral position. The imperial council could help only if all participating parties regarded it as legitimate. The general council could be expected to solve the controversy only as long as the Catholic Church remained integrated as the sole ecclesiastical organisation of occidental Christendom. Charles displayed considerable skill in placating the Lutherans during the 1520s and 1530s. During this period he went to great lengths to lead the Lutherans back into the Catholic Church by peaceful means, against the strong language he had used at the Worms imperial diet. In 1526 he agreed to forestall the Worms ban and to tolerate Lutheran creeds and ritual practices until a general council could decide. He posed as a reformer himself and accepted core points of the Lutheran programme of reforms that they wanted implemented before returning to the Catholic Church. He continued to press for reforms, hoping to restore unity to Christendom. But a setback had already occurred at the imperial diet of Speyer of 1529, when the Catholic estates passed a resolution to revoke the toleration edict of 1526 and voted to enforce the Worms ban. The Lutheran estates submitted a formal protestation claiming that they had a right of self-organisation in religious matters and were henceforth nicknamed 'Protestants'.[35] The protestation of Speyer constituted the claim that, up to the meeting of the general council, territorial rulers and urban governments could decide about religious matters on behalf of their subjects, even though it was not only Lutherans who continued to regard religion as a private matter. With an eye on the ongoing northwards advance of Ottoman Turkish armies, Charles granted to the Lutherans the possibility of submitting a statement of principles underlying their creeds and ritual practices. He assured them that the statement would be considered at the next imperial diet scheduled to take place at Augsburg in 1530. Yet he insisted that it was a matter of his honour to act as the defender of the Catholic faith (Plate 13).[36]

The imperial diet of Augsburg of 1530 marked the peak of Charles's quest for a peaceful solution to the controversy over the 'Lutheran heresy'. He arrived at Augsburg as a crowned emperor with the confidence that the coronation had added to his personal power and honour and that both would help to reduce the Lutherans to subservience by peaceful means. Moreover, he was certain that he could use the shock of the Turkish siege of Vienna in the previous year as a political instrument in his campaign to persuade the estates of the necessity of ending the controversy on doctrinal matters. His argument was that the estates were putting the empire in great danger of a further attack by Ottoman Turkish armies if they failed to restore the unity of Christendom. But the strategy backfired. It gave the Lutherans the leverage to demand concessions in the controversy before they were willing to support the deployment of forces against the sultan. At Augsburg the Lutheran estates produced a lengthy document in which they explicated the theological foundation of their creeds and ritual practices with rigour and confidence. The document received the title *Confession* and obliged the Catholic estates to reply.[37] The Catholic reply became known as the *Confutation* because it was written for the purpose of refuting the Lutheran *Confession*.[38] The two documents stood thus side by side as manifestations of disagreement rather than as bridge-building instruments. Instead of solving the controversy, the Augsburg imperial diet brought to light two incompatible statements of theological doctrine. They established rival confessions, each with its own doctrinal platform. In the same year the Lutheran estates took an important further step and founded their own political and military organisation in the form of the Schmalkaldic League.

For the time being, Charles remained unimpressed by the difficulties and continued to pursue his irenic strategy. If the two confessions existed, a compromise had to be found between them. In the following year Charles released an imperial mandate at the Nuremberg imperial diet, which obliged Catholics and Lutherans to resolve their dispute peacefully within an unspecified period of time. But the mandate did not include the emperor, thereby reserving for Charles the option to use military force. Moreover, the mandate was more easily written than enforced; the Lutherans began to articulate new demands that went beyond the matters explicated in the Augsburg *Confession*. Their key new demand was related to legal matters. Since the Speyer imperial diet of 1529, the Imperial Court of Law had been reviewing cases against Lutheran estates in whose territories Catholic church property had been confiscated. The Catholic Church regarded the confiscations as illegal and sued for restitution and compensation. The Lutheran estates demanded that the Nuremberg peace mandate be extended to waive not only the deployment of military force but also resort to judicial measures. Charles refused to include the latter aspect into the mandate but added a personal statement expressing his willingness to support a suspension of the trials. But Charles read his statement out only to the Lutheran estates, which meant that it was not binding for the Catholics. Moreover, he did not explicitly ask the Imperial Court of Law to adjourn the pending trials. Nevertheless, Charles concluded the Nuremberg imperial diet with success. Although the Lutherans were not completely satisfied with the settlement, they approved of further imperial subsidies for Ferdinand's war against the Ottoman Turkish army operating in Hungary.

Lutherans promote their military and political organisation

Meanwhile, ever more imperial estates converted to Lutheranism, rival Protestant groups grew stronger in Switzerland under the leadership of Ulrich Zwingli and Heinrich Bullinger, and Henry VIII split from the Catholic Church over his divorce issue. The Lutherans received support from Henry's decision not to implement the imperial ban against Luther's works, although Pope Leo X had conferred upon Henry the title *Defensor Fidei* with the obligation to proceed against Luther and his followers.[39] Likewise, Lutheranism benefited from Scandinavian aristocrats who overthrew King Christian II and rejected Catholicism to assert their autonomy *vis-à-vis* the emperor. Lutheranism made headway in the Habsburg hereditary lands, the Spanish kingdoms and the Italian principalities. Much to the dismay of the popes and the Catholic estates, Charles's irenic approach appeared to consolidate rather than to suppress the 'Lutheran heresy'. Charles sensed that dissatisfaction with his strategy was mounting and dispatched his vice-chancellor Dr Matthias Held on a mission of investigation to the empire in 1536. Held was to find out how strong Lutheran loyalty to the emperor was and whether the king of France had serious chances of mobilising anti-Habsburg sentiment in the empire. Held was also instructed to determine the prospects for a settlement of the doctrinal controversy if it should prove to be impossible to convene a general council in the immediate future.[40]

But Held was a staunch Catholic and former judge at the Imperial Court of Law and overstretched his instructions. Instead of seeking to obtain information about political attitudes, he tried to impose a solution straight away. He produced an imperial patent saying that the Lutheran estates were obliged to attend a general council and to provide support for the emperor's war against the Ottoman Turkish Empire. While Charles tried to calm down the controversy, Held fuelled it. While Charles wanted to determine the strength of the French king's political influence in the empire, Held spoke out against the French king. Although Charles continued to act as the bringer of peace between Catholics and Lutherans, Held conveyed the impression that the emperor had made up his mind to strike against the Lutherans. In consequence of Held's mission the Lutheran estates called into question the emperor's neutrality and promoted their own organisation of the Schmalkaldic League. They had good reason to do so because, at his own discretion, Held advanced the formation of a Catholic counter-alliance against the Schmalkaldic League. Indeed, Held's counter-alliance came into existence in 1538 as the 'Catholic Confederation'. Although Charles had no knowledge of Held's plan and was not included in the alliance at its beginning, the Lutherans suspected that Held was acting on the emperor's behalf and denounced the alliance as a way of preparing for war. Held had to acknowledge the failure of his mission but blamed it on the apparent intransigence of the Lutheran estates. Trying to defend himself, he exaggerated the power of the Lutheran estates and placed them at the same level with the sultan and other enemies of the emperor: 'Turks, French, Zapolya and the Lutherans have the same honour and the same good will towards the emperor',[41] he exclaimed rhetorically, implying that, in his view, the emperor's enemies had neither honour nor good will at all.

At the time of Held's mission Charles was unwilling to risk war within the Roman Empire as he was then more concerned with France and the Ottoman Turkish Empire. Hence he agreed to a further compromise in 1539. With the exception of the doctrinal matters that were to be settled at a general council, he was now willing to give in to Lutheran demands. In his Frankfurt peace mandate of 19 April 1539 he granted the suspension of the law suits at the Imperial Court of Law, the freedom of the choice of confession, and the assurance that the mandate was valid even for estates that might convert to the 'Lutheran heresy' in the future. The assurances were subject only to the condition that the Lutheran estates agree to support Charles in his war against the Ottoman Turkish Empire and keep peace within the Roman Empire. If the Lutherans were willing not to expand the Schmalkaldic League, Charles was ready to extend the period of validity of the mandate to fifteen months. The controversy over doctrinal matters was to be settled in a formal disputation between Catholic and Lutheran theologians.[42]

The disputation convened at Hagenau in Alsace on 1 August 1539 and was later relocated to Worms. It took place under the presidency of the elder Granvelle and was ranked as a fruitful debate. But it concluded in the confirmation of the points of disagreement and referred the settlement of the controversy to a future general council. The core factors impeding an immediate settlement were the growth, diversification and radicalisation of the Protestant movement beyond its Lutheran origins in the course of the 1530s. The establishment of the Church of England with King Henry VIII as its head was of serious concern for the pope and the prime reason for Henry's excommunication by Pope Paul III. High-ranking office-holders who stayed loyal to the pope had to give up their office, most notably Cardinal Reginald Pole, archbishop of York. Pole sought the emperor's support against Henry VIII in 1539, but Charles refrained from intervening in

Henry's domestic troubles,[43] and the archbishop had to live the rest of his life in Rome. Anglican theologians were not present at the Hagenau disputation, thus demonstrating their lack of willingness to join the Lutheran camp. Consequently, an accommodation between Lutherans and Catholics would not be binding for the Church of England.

Protestant radicalism

The same obstacle applied to radical Protestant sects that organised themselves under the leadership of Jean Calvin in Geneva during the 1530s. The Calvinists developed theological doctrines that were anathema to the Catholic Church and incompatible with Lutheran creeds. For one, Calvin insisted that humans had been created too weak to have the capability of autonomous decision-making and could do nothing that had not been willed by the divinity.[44] The doctrine of predestination reduced humans to mere executors of divine will. It stood against the tradition of high and late medieval ethics whose principles Catholics and Lutherans continued to accept throughout the sixteenth century. This was formulated in the work of Peter Abelard[45] and became systematised in the writings of St Thomas Aquinas.[46] It suggested that humans should be granted the freedom to decide whether they wanted to commit themselves to good or to evil actions. Abelard and St Thomas used this doctrine in an effort to explain why humans were able to act sinfully. They argued that sinful action ought to be recognised as purposeful action and that unless humans had the freedom to do something wrong on purpose, they were unable to commit a sin. If humans had no capability of committing a sin, the doctrine of redemption was meaningless. In denying to humans the capability of autonomous decision-making, Calvin called into question the theology of redemption as one of the core Christian doctrines. Thus there was no way of accomplishing a settlement on doctrinal matters that included Calvinists.

An even more radical movement was formed by lay clerics in Switzerland in 1526, who admitted only the Bible as a source of theological doctrine, organised their own autonomous congregations, practised their own rituals and appointed their own priests. The so-called Anabaptists took control of the city of Munster in Westphalia in 1534, where they established a divine state under the exclusive control of clerics, and received sufficient political and military support to be able to stay in power for more than a year. Although the movement was local and its political organisation short-lived, Anabaptist groups continued to exist and revealed the revolutionary potential inherent in Protestantism.[47]

In view of these movements and their doings, Charles, the pope, Ferdinand and the Catholic imperial estates became ever more reluctant to seek compromise with the Lutherans. Charles's potential for acting as the supreme judge between Catholics and Lutherans evaporated and, by 1541, was exhausted. The emperor alone was incapable of subduing the 'Lutheran heresy' with his personal power, nor could Charles reintegrate the Lutherans into the Catholic Church through manifestations of his honour. As Charles's power and honour proved insufficient for the solution of the conflict, the general council remained the sole means of restoring unity to Christendom from the 1540s. Indeed, repeated assurances from the imperial side that the council would not be used as a platform for criticism of the pope eventually allowed Pope Paul III to accept the council. He agreed that the council met at Trento, the southernmost city on the territory of the Roman Empire, and invited Catholics as well as Protestants to participate. The main issue on the agenda was the 'reformation' of the Catholic Church. However, by the time the council actually had its first meeting in 1545, it was already clear that most of the Protestant clergy would stay away and ignore the council's decisions. When, in 1547, Pope Paul III transferred the council from Trento to Bologna, which was a city in the papal states, he effectively closed the door to all Protestants. At Bologna, the pope was also head of the civil government, and Protestants felt that their safety could not be guaranteed. Although the pope agreed to recall the council to Trento in 1551, its reformation decrees eventually remained valid only in the Catholic Church. The prospects for a peaceful and equitable solution of the conflict

179

between Catholics and Lutherans looked bleak when the council gathered at Trento. Widening Protestant radicalism, deepening institutionalisation of the Lutheran church organisation and increasing Catholic resilience frustrated the hope that at least Lutherans could return to a reformed Catholic Church.

Principles of Lutheran church organisation

Answers to the second question about the freedom of choice of religious doctrine added to the contentiousness of politics in the empire and, eventually, to the decline of the decision-making capability of the emperor. In establishing himself as the head of the Church of England, Henry VIII added vigour to an already established pattern of behaviour that secular rulers in the empire displayed when converting to Lutheranism. From the 1520s these rulers took the view that it was legal for them to interfere in matters of church organisation and to legislate on theological doctrine. In the aftermath of the Worms imperial diet of 1521 the elector of Saxony, acting as Luther's protector, had ignored the imperial ban and, when he tolerated Luther's frontal attacks on the pope, called into question the legitimacy of the ecclesiastical leadership of the head of the Catholic Church. At that time, however, Luther and his followers insisted that they were articulating their criticism within the still-unified Catholic Church, had no intention of breaking away from it and were simply pressing for its reformation. Yet at the end of the 1520s, when the territorial estates of Hesse, Palatinate, Württemberg and others, together with several imperial cities, joined the Lutheran camp, a separate church organisation came into existence which was drawn on the territories over which secular rulers held sway. Lutheran church organisation was thus particularistic from its very beginning and, in this capacity, stood against the universalism to which the Catholic Church continued to adhere. Lutherans then formed autonomous territorial church organisations, each confined to an imperial estate. Zwingli's and Calvin's followers in Switzerland established their organisation along the same lines. Each of the Lutheran churches appointed its own bishops and priests. The church leadership was closely interconnected with secular rulership in the Lutheran estates. The particularism of the Lutheran church organisation was beneficial for the participating secular rulers because it added to their governing powers. Luther himself developed a strong record of rigorous support for territorial rulers and instructed his followers to obey the rules and laws of their governments.[48] As he campaigned with a pro-government rhetoric against the rebels at the time of the German Peasants' War of 1524/5,[49] rulers recognised the benefit of supporting the particularism of the Lutheran church organisation.

During the 1530s Charles unwillingly added to the political strength of particularism within the empire by seeking to buy support for his and Ferdinand's campaigns against the Ottoman Turkish Empire. Henceforth, interventions in church matters seemed to increase the political benefits for rulers of imperial estates. Not only Lutherans but also Catholics understood this implication and used it against the emperor. Hence the toleration agreements of the imperial diets at Nuremberg (1532) and Frankfurt (1539) could be thrust upon the emperor and his brother by the Lutheran minority with the tacit consent of some Catholic estates, such as Bavaria. The increasing capability for autonomous decision-making of territorial rulers and urban governments became dramatically visible in their engagement with rulers outside the empire, specifically the king of France. The positions that the French king articulated in the 1530s widened the scope of policy options at the disposal of the estates that were willing to consider Francis's arguments. This was the danger that provoked Charles to dispatch his vice-chancellor Held to the empire. Whenever Charles was recognised as interfering in the domestic affairs of imperial estates, such as on the occasion of the investiture of a duke of Milan, Francis I obtained leverage to intervene in the politics of the empire and could hope to draw estates into alliances.[50] Confessions of faith did not play a decisive role in alliance-making. As a staunch defender of the Catholic Church, Francis saw no reason not to cooperate with the Lutheran estates on political matters.

Charles found no means to counteract the French impact beyond the mere contention that Francis I had a notorious record of breaking treaties and was therefore not a reliable partner. Yet in practice, Charles followed the precedent that Francis was setting. In his 1544 campaign against Francis, Charles allied himself with Landgrave Philip of Hesse, one of the leaders of the Schmalkaldic League. Likewise, Charles agreed to confer the title of 'defender of faith' upon Henry VIII in 1543, after Henry had broken with the Catholic Church. Charles did so because he wanted to form another alliance against Francis I. By the beginning of the 1540s the rulers of the Lutheran estates had gained recognition as equals with their Catholic counterparts. If Lutheran and Catholic theologians could debate doctrinal matters on an equal footing at Hagenau and Worms, the Lutherans could no longer be 'heretics'. The personal decision of the rulers of imperial estates to convert to Lutheranism came to be accepted as binding on their subjects. Even though the choice of religious confession was free, the right to make use of the freedom became restricted to the rulers.

The quest for the unity of the empire and the war against the Lutherans

The third question, concerning the unity of the empire, touched upon the imperial constitution. How could Charles combine his staunch support for the Catholic faith with his obligation to act as the representative of all imperial estates and the leader of a comprehensive occidental armed force against the Ottoman Turkish Empire? The longer the 'Lutheran heresy' lasted and the more profoundly it legalised its own particularistic organisation, the more the unity of the empire was in jeopardy. Charles's self-proclaimed position as defender of the Catholic Church did not allow him to acknowledge Lutheran particularism.[51] But if he was incapable of restoring the unity of the Church and the empire, at least he had to provide good government for the empire. To that end the Augsburg imperial diet of 1530 enforced the Imperial Policing Order which set out the principles for the appropriate government of the empire[52] and prepared for a new criminal code,[53] all in Charles's name. The doctrinal controversy between Catholics and Lutherans did not feature prominently on the agenda of the diet.

However, Ferdinand was assuming the role of the effective organiser of the defence against Ottoman Turkish armies, and Charles accomplished his victory at Tunis without imperial forces. Consequently, the emperor removed himself from the imperial agenda in the 1530s and thus could not continue to rely on his personal power if he wanted to promote unity in the empire. The failure of the Algiers expedition, when the emperor's honour was at a low ebb, not only strengthened the power of the sultan and his lieutenants; it also further reduced Charles's grip on the Lutherans. No longer could he hope to be able to rally forces behind him for a future strike against the Ottoman Turkish Empire with the simple argument that he was successful as a crusading warrior. Charles had to act for the purpose of restoring unity to the empire before he could think of more far-reaching strategic goals. In other words, the emperor had to prepare for a showdown against his domestic foes in the empire before he could hope to be able to move against the sultan. The disaster of Algiers and the effect of the Ratisbon imperial diet which appeared to have strengthened the Lutheran position occurred in the same year of 1541 and taught Charles a lesson. He convinced himself that it was necessary to terminate his irenic approach to the Lutherans and to strike forcefully against his enemies within the empire and his rivals beyond its borders.

The first ruler to feel Charles's newly grown wrath was Duke William of Cleves, brother of Henry VIII's fourth wife and a long-term ally of Francis I. Charles's sister Mary complained about the duke's activities in Gelderland and nearby areas in the Netherlands where he seemed to jeopardise Habsburg rule. Francis used Martin van Rossum as a proxy warrior and kicked off a campaign of public resistance to the emperor on the western fringes of the empire. The duke of Cleves supported the Lutherans as well as Martin van Rossum, who threatened the Netherlands militarily. Charles was ready for action in 1543. He departed from the Spanish kingdoms leaving his son Philip as his regent and rushed towards the empire, determined to end the 'Lutheran heresy' for ever.[54] Upon arriving in the Netherlands Charles assembled an army for a strike against the duke of Cleves. The campaign ended in a sweeping victory for the emperor, restored Charles's power and honour, and opened the way towards a new alliance with Henry VIII against Francis I.

Within a year of his departure from the Iberian peninsula Charles gained a position in which he could intimidate the Lutheran camp. His display of determination seemed to work. But meanwhile the general council began its meetings at Trento. Charles decided to wait and to review the council proceedings. He convened a further theological disputation and chaired the Ratisbon imperial diet of 1546 in search of tactical gains. His restored honour not only raised his spirits; it also helped improve his physical condition. For years Charles had suffered from occasional episodes of a disease that he and the medical people at his Spanish courts referred to as gout. The episodes forced him to rest and seriously impeded his movement. Yet having recovered, Charles tried to lead a ruler's normal life, enjoying lavish meals and hunting as his favourite pastime.[55] Shortly before his departure for the empire he even took part in a bullfight, not as a spectator but as a fighter. At Ratisbon, the business of the imperial diet does not seem to have been time-consuming. Charles found opportunity to have an affair with Barbara Blomberg, daughter of a wealthy Regensburg artisan. On 24 February 1547, Charles's birthday, Barbara delivered a boy who became known as Don Juan and whom Charles recognised as his illegitimate son in 1554.[56]

But the scheduled disputation did not take place. Likewise, Charles made little tactical headway as the Schmalkaldic confederates decided to move against the duke of Brunswick. Moreover, Duke Maurice of Saxony deserted the league and joined the imperial camp, due to controversies over succession in the duchy of Saxony. The Saxon ruling dynasty split into two branches at the turn of the sixteenth century, and only one branch held the electorate. Maurice belonged to the branch that was barred from electoral honours and tried to drive the Saxon elector John Frederick, his relative, out of office. He hoped that Charles would invest him with the electorate in the event that the forthcoming war against the Lutherans should end in their utter defeat. The prospects for an imperial victory looked bright as Charles even received reinforcements from the pope. John Frederick and Philip of Hesse, Charles's previous ally, were placed under an imperial ban. In 1546 the war began as a military execution of the ban.

The imperial and confederate armies marched side by side in the upper Danube Valley. Charles led the imperial army in person, while Schmalkaldic troops were under the command of Philip of Hesse and Schertlin von Burtenbach, the veteran of the Sack of Rome of 1527. Philip and Schertlin followed an offensive strategy, seeking battle with the imperial army. But Charles displayed caution and manoeuvred. A propaganda war accompanied the manoeuvres. The imperial party classed the Lutherans as heretics once again, and the Lutherans ridiculed their foe as 'the butcher of Flanders' and 'Charles of Ghent claiming to be emperor'.[57] Contemporary analysts of the campaign engaged in controversy about the wisdom of the emperor's defensive strategy, which appeared to protract the campaign instead of leading to a decision.[58] Eventually, Charles gave in to the pressure and responded positively to demands from Ferdinand and Maurice. In 1547 he instructed his army to move to Saxony as soon as possible and beat John Frederick in his home land. But in the middle of the campaign Pope Paul III decided to withdraw the papal forces and to transfer the general council from Trento to Bologna (Plate 15). Nevertheless, the imperial army marched to Saxony. Its vanguard managed to cross the River Elbe under fire from the confederates at Mühlberg, where John Frederick was waiting. Imperial and confederate forces fought a skirmish on the northern banks of the river, where John Frederick was taken prisoner on 24 April 1547. Exhausted, slightly wounded but stained with blood, he was presented to the emperor. In an improvised ceremony Charles forced John Frederick to kneel before him, pledge loyalty and ask for forgiveness. Reportedly, John Frederick displayed obedience and addressed Charles as emperor. But Charles responded by asking John Frederick why he was doing so, when he had previously sanctioned the use of the phrase 'Charles of Ghent claiming to be emperor'.[59] It is likely that this report of the emperor's arrogance is faithful because Charles continued to act without clemency. He deprived John Frederick of all titles and invested Maurice as the new elector and joint ruler of Saxony together with John Frederick's two sons. Moreover, Philip of Hesse, John Frederick's ally, was persuaded to submit himself to the emperor, who took him prisoner as well. Charles followed his advisers and spared the elector's life.[60] But John Frederick and Philip remained in the custody of the emperor, who treated them as his private property and paraded them in formal processions, such as entries into imperial cities. John Frederick became free in 1552 and died in 1554; Philip also received a pardon and was released in 1552 after another treaty was signed between Charles and the Lutherans. It was impossible for the Lutherans to accept the humiliation of their leaders and to believe that Charles was acting as a ruler with discipline and justice (Plate 14).

Although they were by no means militarily defeated, the Lutheran camp acknowledged the emperor's victory and approached him with respect. Charles was at the pinnacle of his power within the empire, and his honour was greater than ever before. He was determined to use his power and honour to terminate the 'Lutheran heresy' immediately, if necessary without involving the pope and the general council. The conditions were favourable as Ferdinand had signed a truce with the Ottoman Turkish army operating in Hungary in 1547. The next imperial diet was scheduled to meet at Augsburg in 1548. Charles put together an agenda apt to subject Lutherans to obedience, even without assistance from the pope. The diet ran on a busy schedule. It approved new rules of conduct for a reformed clergy, a general peace, statutes for the Imperial Court of Law, a revised version of the statutes for good government and a comprehensive statement of principles of faith.[61] It also promulgated a treaty with the Netherlands defining imperial rights in what was constituted as a united territory of seventeen provinces.[62]

The statement of principles of faith served as the platform of theological doctrine on which Catholics and Lutherans agreed and from which the restoration of the unity of the Catholic Church was to proceed. But it was given the character of an interim statement, which was to be valid only until the general council made the final decisions. As an interim statement it was the instrument that Charles expected to facilitate the temporary coexistence of Catholics and Lutherans until the conclusion of the general council. But it banned the followers of other Protestant creeds, namely the adherents of Zwingli's theology. As a preliminary statement of toleration of Lutheranism the text became known as the *Interim*, and Charles obliged all imperial estates to publish the statement under this title. Lutherans anticipated that tough times would return because the *Interim* was a document of imperial law and obliged Lutherans to return to the Catholic Church. When Luther closed his eyes at Wittenberg in 1546 the future of Lutheranism looked bleak for the moment.

At Mühlberg Charles gained a military victory but humiliated his enemies and soon lost the peace. One of Titian's most famous paintings was completed in 1548. It shows the emperor in full armour speeding forcefully on an armoured horse across an imagined landscape. Titian portrayed the emperor in the pose of St George, the dragon fighter and patron of the knightly order that Frederick III had founded to conduct a crusade. However, the emperor in Titian's picture is no longer fighting his crusade against the Ottoman Turkish Empire but against the Lutherans in the Roman Empire.

THE CONCEPTUALISATION OF TERRITORIAL RULE: THE CASE OF
QUEDLINBURG

There were many estates in the empire beyond Saxony, Hesse, Brunswick, the Palatinate, Bavaria, Brandenburg and Cleves. Most of them were small, some merely with village populations. The free imperial city of Wimpfen on the Neckar, for one, had only about 600 inhabitants and yet ranked as a self-governing polity like the larger territorial estates. Not only the governments of many cities but also abbots and abbesses, bishops and archbishops vigorously defended their autonomy in the face of neighbouring territorial rulers. Ecclesiastical rulers not only exercised control over their institutions in church matters, but also acted as secular rulers whereby the territories over which they held sway differed in size from the institutions over which they had ecclesiastical authority. The archbishoprics and electorates of Cologne, Mainz and Trier were by far the largest and most powerful ecclesiastical estates. But even some less powerful bishops, abbots and abbesses could have a political impact on the government of the empire. The size of territories did not necessarily matter in assessments of political power.

Territories in the empire did not have to be laid out as coherent masses of land within linear boundaries. Instead, the territory of one ruler could be – and frequently was – scattered, bringing together under the rule of the same person different population groups with heterogeneous collective identities and traditions. Thus lay aristocrats, urban governments as well as archbishops, bishops, abbots and abbesses could act as secular rulers over forests and rural farming villages as well as towns and monastic institutions. Obviously, Lutheranism affected the rule of the ecclesiastical territories most strongly. When ecclesiastical rulers converted to the 'Lutheran heresy' they not only reduced the number of religious followers of the pope but, more importantly, alienated the property of the Catholic Church. After their conversion ecclesiastical rulers could merge their territories with those of other rulers or continue as secular office-holders. On the one hand, the territory of the Teutonic Order in Prussia was eventually transferred to the control of the elector of Brandenburg, after the master of the order, Albert of Brandenburg, converted to Lutheranism in 1525. On the other hand, the tiny monastic principality of the nuns of Quedlinburg east of the Harz mountains retained its autonomy when the abbess admitted Lutheranism as the dominant confession and the monastery was converted into a female religious community in 1540. Quedlinburg continued as an imperial estate until 1803, with a seat and ballot on the bench of the Rhenish prelates of imperial diets. At this time, Quedlinburg had an area of 82 sq km and about 11,600 inhabitants.[63] At the turn of the sixteenth century, Quedlinburg's territorial size was the same, while its population may then have amounted to no more than 5,000 people. The perseverance of the convent as a principality deserves a closer look.

In 1477 Abbess Hedwig succeeded in restoring her rights to administer justice in criminal cases other than those leading to the death penalty and to exercise secular authority over the abbey, Quedlinburg Old Town, Quedlinburg New Town, the village of Ditfurt as well as a number of adjacent fields, pastures and fish ponds. The twin cities had been amalgamated administratively in 1327 but remained socially and architecturally separate. Hedwig was able to restore her power with the help of her brothers Ernst and Albert, then reigning electors of Saxony. The electors deployed an armed force of 400 cavalrymen and 200 infantrymen, conquered the cities and subdued the burghers' government. They claimed to protect the rights of their sister on behalf of Emperor Frederick III, whose sister Margaret was their mother.[64] Although Frederick III had not commissioned them to intervene in the internal relations between the abbess and the burghers, Hedwig had indeed requested military support from her brothers. She had done so by appointing them as church advocates to the abbey and its holdings. In their capacity as Quedlinburg's advocates, Ernst and Albert had the tasks of protecting the abbey and acting as judges in criminal cases where capital punishment might be involved. The electors of Saxony retained their church advocacy over Quedlinburg until 1698, when they sold it to the elector of Brandenburg. Hedwig and her successors thus paid for the support from the electors of Saxony by investing them with essential governing rights over the abbey's holdings.

The abbess was not only struggling with the burghers of the twin cities but also with the bishop of neighbouring Halberstadt in whose diocese Quedlinburg was located. Although the abbey and its holdings were exempt from episcopal control, being placed directly under the ecclesiastical jurisdiction of the pope, the bishops of Halberstadt quarrelled with the abbess about rights over lands in the vicinity of the twin cities. Hedwig's predecessors had acquired these lands in the course of the Middle Ages under circumstances that remained contested. At the turn of the sixteenth century the incumbent bishop was Ernst II, son of Elector Ernst of Saxony (1480–1513). In turn, Halberstadt lay in the archdiocese of

Magdeburg, and Ernst of Halberstadt united in his person the position of archbishop of Magdeburg (1476–1513). This union continued under Ernst's successor Albert IV, brother of Joachim I, who was elector of Brandenburg.

Ecclesiastical and secular estates in the empire were thus closely interconnected through networks of kin ties among their rulers. The emperor was thereby forced to cooperate with powerful multiple alliances of territorial rulers. While the abbess of Quedlinburg was in charge of all ecclesiastical matters, she shared secular authority over the abbey and its holdings with her advocates. The advocates had their own representatives in the cities and pursued their own interests in the relations with the bishops of Halberstadt and the archbishops of Magdeburg. As a consequence of the conquest of 1477 the burghers, who were members of the Hanseatic League until 1476, agreed to swear allegiance to the abbess and her advocates, left all leagues, revoked all alliances, paid an annual rent of 500 guilders to the abbess and the amount of 1,000 guilders as a compensation for their alleged insubordination, pledged to enforce rules only with consent of the abbess and her advocates and agreed to elect any burgher into the cities' governing council only after the abbess had approved the candidate. The cities were thus fully subjected to the territorial rule of the abbess and her advocates.[65] Moreover, the abbess exercised direct control over the residential palace of the abbey itself, two monasteries, some buildings lying outside the city walls and four courts in the Old Town. These buildings were considered to have immunity even against the advocates. Persons indicted for acts involving capital punishment and living in these buildings could not be arrested directly by the representatives of the advocates but had to be extradited by the abbess upon request.

In 1485 Ernst and Albert agreed to divide their realms. In consequence of the partition Ernst assumed the dignity of elector while Albert gained the title of duke and became the sole advocate for Quedlinburg.[66] Albert passed the advocacy to his son George, who succeeded in 1500. George of Saxony pursued more rigorously the interests of his dynasty than his father. He pressured Hedwig into subordinating herself to his secular rule. Hedwig appealed to

Pope Julius II for protection against her advocate, and the pope asked the archbishop of Magdeburg to protect the abbey. Indeed, Ernst of Magdeburg and Halberstadt tried to counterbalance his cousin George but charged his own price. He demanded that Hedwig return the lands whose ownership had been controversial. The pope confirmed Ernst's rights and imposed a ban on Hedwig. But the abbess died before the papal edict reached Quedlinburg. The convent elected Magdalen of Anhalt as Hedwig's successor, much to George's dismay. Duke George of Saxony was determined to admit only a subservient abbess at Quedlinburg. Because Magdalen's family, the house of Anhalt, was another powerful dynasty, she appeared to become a difficult partner. George's bullying techniques convinced Magdalen that Quedlinburg was the wrong place for her. She retreated to the monastery at Gandersheim where she died in 1514. George made up his mind not to tolerate another autonomous election by the Quedlinburg nuns and approached Count Botho of Stolberg in the Harz mountains, who was the court master of the archbishop of Mainz. Botho's daughter Anne was twelve years old and seemingly ready for the position of abbess at Quedlinburg. When Albert of Mainz succeeded as archbishop of Magdeburg and bishop of Halberstadt in 1514, the deal was struck. Anne was duly elected in 1515 and received her papal consecration in 1516.[67] The burghers of Quedlinburg swore loyalty to the new abbess and her advocate. Anne presided over the convent until her death in 1574.

With Luther's rise to prominence as a reformer and leader of a 'heretical' sect, politics in Quedlinburg became even more complicated. There were monasteries of Luther's Augustinian brethren in the twin cities as well as in the neighbouring towns of Eisleben, Sangerhausen and Himmelpforten (near Stolberg). The Augustininans followed their prominent brother, welcomed his reformation movement and left the monasteries one after the other. In 1523 the Augustinian monastery at Quedlinburg had only one resident, a lay brother. In the beginning of the movement, the Saxon rulers were equally well disposed to the Lutherans. Elector Frederick, Ernst's son, was Luther's protector at Worms. Likewise, George was on good terms with Luther. The two men respected each other and exchanged letters until 1519, when Luther's radicalism began to shock the duke. He had the Leipzig bookseller Herrgott decapitated for distributing Luther's writings and expelled about 800 Leipzig inhabitants who were suspected of adhering to the 'Lutheran heresy'. But George soon became aware of the fruitlessness of his sanctions. While visiting Quedlinburg in 1523 he wrote a letter to King Henry VIII, with whom he then felt united in his hatred of Luther. George asked the English king for support and warned:

> If the destructive seed is not exterminated with the sickle right in the beginning, Luther will first conquer the nations of Germany and soon the remaining nations in the Occident. Whatever direction things may take, I want to make sure that, if everything turns against the demands of the benefit of the Church, everyone can realise that I lacked capacity, not determination.[68]

Abbess Anne left it to her church advocates to take a stand against the Lutherans. In the same year, 1523, angry burghers stormed the Augustinian monastery and drove the resident Franciscans out of the cities. Worried about his daughter's safety, Count Botho of Stolberg called on Duke George for help. But George failed in his attempt to restore the two monasteries. In 1524 he censured the city council for having allowed a Lutheran preacher to visit the cities. But the Lutherans in the cities were already strong enough to mount resistance. When the German Peasants' War ravaged the areas south of the Harz mountains in spring 1525, angry crowds plundered monasteries, including those under the rule of the abbess of Quedlinburg. George requested a formal investigation, which accused the abbess of having tried to share the monasteries' property with the city council. But the accusations were weak. The duke stopped the case and apologised to the abbess for having intervened in her rights. After the imperial diets of Speyer (1529) and Augsburg (1530), the duke enforced the Catholic position and banned Lutherans. Nevertheless, the number of practitioners of the 'Lutheran heresy' grew steadily until George's death in 1539. He was succeeded by his brother Henry who, immediately upon acceding to the throne, followed his relative Elector John Frederick of Saxony and converted to Lutheranism. In 1540 Duke Henry dispatched a commission of five leading Lutherans to Quedlinburg for the purpose of promoting conversions and enforcing Lutheran theological doctrine. Abbess Anne was bitterly opposed to the work of the commission and refused to accept its presence in the cities. She even forbade the burghers to support its work. Sandwiched between their two lords and anyway leaning towards Lutheranism, the city council opted for the ducal position and implemented the decisions of the commission against the will of the abbess. The abbess then gave in and accepted Lutheranism.

Once Lutheranism had been introduced in Quedlinburg the dukes lost their interest in the advocacy and returned authority to the abbess. In 1547 the emperor confirmed the ancient privileges of the monastery and demanded that the city council be obedient to the abbess and acknowledge her rights.[69] Nevertheless, Duke Henry and his successors, the electors of Saxony and subsequently the electors of Brandenburg, did retain their privilege to approve the election of a new abbess. Upon the election of Abbess Elizabeth as Anne's successor in 1574, Elector August I of Saxony forced the new abbess to sign the promise that she would tolerate only the Augsburg Confession of 1530 and remain in the Saxon church organisation.[70]

Lutheranism thus helped promote the integrity of territorial rule as it was evolving in the course of the sixteenth century. The electors and dukes of Saxony benefited from Lutheranism and acquired the competence to interfere in the internal affairs of the Church and establish their own church organisation. They did so as secular territorial rulers in their own domains. The electoral branch of the dynasty went ahead in the early decades of the sixteenth century, and the ducal branch followed suit in 1540. The abbess of Quedlinburg suffered a temporary reduction of her rights over the abbey and its holdings. But, in the long run, Lutheranism helped the abbess to regain control over the Quedlinburg burghers, who defended their convictions successively against the duke of Saxony and the bishops of Halberstadt. When Abbess Anne eventually accepted the change she could no longer prevent anyway, she was restored to her position as the secular ruler over a population that was more thoroughly integrated and had developed a more solid collective identity as Quedlinburg burghers than ever before. Only on this condition could the abbey continue to exist as an imperial estate until 1803. Local politics at Quedlinburg were thus high politics in the empire, while Charles was fighting against the 'Lutheran heresy'. When Charles purged Elector John Frederick after his victory at Mühlberg in 1547, he transferred the office of the elector to John Frederick's cousin and rival Maurice, who was already advocate of Quedlinburg at the time. In 1547 Lutheranism was already so firmly entrenched in the lands of the new elector and incumbent advocate that the transfer of the electoral title within the Saxon ruling dynasty no longer entailed a change of the distribution of the confessions in this part of the empire. A year later, Charles had no trouble enforcing the *Interim* in Quedlinburg. Again, in this respect, Quedlinburg was peculiar. Elsewhere, namely in Magdeburg and Bremen, burghers refused to accept the *Interim* and did not restore Catholic church property. Charles classed the refusal as insubordination against the empire and responded with a ban. He ordered Maurice to execute the ban by military means. But Magdeburg and Bremen remained defiant, and Charles left the issue pending.

CHARLES AS OVERLORD OF IMPERIAL CITIES

That territorial rulers and urban governments in the empire were ready to enhance their autonomous decision-making capability *vis-à-vis* the emperor was not a surprise. That the pope strove to solidify his position among the territorial rulers in the Italian peninsula by extending his rights to exercise control over land and people in the central part of the peninsula made sense, because this strategy did not jeopardise the position of the pope as the head of the Catholic Church. But that Charles made substantive efforts to enforce his rights as a lord over cities warrants an explanation. Charles did so on several occasions with regard to cities in the

Netherlands and in the empire. Obviously, Charles as emperor needed the cities as his source of revenue. But it was a far-fetched expectation that the revenue would flow more easily if Charles subjected the cities to strict surveillance and coerced obedience by military means and ceremonial displays of power, particularly as he treated Lutheran and Catholic cities with like rigour.

Procedures were difficult and success limited. In 1540 Charles had given a dramatic example. Moved by the news of the rebellion in Ghent he rushed to Flanders to help his sister Mary subdue the protest. The situation was serious because the rising grew out of discontent about excessive taxation: much to Mary's dismay, Charles relied heavily on extraordinary taxes levied from the Flemish cities for funding his wars. On the occasion of the war between Charles and Francis in 1536 the burghers of Ghent refused to send the requested contributions. Even after Mary had signed a special truce with Francis for the Netherlands on 30 June 1537, Ghent remained defiant and ignored Mary's order to pay its share of the war costs. Even her pleas that contributions were necessary to improve defence works for the future could not change the minds of the burghers, who pointed to ancient privileges as the basis for their complaints. The matter remained unsettled, resistance unbroken. Indeed, it increased. The burghers tore to pieces the *calfvel*, the piece of parchment containing the city law that Charles had issued as duke of Burgundy in 1515. Through this dramatic action they confirmed their determination to continue the rebellion. In 1539 the rising spilt over into neighbouring Flanders, while Francis stayed calm.

Charles entered Ghent in a triumphal procession on 14 February 1540 in the company of his sister, the papal nuncio, a number of dignitaries and a military contingent. As in the times of Philip the Good, Charles the Bold and Maximilian, the 1540 entry was styled as a demonstration showing that the territorial ruler could enforce his will upon the burghers. Charles succeeded in impressing the burghers of Ghent, who tried to justify themselves. But he ignored their pleas and sentenced the leaders of the uprising to death. On 29 April 1540 he released the verdict that Ghent should lose all its rights and privileges. All public property was confiscated and the burghers had to pledge loyalty to the duke and his regent. This ceremony took place on 3 May 1540. On the following day Charles enforced a new constitution that placed the city under the direct control of his regent. A citadel was built as a lasting and visible manifestation of Charles's power.[71] The move was successful from Charles's point of view: Ghent remained calm for the rest of Mary's regency. Yet from her side, Mary took every opportunity to remind Charles of the volatility of politics in the Netherlands and the necessity of searching elsewhere for funds to finance his wars.

While there had been a long history of disagreement and conflict between Flemish cities and the territorial rulers in control of the adjacent areas from the fourteenth century, the relations between the emperor and the cities in the empire were usually less prone to conflict. For example, relations between the emperor and the imperial city of Nuremberg were amicable. Charles followed his grandfather in confirming ancient privileges to the city of Nuremberg in 1520.[72] Ferdinand visited the city on two occasions, in 1521 and 1540, while Charles received a triumphal entry in 1541.[73] Nuremberg was an important city for the emperor, not only because the imperial insignia were kept there, but also because it had a constitution that gave plenty of power to the patriarchate of wealthy traders and outlawed artisans' guilds. Christoph Scheurl von Defersdorf, a learned jurist in imperial service, professor of law at Wittenberg and legal consultant to the Nuremberg city council, described the Nuremberg constitution in 1516 as a model of stability and good government.[74] Nuremberg remained loyal to the emperor even after the 'Lutheran heresy' took root there in the 1530s. After the Ghent rebellion Charles was advised to use the Nuremberg constitution as a model for other imperial cities. Unlike Nuremberg, many imperial cities had constitutions similar to that of Ghent, admitting artisans' guilds and stipulating some form of participation for all groups of resident burghers in the government of the cities. The Nuremberg constitution served as a counter-model to these normative frameworks and was expected to prevent the rise of radicalism.[75]

In most imperial cities politics was complicated. The 'Lutheran heresy' spread rapidly in the urban landscapes of Alsace, Swabia and Franconia, and produced unstable situations in which Charles and Ferdinand faced opposition on several occasions. The establishment of the Schmalkaldic League was one of them. From the thirteenth century confederations and leagues among cities or between cities and territorial rulers (such as the Hanseatic League or various short-lived leagues among Rhenish, Swabian and Upper Italian cities) belonged to the most important means of urban diplomacy and political strategy. During the early years of Charles's imperial reign, the Swabian Confederation, established in 1488 under imperial leadership, continued to be the most important league within the empire. The Lutheran Schmalkaldic League impacted on the Swabian Confederation because Lutheranism took root in Swabian imperial cities which were members of the Swabian Confederation. In 1533 the cities of Augsburg, Nuremberg and Ulm established an alliance for mutual military assistance. The involved city councils as well as non-involved members of the Swabian Confederation understood that the tripartite alliance had been established because the concluding parties were convinced that the Swabian Confederation could not provide sufficient safety for them. Hence the alliance of 1533 was understood to foreshadow the collapse of the Swabian Confederation. This was to be expected because the existing confederation pact was to expire in the following year. Indeed, when the members of the confederation met at their regular convention in 1534, the confederation pact was not renewed. In 1536 Dr Matthias Held, Charles's vice-chancellor, toured the empire for the purpose, as he believed, of establishing a successor to the Swabian Confederation and a counterbalance to the Schmalkaldic League under the leadership of the emperor. But Held's plans failed to attract support.[76] As a result, many imperial cities opted for membership of the Schmalkaldic League after having converted to the 'Lutheran heresy'.

Charles was thus not merely losing ground in his quest for the restoration of the unity of the Church and the empire; he was also in danger of losing access to the credit markets controlled by bankers in the southern German imperial cities. But at least for the time being, he could not hope to overcome the difficulties by responding in the same way as he had done in Ghent. He had neither the military forces nor the legal title to intervene in the imperial cities as he had been able to do in the Netherlands. Hence Charles's choice of for an irenic approach to the settlement of the doctrinal controversy between Catholics and Lutherans in the course of the 1530s was also motivated by his lack of ability to impose his will on the imperial cities. If the imperial cities rose against the emperor as the burghers of Ghent had rebelled against the count of Flanders, the empire was in serious danger.

The cities responded favourably to Charles's irenic overtures and welcomed him whenever he was on the move in the empire during the 1530s. Augsburg, for one, voluntarily gave him a triumphal entry when he visited the city after having been crowned in Bologna.[77] As late as 1538 the Ulm city council joined their colleagues from Strasbourg in a pledge not to support the king of France in the ongoing campaign over Milan. Both councils agreed that an alliance with Francis was out of the question because the French king was allied with the sultan and had a strong record of breaches of earlier treaties. The city councils were also ready to implement Charles's repeated mandates that prohibited the entry of the emperor's subjects into French military service.[78] Even in 1543, when Charles visited Ulm, the burghers swore allegiance to the emperor and obliged themselves to promote the unity of the empire.[79]

But the supportive mood turned into defiance once Charles revoked his peace-preserving strategy and decided to move against the 'Lutheran heresy'. The cities felt the emperor's military pressure while he was campaigning in the Danube river valley in 1546. Many smaller members of the Schmalkaldic League, namely the cities of Giengen, Nördlingen, Aalen, Bopfingen, Dinkelsbühl, Rothenburg ob der Tauber, Schwäbish Hall and Heilbronn, switched sides and joined the emperor because they felt that they were too weak to resist his forces.[80] Even Ulm considered turning away from the Schmalkaldic League for fear that the emperor's soldiery might invade Ulm territory. Late in December 1546 the city council once more corresponded with their Strasbourg colleagues in an attempt to establish a common policy towards the emperor. The attempt was unsuccessful. Strasbourg remained in opposition while Ulm pledged loyalty on 28 December 1546.[81] Augsburg changed sides as well and joined forces with Charles in 1547.[82]

Yet Charles classed membership of the Schmalkaldic League as an act of insurgency and responded without clemency. After his victory at Mühlberg he felt strong enough to intervene in the domestic affairs of Augsburg and Ulm to state examples of his power and his determination not to tolerate opposition on the part of the imperial cities. Charles demonstrated his rage as he had done at Ghent, though with less fatal rigour. The burghers of Augsburg had to prostrate themselves before the emperor when he arrived in the city to hold the imperial diet there in 1548. After the diet had approved of the *Interim* it was communicated to the burghers as a temporarily valid legal framework of theological doctrine. While the *Interim* guaranteed the coexistence of Lutherans and Catholics for the time being, it obliged city councils to act against adherents of Zwingli's theology. In practice this meant that preachers of Zwingli's theology had to be expelled from the cities. The Augsburg city council acted accordingly.

On 3 August 1548 Charles went a step further and cancelled the Augsburg city constitution, purged the city council, abolished the guilds, appointed a new, seemingly more obedient council and enforced a new constitution drawn on the Nuremberg model.[83] He then quickly proceeded to Ulm and repeated his actions. Again, the burghers had to prostrate themselves before Charles and swear allegiance. From 15–16 August 1548 Charles revoked the Ulm constitution, abolished the guilds, and enforced a new constitution on the basis of the Nuremberg model. Two days later he sacked the old and appointed a new, seemingly more serviceable council. At Ulm Charles was more rigorous than at Augsburg in that he had Lutheran preachers arrested on 20 August under the allegation of disobedience against the *Interim*.[84]

Charles left Ulm and continued to the Netherlands. But at Ulm the dramatic changes did not last long after the emperor's departure.

In the following year many of the old guard were back in power, the guilds started to restore their organisations, and the old constitution was recovered from the archive. It was laid down in a charter dated 1397. The charter contained a mutual promise by which the mayors and the patriarchate on the one side and the commoners on the other swore loyalty and obliged each other to provide security and to respect the law. Ulm's chronicler Fischer praised the charter as an instrument enforcing domestic peace: 'In the chronicles of hardly any city has one ever seen a city that has been governed more peacefully and has had less numerous wars than Ulm. She has never gone to war except when she had to do so.'[85] He then lamented the disaster of the war against the Schmalkaldic League and criticised the Ulm city council for having joined the confederation. Fischer then reported Charles's intervention as a legal response against insubordination for which he blamed the city council. But at the same time he insisted that the old constitution was not in need of revision. Indeed, the charter was restored as the platform for a public ceremony in which all parties engaged in the government of the city swore allegiance to each other once a year, but did so on a day that differed from the one that had been stipulated in the charter.[86] The ceremony evolved into an annual festival that has continued to be celebrated until today.

At Augsburg, which was not merely a centre of production and trade but also an episcopal see, Charles's reforms received a warmer welcome. The Augsburg patriarchate of wealthy traders and the resident Catholic clergy accused the old city council of selfishness and ineptitude. The new council, consisting of a merchant patriarchate, paid an indemnity of 95,000 guilders to the Catholic Church and gave assurances of security to the bishop, the chapter, the monasteries and the Catholic clergy. With the exception of a brief rebellion of the suppressed guilds in 1552, the new regime remained stable, and Catholicism coexisted with Lutheranism in the city.

Yet Charles did not only intervene in imperial cities that were strongholds of Lutheranism. He also sought to strengthen his influence in cities that continued to adhere to Catholicism. A case in point was Cologne. On his way to the Netherlands in 1548 Charles stopped briefly in the city to settle an issue of potentially disruptive effects. At Cologne a self-governing institution for the city existed side by side with the centre of the administration of the archbishopric as an ecclesiastical electorate. The relations between the city and the archbishop were often antagonistic. In June 1548 a round of controversy opened over a request by the newly installed Archbishop Adolf III of Schaumburg. The new archbishop wanted to receive a formal entry into the city as a sign that the burghers welcomed their new shepherd. The city council considered the request and expected that the archbishop intended to use the entry as a formal act of making manifest his rule over the burgers. But the burghers of Cologne were subject to no one other than the emperor, and thus the council was determined to refuse to grant the entry to the archbishop. The council searched its archive and claimed to have found that since the beginning of Christianity at Cologne, there had been sixty-four archbishops, and only four of them had received an entry. Records also appeared to confirm that these four archbishops had been particularly controversial and on bad terms with the city. The council concluded that the archbishop held all legal rights without an entry into the city and that, for the sake of maintaining good relations with the city, the archbishop should waive his request.[87]

But the archbishop would not give in easily. Adolf III was an ardent supporter of the *Interim*; he was present at the Augsburg imperial diet of 1548, where he received his consecration. He agreed with Charles's quest for church reformation but would not touch essentials of Catholic theological doctrine. To the end of imposing his will upon the obsessive burghers, he asked the emperor to intervene in his favour, and Charles was ready to support the archbishop. He instructed the city council to grant the entry, while assuring the city council that it would be able to keep all its rights and privileges.[88] Against Charles's expectation the city council remained stubborn and ignored the emperor's will. Charles then decided to settle the issue himself during his visit to the city, where he was scheduled to arrive on 7 September 1548. At Cologne the emperor was highly unwelcome. During the formal entry bystanders yelled in protest and had to be sent to prison.[89] Inside the city Charles discussed the issue with the council. The council agreed to consider the issue again and submit its final decision to the emperor. On 17 September 1548 Charles continued his journey to Brussels. Deliberations at Cologne lasted for a considerable period of time. In the spring of the following year the council dispatched a delegation to Brussels for negotiations. Charles continued to insist that the archbishop should be granted a formal entry and specified 4 October 1549 as the date on which the entry was to be held. Until then a commission of two mediators was appointed, namely Earl William of Nassau, prince of Orange, and Earl William of Neuenahr. The delegation returned to Cologne with two draft proposals that the mediators had submitted in the meantime. The delegation reported to the council on 6 April 1549. The council accepted the proposals and sent the delegation back to Brussels. Eventually the entry took place on the scheduled day.[90]

The Cologne incident shows that the emperor's control over the cities was limited in terms of practical administration, irrespective of confessional affiliation, and could be enforced only after lengthy negotiations. According to constitutional theory the emperor was lord of the imperial cities, and Charles seems to have taken his privilege seriously. But the practice was different. The emperor could impose his will through his personal presence in a city or with the threat of using military force. As an itinerant ruler his ability to enforce long-term regimes was limited and subject to agreement by the local elites. The imposition of imperial decrees against the declared will of local power-holders or resistance on the side of the burghers was costly. While the councils, the patriarchates and the commoners in the cities might yield to the emperor's momentary military supremacy, respect his will, swear allegiance and even prostrate themselves, they would do so with reluctance and grudgingly, and try to reverse their awkward position once the emperor was gone. As a result of short-term demonstrations of power Charles faced the long-term alienation of his subjects. By late 1540 the alienation of burghers from their imperial lord had advanced to the degree that they were seriously considering withdrawing their financial support. At this time, the decision to do so was not merely motivated by political grudges but also by financial constraints. Bankers were losing confidence in the emperor's ability to repay loans with interest and were running short of funds as the cash flow from the imperial coffers thinned out. Some, like the Fuggers, agreed to further credits only because they were fearful of losing all rights to previous loans and had to write off all previous investments if they denied further credit. At the end of 1548 Charles restored his honour, succeeded in a show of military strength and imposed his will upon the imperial estates. But he alienated more of his subjects than ever before, Catholics and Lutherans alike. His strike against the cities was an attempt to enforce loyalty against rising opposition, specifically among the urban elites. The effects of his showdown against the Lutherans were as short-lived as his triumph against Tunis. He postponed the war against the Ottoman Turkish Empire with the argument that he had to put down the 'Lutheran heresy' before being able to strike against the sultan. In the end Charles had to acknowledge that Lutheran theological doctrine was equal to the Catholic faith, and the war against the Ottoman Turkish Empire never took place.

SEVEN

Exeunt: *Succession Issues, the Settlement of 1555, Abdications, Retirement, Death (1549–58)*

ENDING THE STRUGGLE

Succession issues

Old age coming with frailty brings despair and loneliness. This medieval wisdom was also Charles's experience.[1] From 1545, when reports about attacks of gout became notorious, the emperor's health was visibly failing. Reports about rulers' illnesses were good news for diplomats, who were eager to produce scenarios of possible or probable succession arrangements. Charles was aware of his plight and tried to stem the tide. At the Ratisbon imperial diet of 1546 and the Augsburg imperial diet of 1548 we find him rejuvenated by recent military successes against the 'Lutheran heresy'. But it was undeniable that Charles became a lonely figure after his rival friends Francis I and Henry VIII had passed away. Francis's son Henry II was known to have disagreed with his father's policy of maintaining friendly relations with the emperor. Henry's sickly son Edward VI was too weak to exercise full control and left politics to the virtual dictatorship of the duke of Northumberland. By 1549, when he took a rest in the Netherlands, Charles was ready for succession talks.

The essential problem was the redistribution of rights to rule over Charles's many lands. The stakes were the empire, the Spanish kingdoms and their dependencies, the recently amalgamated provinces of the Netherlands, the Habsburg hereditary lands, and the northern part of the Italian peninsula. The Spanish kingdoms and

204

their dependencies posed the least difficulty because Charles's son Philip was regent and the recognised heir apparent. In the Habsburg hereditary lands Charles's brother Ferdinand was the unquestioned ruler. But in both respects, the open question concerned the longer perspective, namely who was to succeed after the heirs apparent. After the victory at Mühlberg, Charles seems to have wanted to demand more for his son Philip than merely the succession to the Spanish kingdoms, and placed the question of the succession in the Netherlands on the agenda. He proceeded with skill and caution, ordering Philip to come to the Netherlands on a grand tour of good will. The tour was to create an atmosphere of support for the emperor's son, subdue local resentment against Habsburg rule and exclude rival claims from elsewhere in the dynasty.

Philip complied. He invested his sister Mary and her husband, Ferdinand's son Maximilian, as regents and embarked on his first journey outside the Iberian peninsula on 20 October 1548. He travelled via Genoa, Milan, Trento and Innsbruck, and reached Brussels on 1 April 1549. Meanwhile Charles enforced the so-called Pragmatic Sanction of Augsburg, stipulating that the amalgamated provinces of the Netherlands had to remain united beyond Charles's rule. The sanction implied that only one ruler would follow Charles in the Netherlands. It effectively thwarted ambitions by local aristocrats and urban governments who were looking for an opportunity to have their ancient privileges restored after Charles's death. Philip's journey to and in the Netherlands was a triumphant success. The northern Italian cities gave him a warm welcome with ceremonial entries. Cities in Brabant and Flanders did not want to lag behind, and built triumphal arches, organised pageants and gave pledges of loyalty to the emperor's son.[2] The positive impression that Philip's tour left behind convinced Charles that he should push forward and establish Philip as his successor in the Netherlands and in the northern Italian principalities over which the emperor held suzerainty. On this occasion the burghers of Ghent tried to avoid all risks and did everything to demonstrate their agreement with Charles's plans: one of the triumphal arches that they erected for Philip featured a sculpture of the emperor's ninth-century predecessor and namesake Charlemagne designating his son Louis the Pious as his heir (Plate 16).[3]

The next step was to raise the issue of the succession in the empire. Following the precedent that Frederick III had established for his son Maximilian in 1486, it was clear that Ferdinand, anointed king of the Romans, was Charles's successor at the helm of the empire. But, contrary to the designation of 1486, Ferdinand was merely three years younger than his brother, perhaps of more robust health but reaching old age as well. Hence, even if Ferdinand's succession was uncontroversial, the question remained who was to succeed after Ferdinand's death. Charles decided to proceed in the same way with regard to the empire as he had done in the Netherlands. He presented his son and tested responses. As the mission in the empire was more complicated than it had been in the Netherlands, Charles used the Augsburg imperial diet of 1550 to present Philip to the assembled estates. Philip thus accompanied his father on the journey from Brussels to Augsburg, where Charles introduced his son. While the diet debated the issue of Lutheran participation in the general council, Charles deliberated the imperial succession with his brother, who was also present. The issue was whether Charles's son Philip or Ferdinand's son Maximilian should have priority as successor to Ferdinand. The real problem was not merely one of personal qualifications and aspirations but whether the Habsburg family would remain an integrated dynasty of rulers or break apart into an imperial and a Spanish branch. If Ferdinand's son Maximilian succeeded his father in the empire, the split of the dynasty was manifest.

In principle the two brothers agreed that this outcome should be avoided and could thus easily agree between themselves on a compromise. The compromise envisaged the alteration of the two lines and found support even from Mary of Hungary. She was fearful that the relations between the Netherlands and the empire would be strained if Philip succeeded in the Netherlands and Maximilian in the empire. Hence the two brothers and their sister agreed that Philip should follow Ferdinand in the empire and Maximilian should succeed Philip. With the aim of tightening the deal, Maximilian's marriage with Charles's daughter Mary was to be complemented by Philip's marriage with one of Ferdinand's daughters. At least one of the two couples would then produce a single heir for all branches of the Habsburg dynasty. Ferdinand accepted the deal but presented his bill. He insisted that Philip could succeed neither in the Habsburg hereditary lands nor in the northern Italian principalities. He obliged Philip to contribute to the campaigns against Ottoman Turkish armies and claimed control over the Habsburg lands south of the Alps for himself, where Philip could serve as his regent when he was absent. Grudgingly Charles seems to have accepted the demands but did not commit himself to an explicit agreement in writing.[4] Nevertheless, Philip appeared at Augsburg as unofficial heir for the empire.

The resumption of warfare against the Lutherans and France

The Augsburg imperial diet of 1550 decided that Catholic and Lutheran estates should dispatch delegations to the general council, now relocated to Trento. Philip stayed on at Augsburg until May 1551, when he bid farewell to his father and returned to the Spanish kingdoms. At the end of August 1551 Charles moved to Innsbruck, where he remained until 1552. During his stay at Augsburg Philip failed to generate the positive impression that had resulted from his journey to the Netherlands. The imperial estates regarded him not merely as a ruler of remote origin: more importantly, Catholic and Lutheran estates were equally fearful that the Habsburgs were trying to reduce the decision-making competence of the Electoral College by presenting Philip as a candidate for the imperial election after Ferdinand's death. A propaganda campaign began that accused the Habsburg dynasty of attempting to transform the empire into a hereditary monarchy. The suspicion was not unfounded, as Charles and Ferdinand were both aware of the possibility that the electors might vote for a non-Habsburg candidate after Ferdinand's death. When Philip returned to the Iberian peninsula it was obvious that the two Habsburg brothers had made their bill without the host. The succession scheme was in tatters.

Moreover, Lutheran opposition to Charles gained strength in February 1550 when Margrave Hans von Küstrin, Duke Albert of Prussia and Duke Albert of Mecklenburg entered into a defensive alliance against the emperor. In March 1550 King Henry II of France signed a peace treaty with Edward VI and began to resume his father's attempts to support Charles's enemies in the empire. At the same time, Henry tried to mobilise Ottoman Turkish forces against the emperor. In May 1551 Maurice, elector of Saxony and hitherto a prominent supporter of Charles's cause, used his military strength as the executor of the imperial ban against Magdeburg to accede to the alliance with the group of north German Lutheran rulers who already stood in opposition to the Habsburgs. The alliance was directed against Charles but not against Ferdinand. The revolting Lutheran rulers reserved for themselves the option of cooperating with Ferdinand when they could expect advantages. Although himself a staunch defender of the Catholic Church, King Henry II of France responded favourably to the alliance and posed as a guarantor of the liberties of the imperial estates *vis-à-vis* the emperor. In 1552 Maurice openly switched sides and turned against Charles. The so-called 'war princes' signed an alliance treaty at Chambord on 15 January 1552 to which Henry II acceded. The signatories declared the restoration of ancient freedoms as their goal, promised to surrender Naples, Flanders and Artois to the French king and pledged to support a French candidate at the next imperial elections.[5] They envisaged that Henry II would be the candidate whom they intended to support.

In the meantime, Pope Julius III, who had succeeded Paul III in 1550, suspended the deliberations of the general council at Trento and sent the delegates home on 24 April 1552. The 'war princes' immediately launched a coordinated diplomatic and military action. Maurice led a fighting force to Innsbruck where Charles was residing and simultaneously submitted a list of complaints to Ferdinand. Negotiations about the complaints were taking place at Linz in April 1552, while Maurice reached Innsbruck and forced Charles to flee from the city rather than become Maurice's prisoner of war. In fact, Maurice had the opportunity to capture Charles but, most probably, intended merely a demonstration of his military strength. In any case Charles experienced the shame and humiliation of having to escape across the Alps to Villach in Carinthia.

At Linz the 'war princes' accused Charles and Ferdinand, among other things, of planning to convert the empire into a hereditary monarchy and of presenting a 'foreigner' as a candidate for future elections. They insinuated that Charles was articulating his concerns for the well-being of Christendom merely as a pretext for trying to aggrandise his own power, and that the emperor was unwilling to conduct the crusade because he wanted to strengthen his positions elsewhere.[6] Through their verdict the 'war princes' reminded Charles of his own post-election promises when he had assured the imperial estates that only German office-holders would be allowed to take charge of imperial affairs. In view of the promise that the 'war princes' had earlier extended to Henry II, the accusation appears as straightforwardly treacherous. But it reflected the poor impression that Philip had left behind at Augsburg and simply used the 'proto-nationalist' ticket on which Charles had himself campaigned more than thirty years before. Ferdinand used the military attack on Charles as a pretext for interrupting the negotiations.

Helpless in his anger, Charles responded from Villach that the accusations were unfounded; that Ferdinand had ample evidence to the effect that they were untrue; and that the Habsburg brothers were not trying to convert the empire into a hereditary monarchy. Yet the 'war princes' would not give in to imperial pressure. They insisted that the negotiations should continue and received support from seventeen delegations from Catholic as well as Lutheran estates. Ferdinand complied and agreed to the resumption of the negotiations at the Bavarian episcopal city of Passau. At Passau, the 'war princes' cast their demands in the form of three requests: first to guarantee the liberties of the estates, second to revoke the *Interim*, and third to grant a general amnesty for all rulers who had fought against the emperor during the Mühlberg campaign and to release Landgrave Philip of Hesse from imperial custody. Ferdinand travelled to Villach to persuade Charles of the urgency of accepting the demands. But Charles remained stubborn. He angrily protested against Ferdinand's plea and refused to accede to the first two demands. He argued that, for him, support for the Catholic Church was not negotiable. Charles's reservations led to further deliberations but, in the end, all parties accepted a treaty that ratified the third demand and postponed the decision about the other two to another imperial diet scheduled to be convened within six months. Charles hesitated to sign the treaty but Ferdinand's mounting pressure seems to have compelled him to do so. On 15 August 1552 the treaty came into force. It has since then been known as the treaty of Passau.[7]

Having been relieved of his most immediate threats, Charles resumed the offensive and assembled an armed force to punish Henry II for having intervened in imperial affairs. The conditions were favourable as the 'war princes' were neutralised for the time being and the Ottoman Turkish armies were not responding to Henry's call to arms. But, once again, Charles's army was hastily and poorly equipped. Moreover, on this occasion, a dubious character supported the campaign. This was Margrave Albert Alcibiades II of Brandenburg-Kulmbach, ruler over some scattered territories in Franconia. Charles had publicly reprimanded him after an unwarranted attack on the Franconian bishoprics of Bamberg and Würzburg as well as on the city of Nuremberg. During the attack, Albert Alcibiades had forced the bishops and the city council to sign treaties ceding property to him, and Charles declared the treaties null and void. But Albert had an effective fighting force at his disposal, and Charles intended to use this force for his war against Henry II. Thus he agreed to indemnify the margrave on condition that he joined the emperor's campaign. Indeed, Albert entered imperial service in October 1552. The army moved ahead to the French city of Metz and laid it under siege. But the French garrison defended the place well and bad weather forced the emperor to withdraw in January 1553. Observing the spectacle, the burghers of Metz mocked the retreating emperor with a banner reading 'Non ultra Metas' (No further than Metz), a pun on the emperor's motto PLVS VLTRA.[8] Elector Maurice of Saxony eventually defeated Albert Alcibiades in the battle of Sievershausen on 9 July 1553. But during the battle, the elector received a wound from which he died three days later. Charles did not return from Metz to the empire but proceeded to the Netherlands.

Succession problems in England and a new marriage arrangement

Before holding the scheduled imperial diet Charles intended to play one further trump card. This was Mary, daughter of King Henry VIII by Catherine of Aragon. In 1553 Charles's ambassador to England sent reports that Mary continued to adhere to the Catholic faith, was popular among the English people and would soon succeed the sickly Edward. Charles had once been betrothed to Mary himself but, for obvious reasons, was no longer available. Presenting his son as the bridegroom was an ideal solution because it could help settle old bills with the English royal dynasty and set up a third Habsburg family next to the Austrian and Spanish branches. If Charles and his heirs controlled the Spanish and future English branches they could gain a majority over Ferdinand and his heirs even if they could not gain direct access to the helm of the empire. These calculations induced Charles to conduct negotiations with the English court discreetly, without providing clear information to Ferdinand. Charles rightly anticipated that Ferdinand was also casting an eye on Mary, whom he wanted to marry to his son.[9] Charles forced Philip, who was widowed at the time, to break off negotiations with the Portuguese court about his remarriage. But Charles's secret diplomacy added to the growing distrust between the two brothers, both of whom grew increasingly sceptical about being able to agree on succession issues.

But the English succession evolved into a drama. When Edward fell fatally ill in spring 1553, the duke of Northumberland saw the end of his virtual dictatorship approaching and decided to take preventive action. Propagating the fear that Mary would reintroduce Catholicism, he summoned the royal council and talked them into accepting Lady Jane Grey, great-niece of Henry VIII, as the new ruler. Because she had long been considered as Edward's future wife,

Lady Jane had received a Protestant education. In May 1553 Northumberland forced Lady Jane to marry his son Guildford Dudley and persuaded the dying Edward to declare illegitimate his half-sisters Mary and Elizabeth. When Edward was dying on 6 July 1553 Northumberland summoned Mary and Elizabeth to the king's deathbed, intending to arrest them and proclaim Lady Jane as the new ruler. However, Elizabeth stayed at home pretending to be ill, and Mary was warned off on her way to Edward. Northumberland remained determined to accomplish his goal even though Henry's two surviving children could not be removed straight away. He proceeded with Lady Jane's proclamation, while Mary sent a letter to the royal council asserting her rights and Elizabeth stayed in bed. As popular support for Mary grew, the royal council turned against Northumberland. All members except three deserted the duke and asked the mayor of London to proclaim Mary on 19 July 1553. Mary entered London on 3 August and received a welcome in which Elizabeth joined. Immediately afterwards Mary officially informed the emperor of the death of her brother and her accession to the throne.[10] She had Northumberland executed in August 1553 and subjected Lady Jane and her husband to the same fate on 12 February 1554.

Sad as these events may have been, Charles's ambassadors welcomed them and gave optimistic reports on the prospects for the marriage plan.[11] Indeed, Philip set off for England in the summer of 1554, leaving the Spanish kingdoms to the regency of his sister Juana, whose husband King John of Portugal had died the same year. Ferdinand's son Maximilian and his wife Mary eventually returned to the Habsburg hereditary lands in 1556. Philip married Mary at Winchester on 25 July 1554. In England opposition forced Philip to abandon his plan of receiving his own coronation as king of England and, with it, the possibility of establishing his right to succeed. Moreover, it soon became clear that the couple would remain without offspring. Hence, if he survived Mary, Philip would have to return to Spain with empty hands. Charles's last dynastic plan was about to collapse. Indeed, Philip left England alone in 1555.

Getting ready for a settlement: the Augsburg imperial diet of 1555

There was little else that Charles could do about the succession issue. He sensed that a settlement was approaching along lines to which he objected, feared that the forthcoming imperial diet at Augsburg would ratify the treaty of Passau and notified his brother that he would not attend, pretending that he was too ill for the journey. He authorised Ferdinand to preside over the diet in the emperor's absence but was unwilling to give complete authority to his brother. He dispatched commissioners although he assured Ferdinand that they would not interfere with his agenda. In his correspondence with Ferdinand, Charles revealed the reason for his absence:

> To tell the reason honestly, as it has to be done between brothers (while asking not to imagine any other reason): it is merely with respect to religion that I continue to hesitate to attend, as I discussed with you in detail and at length while we last met at Villach. I have no doubt that, good and Christian ruler that you are, you will be on your guard not to agree to anything at the diet that might impinge on your conscience or could be the cause for even greater dissent about the matter of religion.[12]

The message was clear: Charles was unwilling to take the final responsibility for decisions that, in his view, were going to legalise Lutheranism within the empire.

Ferdinand was now ready to grant precisely this. He feared that the struggle with Ottoman Turkish armies over Hungary might resume and that he needed Lutheran support in this eventuality. Moreover, Charles had done a bad service to everyone in attempting to enforce a general peace in the empire; he had granted impunity to Albert Alcibiades although the margrave had acted in open breach of imperial peace and the treaty obligations of the estates. Seeing that actors like Albert Alcibiades were a threat to their own safety, the estates were willing to enact a settlement through which they obliged themselves to cooperate militarily against rulers who were responsible for blatant breaches of peace.

After the diet had been postponed twice, Ferdinand eventually convened it at Augsburg and declared it open on 5 February 1555. Attendance was low. Not only was the emperor absent; so were all six electors and rulers of many powerful estates. Yet Ferdinand displayed strong leadership and persuaded the delegates to accept a settlement. He tried to prevent the doctrinal controversy from resurfacing on the agenda by repeating the proposal to organise a theological disputation. When this proposal failed to materialise once again, he pursued the strategy of 'dissimulating' the doctrinal differences between Catholicism and Lutheranism. This meant that he urged the delegates to act as if there were no controversy over doctrine. The latter strategy paved the way for a peace settlement that could include Catholic as well as Lutheran estates as allies in pursuit of the common goal of maintaining peace in the empire.

Indeed peace, not religion, was the main topic of the deliberations at the diet. Only thirteen out of 141 articles of its final act combined peace with matters of religion. These articles related to: the inclusion of Lutherans into the peace (whereby Lutheran estates were defined as the adherents to the Augsburg Confession of 1530) and the prohibition of the use of military force against Lutherans (Art. 15); the inclusion of Catholic estates, defined as adherents to the 'old religion', into the peace and the guarantee of their safety (Art. 16); the exclusion of all other religious faiths, that is, the confessions supported by the followers of Zwingli and Calvin (to whom the Augsburg settlement was extended only in 1648)[13] (Art. 17); the proviso that if office-holders of the Catholic Church converted to Lutheranism, they must vacate their offices to make room for Catholic successors (Art. 18); the restitution of monasteries and other property to the Catholic Church, if they had been alienated after the conclusion of the treaty of Passau (Art. 19); the suspension of Catholic ecclesiastical jurisdiction over Lutherans (Art. 20); the guarantee of all revenues to estates adhering to the 'old religion' (Art. 21); the peaceful arbitration of controversies about revenue regulations in accordance with Art. 21 (Art. 22); the pledge that no estate would use force to effect the conversion of another estate (Art. 23); the right of emigration for population groups who chose to adhere to the 'old religion' in the case of the conversion of their ruler (Art. 24); the mutual pledge to seek the restoration of the unity of Christendom through the general council, a national council, theological disputations or acts of imperial law, and to accept the current settlement as a permanent peace (Arts 25, 139, 140).[14]

The settlement became possible because it left the doctrinal controversy pending and focused on peaceful coexistence until the eventual future restoration of the unity of Christendom. The Augsburg imperial diet did not act as a national council deciding on matters of doctrine, even though it did re-establish the possibility of convening such a council as a possible way to end the controversy. The settlement did not constitute an explicit legal right that allowed rulers to make authoritative decisions about the confession of their subjects. But it did grant to Lutheran estates, and only to Lutherans, the right to act in accordance with their theological doctrines for the time being and thereby implicitly accepted the pivotal role of estate rulers in initialising and steering conversion processes wherever they might occur. The celebrated formula *cuius regio eius religio* (whoever rules a territory decides about religion) is conspicuously absent from the text of the Augsburg settlement and, in fact, has no place in it.

The settlement was a compromise that slightly favoured Catholics. On the one hand, Ferdinand talked the Lutheran estates into accepting the proviso of Article 18, which blocked Lutherans from taking control of ecclesiastical estates after their conversion. He argued that if Lutherans were unwilling to accept the proviso, they were liable to the suspicion that they were merely interested in confiscating church property, as Henry VIII had done. On the other hand, Ferdinand convinced the Catholic estates that it was in their interest to grant dissenters the right of emigration. This right could only be granted to persons who had done nothing wrong, while wrong-doers, such as heretics, had to be punished and could not be granted the right to leave. Hence the Catholic concession was important because, implicitly, the Catholic Church thereby renounced its claim that Lutherans were 'heretics'. Nevertheless, the concession that Lutherans gave weighed more heavily in terms of power politics.

The final decision: Charles abdicates

Waiting in Brussels for the results of the deliberations, Charles received the news that his mother Juana had died at Tordesillas on 13 April 1555. The news added to his grief over the diet proceedings. He was unhappy with Ferdinand's diplomacy and suspected him of mishandling the proceedings. He complained that the diet was in a condition which, 'unless God intervenes and opens the eyes of princes and estates, one could only conclude that they were ready to precipitate their downfall'.[15] To prevent this seemingly impending disaster Charles decided to step on the brakes. At the very end of the diet sessions, after all deals had been finalised, he tried to defer the settlement by presenting two unexpected and most dramatic demands. The first demand was that he wanted the diet to continue its meetings until his special commissioner arrived to announce his abdication as emperor. The second demand was that the settlement should be written out in Ferdinand's name. Indeed, Charles's secretary Paul Pfintzing presented the emperor's demands at Augsburg on 25 September 1555, when the diet was about to conclude. Pfintzing requested that the diet should continue in session until the formal abdication papers with Charles's signatures arrived and could be approved by the delegates. But Ferdinand ignored both demands and closed the diet on schedule. The settlement went into force in Charles's name.

Charles's final decision may have been ill considered but it was not rash. In August 1555, he had ordered Philip to leave London and move to Brussels as quickly as possible.[16] Charles had made up his mind to return to the Iberian peninsula and intended to invest Philip as ruler over the Netherlands before his departure. Looking back on his life in October 1555 he admitted that he had long considered abdicating.[17] But he made no announcement concerning his position in the Iberian and Italian peninsulas. He scheduled a formal investiture ceremony for his son Philip as ruler over the Netherlands but left the succession to the Spanish kingdoms and the Italian principalities unmentioned. The ceremony took place in the hall of the Great Palace in Brussels on 25 October 1555, where the States General of the Netherlands had been convened. Charles had announced his maturity as duke of Burgundy in the same hall forty years before. He passed on to Philip the rights to rule over the now united provinces of the Netherlands, expressed the wish that he should soon have a son and blessed him.[18]

With regard to Spain Philip did not have to wait long. On 16 January 1556, while still at Brussels, Charles abdicated as ruler of the Spanish kingdoms and their dependencies and invested Philip with control over Castile, Aragon, the Two Sicilies, the islands in the western Mediterranean Sea, Tunis and the New World. But Charles's retirement from the remaining Habsburg territories in the Italian peninsula was more complicated. Philip first had to waive his candidacy for succeeding Ferdinand as king of the Romans and heir apparent to Ferdinand as future emperor. Philip did so, thereby annihilating the essence of the 1550 arrangements between Charles and Ferdinand. In order to compensate for his concession, Philip demanded that he be invested as imperial vicar over those parts of the Italian peninsula that he did not control in his capacity as king of Aragon. This privilege would have allowed him to rule over the Habsburg territories in the peninsula in his own right and not by delegation from Ferdinand. But Ferdinand flatly rejected the demand. Philip had to accept the 1550 arrangement with regard to these territories over which he obtained control as Ferdinand's regent.

These decisions were crucial because they paved the way for the succession in the empire according to principles that Charles was keen to avoid. Charles still hoped to tie the diverse lands under Habsburg control more closely together by moving rulers back and forth within the dynasty or keeping them itinerant. But the agreement between Ferdinand and Philip foreshadowed the break-up of the dynasty into two branches. Whereas Charles continued to conceive of rule as the range of activities of persons gifted with power and honour, Ferdinand and Philip were less concerned with honour than Charles and defined power in terms of control over territories and the people inhabiting them. While Charles expected that rulers would compete for the maximisation of their power and honour as personal gifts, Ferdinand and Philip sought to aggrandise their control over the largest possible compounds of adjacent territories. Hence Ferdinand was not interested in his nephew's now-united Spanish kingdom and its overseas dependencies, but forced Philip to retreat from the empire and the northern Italian Habsburg dependencies. Philip accepted the demand that he had to reduce his impact on the northern Italian principalities in return for Ferdinand's concession that the Netherlands should remain under Spanish control. Much to Mary's dismay, Philip did not return to England to accompany his consort but stayed in the Netherlands where he was needed to manage rising unrest among the estates.

The final decisions about the imperial succession were made in the Electoral College in accordance with the imperial constitution. Charles eventually abdicated as emperor on 3 August 1556. He dispatched William of Orange and vice-chancellor Georg Sigmund Seld as his commissioners to Ferdinand to make three proposals. In the first place they were to suggest that Charles resigned from all titles and activities and that the estates transferred their loyalty to Ferdinand. If this suggestion was rejected they were to propose that Ferdinand took over effective government and left to Charles merely the imperial title. If Ferdinand refused to do so the commissioners were to ask him to administer the empire as if Charles were absent. Because the Golden Bull of 1356, the most important legal document relevant to the imperial constitution, did not include any rule concerning abdications, the electors had to decide about procedural matters before being able to accept any of Charles's requests. On 12 September 1556 Charles dispatched a letter to his brother through which he handed the imperial office over to Ferdinand and left it to him to decide about the day of the actual transfer. Eventually, the estates accepted Charles's complete abdication on condition that Ferdinand agree to the transfer of the imperial title upon him during Charles's lifetime. Only after Ferdinand explicitly agreed to the transfer, rather than to a formal election, did the electors ask him to swear his own promise as Charles's successor. The complicated procedure was completed with Ferdinand's eventual proclamation as emperor in Frankfurt on 14 March 1558.[19] The transition from Charles to Ferdinand was unique in the history of the Holy Roman Empire as Ferdinand was neither elected nor crowned.

Departure for Yuste

Charles left Brussels for Spain on 8 August 1556. His sister Mary followed him after Philip had taken over her tasks. Charles's other sister Eleanor returned to Spain from France, where she had stayed as a widow since Francis's death. On 3 February 1557 Charles took up residence in a villa that had been built for him near the monastery of Yuste in Estremadura. A court of about fifty advisers, priests and servants accompanied him there. Charles brought with him a small collection of books. He also had several pictures around him, among them Titian's portrait of the late empress, a portrait of Catherine of Aragon as queen of England and three volumes of sketches of the West Indies.[20]

At Yuste Charles remained active as much as he could. He treated Philip as an apprentice and tried to direct the governments of the Netherlands and Spain. When Henry II of France concluded an alliance with Pope Paul IV and resumed war in 1556, he pressured his reluctant son to take up the challenge and was pleased to see that his insistence paid off with Spanish victories over French armed forces at Saint-Quentin in 1557 and at Gravelines in 1558. He continued to intervene in dynastic relations, trying to secure the succession rights for his descendants. He also advised his daughter Juana, acting as regent for Philip, to take a strong stand against the Lutherans whom the Inquisition had detected at Valladolid, Seville and in surrounding Andalusia. He wrote angrily to Juana on 25 May 1558:

219

Believe me, daughter, that this task has given me concern and has inflicted pains on me to a degree that I am unable to communicate to you. For I had to see that these realms were so calm and free from this bad fortune during the absence of the king and myself but that right now, after I have arrived here to retire and take a rest, to serve Our Lord, in my and your presence such big and shameless acts of banditry are happening and that persons are involved in them who know that I have suffered so much labour and expenses and have lost such a large part of my health fighting against them.[21]

Even after he had retired Charles continued to expect that he could exercise power merely through his physical presence. Furthermore, he ignored the Augsburg settlement of 1555 and deeply deplored not being able to supervise the punishment of those accused of support for the 'Lutheran heresy'.

Charles also went out hunting when his health allowed him to do so and received information about political matters. He spent much of his remaining time in conversation about religious issues with Juan de Regla, his father confessor. Eleanor, Mary and Juana visited him on occasion. Eleanor died at Talavera on 14 February 1558. In August 1558 Charles grew weaker from fever, fits of gout and further pains. On 19 and 20 September he received the sacraments and died on 21 September 1558. Mary of Hungary passed away at Valladolid on 18 October 1558, and his daughter-in-law Mary of England followed them on 17 November 1558. Only Charles's sister Catherine, who was consort to the Portuguese king, lived on until 1573. The dead emperor received pompous funeral processions, the most elaborate one at Brussels on 29 December 1558.[22] In accordance with his last will Charles was put to rest under the high altar of the church at Yuste until his remains were interred in the Escorial, Philip's royal monastic residence outside Madrid, together with those of his mother Juana, his wife Isabel and his sisters Eleanor and Mary in 1574. The time was approaching for Philip II to terminate the years of apprenticeship and assume his role as the 'gendarme of Europe'.

INVENTING RETIREMENT

That the Golden Bull of 1356 did not contain rules on the retirement of rulers was not a contingent deficit but a consequence of the medieval conceptualisation of rulership. In the Middle Ages holders of high secular as well as ecclesiastical offices hoped to be able to lead an active life right to the moment of their death. Thus the Venerable Bede was hailed for having fulfilled his duties as a teacher right up to his death, and Abbot Egil of Fulda was revered for having begun to dig his own grave immediately before he became incapacitated and passed away.[23] William the Conqueror was renowned for having been completely capable of speaking and using his senses fully during the six weeks of his illness before his death.[24] Thus the old, as members of kin groups and as holders of high offices, seem to have been respected when and as long as they could perform their duties. By contrast, the frequent laments about old age[25] seem to have been generated by the fear that frailty might prohibit an active life, as requested from the young as well as from the old. Early in the sixteenth century Maximilian shared the same belief, tried to remain active and in control of his offices even after he became confined to his bed at Wels, and was incapacitated merely for a few days before he died.

Charles broke with an age-old tradition when he requested that he should be relieved from his duties. The demand that he should be allowed to abdicate entailed much more thorny questions than the usual problem of reaching agreement about monarchic succession. Ferdinand in particular was unhappy with Charles's request and made efforts at Augsburg to change the emperor's mind. Ferdinand was fearful that the empire might plunge into a constitutional crisis because there was neither a legal rule nor a precedent for an abdication. Yet the emperor was determined to remove himself from the scene and would not change his mind.

The way and the timing that Charles chose to articulate his request aggravated the difficulties. When Charles pressed for Philip's investiture as ruler of the Netherlands he effectively forced his sister Mary to resign from her regency. Moreover, Charles's ill considered

221

move at the end of the Augsburg imperial diet of 1555 alienated him from his brother, whom he had last met at Villach in 1552. Ferdinand had to overturn the succession arrangements of 1550, unless he wanted to face an open rebellion by his son Maximilian. Maximilian had long complained about his father's obedience towards the emperor and was unwilling to accept a succession rule that placed him behind Philip. Concerning the Spanish kingdoms, timing was bad because Philip, the heir apparent, was away in England, while Maximilian, Ferdinand's son, and his wife Mary, Charles's daughter, were still present in the Iberian peninsula. Charles's declaration that he was willing to abdicate as Spanish ruler came last in the series of abdication announcements,[26] and the delay raised the suspicion that the previous announcements were either insincere or not meant to include the Spanish kingdoms. When Charles eventually clarified the situation and announced his abdication as Spanish ruler in January 1556, he left the position of the regent undetermined and removed himself from the debate. Philip reached agreement with Ferdinand and Maximilian about his withdrawal from the imperial succession without involving Charles. Charles summoned Ferdinand to Brussels. But Ferdinand excused himself, saying that he was too busy to be able to travel to Brussels and left it to Maximilian and Mary to communicate the decision to the emperor. Maximilian and Mary left the regency to Charles's daughter Juana, widow of the heir of Portugal, and executed their task of informing the emperor about the new arrangement while visiting him at Brussels in August 1556. At that time Charles could only accept the *fait accompli*.

Philip's kingdom had to receive one abdicated ruler, one retired regent and one ruler's widow. Charles and Mary had no income of their own and thus depended on the mercy of the younger generation. Already fifteenth-century educational theorists knew that the generational contract was one-sided. Parents had the inescapable obligation to educate their infant children. They could expect that the children would care for their parents in old age but had no leverage to actually receive the necessary care.[27] Charles was similarly aware of his lack of security and obliged Philip to allocate an annual subsidy of 20,000 guilders. He felt that this request was a burden. At the end of the Brussels speech by which he abdicated as ruler of the Netherlands and invested Philip as his successor on 25 October 1555, Charles addressed Philip directly:

> Had you taken possession of these provinces through my death, this beautiful inheritance might have secured me a fair claim to your gratitude. But now that I pass them on to you voluntarily, so to speak dying before my time to your advantage, I expect that the love and care that you have devoted to your subjects will honour me to the degree that I deserve for the sake of such a gift.[28]

The slight irony in Charles's words hardly concealed his public request for support during the rest of his life. He displayed consciousness that his abdication was unusual and demanded that Philip should act with wisdom in order to retrospectively receive praise for his father's decision. Charles thus understood that retirement meant social death. Why did Charles abdicate nevertheless? The answer is difficult because Charles did not disclose his real motive. He admitted in his private correspondence with Ferdinand that illness was a pretence. Perhaps Charles realised that the only possibility for him to continue his struggle against the 'Lutheran heresy' was through meditation in the vicinity of the monastery at Yuste and occasional interventions in the world of politics rather than through ruling offices.

BIDDING FAREWELL: CHARLES'S BRUSSELS ABDICATION ADDRESS

There were two occasions on which Charles reflected on his own life. One was an autobiographical account that he narrated to his secretary Willem van Marle while cruising on the Rhine on his way to the Augsburg imperial diet of 1550.[29] The other was the Brussels address of 25 October 1555.[30] Both records bear remarkable similarities in terms of style and content, despite fundamental differences in textual genre. Philip was the recipient of the autobiographical account whose manuscript Marle completed during Charles's stay at Innsbruck in 1552. The account, to which Charles gave the title *Commentaires*, contains the narrative of Charles's travels. The lost original was written in French and soon rendered into a Portuguese version that is extant. It begins with the voyage from the Netherlands to the Iberian peninsula in 1517 and concludes with the journey through France and Flanders into the empire in 1539. Marle then added a report on the emperor's experiences to the year 1548. The *Commentaires* count the journeys and list them in chronological order. They also enumerate Charles's excursions on the Rhine, and the occasions on which Charles departed from his wife Isabel and his sister Mary.[31] He insisted that the wars against France had been forced upon him as part of the inheritance from his grandfather Maximilian; for Maximilian had been Henry VIII's partner in an anti-French alliance. Indeed Charles claimed to have accomplished and maintained peace with Francis I and friendship with Henry VIII.[32] Luther is conspicuously absent from the report on the second journey to the empire and Flanders (1520–22). But a reference to the 'Lutheran heresy' appears in the account of the third journey to the Italian peninsula and the empire (1529–31), which Charles purports to have undertaken for the purpose of bringing peace. He also mentioned the triumph of Tunis and a visit to his mother on his return to Castile in 1537.[33] He concluded with a detailed report on his negotiations with Francis I at Nice and Aigues-Mortes in 1538 and 1539 as well as the ensuing journey to Flanders and the empire.[34] Lutherans have a low profile in the entire account and crusading rhetoric is completely absent. References to the Spanish conquest of America are lacking, as Charles did not regard the establishment of Spanish rule in America as the result of his own activity. Instead, he recorded his intention to maintain good ties with the core members of his kin group, to his mother as well as his brother, his sisters and his son. He denied any responsibility for the wars against France while dwelling at length on his peace-making efforts and his willingness to provide good government.

The title *Commentaires* seems to have been chosen on purpose, as Charles developed an appreciation of Julius Caesar and, in his later life, appreciated being likened to ancient Roman rulers. When Charles entered Naples, returning from Tunis in triumph, he stepped through a triumphal arch decorated with sculptures of ancient Roman emperors.[35] In his contemporary report on the battle of Mühlberg, Luis Avila y Zuniga compared Charles's crossing of the River Elbe with Caesar's crossing of the Rubicon.[36] Copies of Avila's text and of Caesar's *Commentarii in bellum Gallicum* were among the few books that travelled with Charles to Yuste.[37] In his last instruction to Philip, dated Brussels, 25 October 1555, Charles recommended Roman military organisation and tactics as the model that Philip should use for his own armed forces and urged him to pursue a defensive strategy.[38]

The *Commentaires* do not merely relate Charles to Caesar but also compare both rulers and thereby belong to the then popular genre of texts juxtaposing Greek and Roman antiquity with the contemporary period. This genre of the *querelle des anciens et des modernes* usually resulted in praise of the present. Charles's *Commentaires* were no exception. Whereas Julius Caesar had gone on a single expedition to Gaul, Charles accomplished five journeys through France. Whereas Caesar had conquered nearby Gaul, Charles sacked distant Tunis. In other words, Charles credited his dynastic empire with more power than the Roman imperial institutions.

The same preference for dynasticism over institutionalism formed the background for Charles's Brussels abdication address. The text is extant in a verbatim report by an unidentified witness.[39] Charles portrayed himself as the owner of inherited rights to rule, mentioning Ferdinand of Aragon, Maximilian and his mother Juana as the ancestors from whom he had received these rights. He insisted that he had not campaigned for his election as emperor for the purpose of enlarging his realms but to be able to work for the benefit of the empire and his kingdoms in the eventual hope of defending Christendom against the Ottoman Turkish Empire. He deplored not having been able to conduct a successful crusade and apologised with the argument that he had to fight against the 'outbreak of the German heresy and the jealousy of competing powers', that is, the activities of the Lutherans and the kings of France. Again, he counted his military campaigns and listed the total number of forty journeys. He did not forget to make an implicit reference to the Ghent rebellion of 1540 and praised his sister Mary for having been his faithful regent. He expressed regret about having been compelled to conduct many wars but insisted that they had been forced upon him. He admitted not having been able to accomplish a 'firm and secure peace' but maintained that this had always been his overall goal. He obliged the estates of the Netherlands to continue fighting against 'heretic sects' even after his abdication. He assured them that he had always been determined to avoid acts of injustice and force while deploring the occasions when he had not succeeded in acting with justice and fairness.

Charles's tearful address was a rhetorical masterpiece and did not fail to have effects on the audience. He repeated statements of loyalty to his kin, of adherence to the Catholic faith, of his concern for peace and good government. While he mentioned the war against the Ottoman Turkish Empire on this occasion, he refrained from using radical crusading rhetoric and made no reference to the conquest of America. He continued to treat Lutherans as heretics and demanded the continuity of defensive efforts against Turkish armies. At the end of a warlike period the quest for peace and good government resurfaced as the emperor's core goals. Contrary to the *Commentaires* of 1552, the Brussels abdication speech of 1555 no longer revealed the buoyant optimistic emperor but an atmosphere of doom. When launching his series of abdications, Charles wanted to be remembered as a ruler who, although he had failed, had tried to do his best.

After Charles's abdications people in the world of politics would no longer listen to an old and remote man. Ferdinand assumed full control of the empire and speeded up a process that eventually transformed the empire into a territorial polity and which eighteenth-century intellectuals, such as Jean-Jacques Rousseau, could consider as a stabilising factor in the European balance of power.[40] Ferdinand established a dynasty of rulers who remained at the helm of the empire until 1806 with the single interruption of three years. Philip strengthened his grip on the Iberian peninsula by imposing himself as Portuguese king in 1580 but lost control over the northern Netherlands. Nevertheless, Spain has remained a united kingdom and continued to be ruled by Philip's descendants until 1700. The Italian peninsula retained the pluralism of its political organisation even though Spanish influence continued to be strong well into the eighteenth century. The controversies between Catholics and Lutherans as well as between Catholics and other Protestant sects persisted and formed the background for much war propaganda down to 1648. But, in the end, the Westphalia peace treaties concluded in that year made explicit reference to the treaty of Passau of 1552 and the Augsburg settlement of 1555, that is, the two agreements that Charles had most despised. They became the cornerstones of a European political order against the departing emperor's determination.

Charles's contemporaries feared or venerated him as a powerful ruler. They feared his military power and venerated his peace-bringing efforts. They accused him of striving for universal rule during his lifetime and feared him for his ambition. They obeyed him as the territorial ruler over the Spanish kingdoms and their dependencies. Upon his death, fear necessarily gave way to veneration. Educated as an aristocrat, Charles took for granted that his subjects had the duty to support him and consequently, pursued his foes relentlessly. By positioning war as a condition for the accomplishment of peace he resolved the medieval conflict between rulers' and warriors' tasks in a paradoxical way that, nevertheless, has attracted support until the present time. In the end, he refused to give support to the peace settlement of 1555, although it came into force in his name. While trying to rule with justice he made many enemies: Lutherans and other religious dissenters, whom he inadvertently classed as heretics; most of the popes from Leo X to Paul IV, whom he approached with often exaggerated mistrust; and the Ottoman Turkish sultan, to whom he applied the conventional occidental anti-Muslim sentiments.

Charles's perception of the world and the normative framework for his political decisions differed widely from those of modern

Europeans. Charles was not a world ruler in the sense that he tried to establish himself as the head of a government of the entire world. Africa did not feature in his mental map, he cared little about the Spanish conquest of America and less about the Pacific. Charles acknowledged the new European world picture as a factor of policy-making and thus broke with some medieval traditions. However, Charles's idea of empire was based on dynastic relations rather than on institutions. He tried to use his dynastic relations to stem the rising tide of territorialisation in a bid to continue the legacy of other medieval traditions. Although contemporaries used the imagery of the balance of power as part of their political diction, Charles was far from subscribing to the nineteenth-century idea that stability was given whenever and wherever alliances could be formed that were stronger than the strongest single power. Instead, he insisted that stability existed if and as long as he was the holder of the predominant power. He was free from the twentieth-century geopolitical fancy about continental unity and did not conceive of Europe as a set of secular polities, because his notion of Europe was identical with the medieval concept of Catholic Christendom. He failed because he was innovative merely to the end of preserving traditions of the past in a more effective way. The reason for his failure was lack of sincerity of commitment.

Notes

One

1. For the tapestries see: Florens Deuchler, *Die Burgunderbeute* (Bern, 1963).
   Traditions of descent in Burgundy and the Netherlands are recorded in:
   Philippe de Commynes, *Mémoires*, ed. Joseph Calmette, vol. 1 (Paris, 1924),
   p. 139. Johannes Knebel, *Diarium*, ed. Wilhelm Vischer and Heinrich Boos
   (Leipzig, 1880), p. 33. Ms. Biblioteca Apostolica Vaticana, Cod. Vat. Reg. Lat.
   947, fols 1r–75r (Genealogy of the dukes of Brabant to Philip the Fair), partly
   printed in Gert Melville, 'Geschichte in graphischer Gestalt', in:
   Geschichtsschreibung und Geschichtsbewußtsein im späten Mittelalter, ed.
   Hans Patze (Sigmaringen, 1987), pp. 97–8, 230–1 (Vorträge und Forschungen,
   herausgegeben vom Konstanzer Arbeitskreis für mittelalterliche Geschichte 31).
   Edmond de Dynter, *Chronique des ducs de Brabant*, cap. I, ed. P.F.X. de Ram,
   vol. 1 (Brussels, 1854), pp. 3, 5, 7–8. On the negotiations see: *Aktenstücke und
   Briefe zur Geschichte des Hauses Habsburg im Zeitalter Maximilians I*, ed.
   Joseph Chmel (Vienna, 1854), no. 9, 12–16, S. 30–41, 49–62 [repr.
   (Hildesheim, 1968)].
2. See: L. Berthalot, 'Ein neuer Bericht über die Zusammenkunft Friedrichs III.
   und Karls des Kühnen zu Trier 1473', in: *Westdeutsche Zeitschrift für
   Geschichte und Kunst* 30 (1911), p. 425.
3. Maximilian's appreciation of Burgundian administration is shown by the fact
   that he obtained a copy of the handbook of court administration by Olivier de
   La Marche, the influential Burgundian administrator under Charles the Bold.
   See: Olivier de La Marche, *Mémoirs*, vol. 4, ed. Henri Beaumont and J.
   d'Arbaumont (Paris, 1888). For his praise of Mary see: Emperor Maximilian I,
   Theuerdank, in: *Jahrbuch der Kunsthistorischen Sammlungen des
   Allerhöchsten Kaiserhauses* 6 (Vienna, 1888) [repr. (Plochingen and Stuttgart,
   1968)].
4. Jean Molinet, *Chroniques*, ed. Georges Doutrepont and Omer Jodogne, cap.
   151–4, 169–70, vol. 1 (Brussels, 1935), pp. 587–601, vol. 2, pp. 14–31.
5. For Frederick's proclamation concerning the election of his son as Roman king
   in 1486 see the paraphrases in: Johann Joachim Müller, *Des Heiligen
   Römischen Reichs Teutscher Nation ReichsTagsTheatrum wie selbiges unter*

Maximilians I allerhöchster Regierung gestanden, cap. I, vol. 1 (Jena, 1718), p. 5. See also the letter by Frederick III, dated 25 November 1486, in: *Maximilians vertraulicher Briefwechsel mit Sigmund Prüschenk Freiherrn zu Stettenberg*, ed. Victor von Kraus (Innsbruck, 1875), pp. 56–7.

6. Francesco Guicciardini, *Storia d'Italia* [first published posthumously in 1561], in: Guicciardini, *Opere*, ed. Vittorio de Caprariis (Milan and Naples, 1961), p. 374.

7. See: *Quellen zum Verfassungsorganismus des Heiligen Römischen Reiches Deutscher Nation. 1495–1815*, ed. Hanns Hubert Hofmann (Darmstadt, 1976), pp. 9–14.

8. A manuscript fragment of the Latin original of Müntzer's letter is preserved in the papers of Hartmann Schedel in Munich, Bayerische Staatsbibliothek, Incun. C.a. 424. A translation of the letter into Portuguese is preserved in an appendix to an undated edition of John of Sacrobosco's *Opusculum de sphaera* (Vienna, 1518). The Portuguese version has been edited by Henry Harrisse, *The Discovery of North America* (London, 1892), pp. 393–5 [repr. (Amsterdam, 1961)]. A German version is in: Harald Kleinschmidt, *Geschichte der internationalen Beziehungen* (Stuttgart, 1998), pp. 405–7.

9. On the discussions about Columbus's proposals at the Portuguese court see: João de Barros, *Da Asia*, Dec. I, lib. I, cap. 1 and lib. III, cap. 11, ed. Antonio Baião (Coimbra, 1932), p. 112. Fernando Colombo, *Le Historie della vita e dei fatti dell' Ammiraglio Don Cristoforo Colombo*, lib. I, cap. 12, 21, ed. Paolo Emilio Taviani and Ilaria Luzzana Caraci, vol. 1 (Rome, 1990), pp. 64–6, 85. Bartolomé de Las Casas, *Historia de las Indias*, ed. Agustín Millares Carlo, vol. 1 (Madrid, 1957), pp. 153–61, 195–200.

10. For the sources see: Leo Santifaller, *1100 Jahre österreichische und europäische Geschichte in Urkunden und Dokumenten des Haus-, Hof- und Staatsarchivs*, vol. 1 (Vienna, 1949), no. 30, pp. 45–9. Peter Krendl, 'König Maximilian I. und Spanien. 1477–1504', Ph.D. Diss. (University of Graz, 1970), pp. 29–50.

11. Moralists would use Juan's fate as a warning against excessively ambitious marriage plans. Among others see: Desiderius Erasmus, *Institutio principis Christiani*, ed. Otto Herding, in: Erasmus, *Opera omnia*, vol. 4, 1 (Amsterdam, 1974), p. 187.

12. On Philip's diary see: Ferdinand of Aragon [Letter to Louis Ferrer, his ambassador to Philip, 29 June 1506], in: *SP Spain*, vol. 1, no. 470, pp. 389–90. Pontus Heuterus, *Opera historica* (Louvain, 1643), p. 246. For Juana's determination to succeed her mother see: Vincenzo Quirino [Dispatch to the Senate of Venice, 11 July 1506], ed. Constantin von Höfler, 'Depeschen des venetianischen Botschafters bei Erzherzog Philipp, Herzog von Burgund, König von Leon, Castilien, Granada, Dr Vincenzo Quirino, 1505–1506', in: *Archiv für österreichische Geschichte* 66 (1885), no. 121, pp. 241–2.

13. A standard source for female self-reliance is the original of Giovanni Boccaccio's *Decamerone* of the middle of the fourteenth century, that is,

before the *novellae* that it contains became the proverbial source for allegations of women's sexual lust. For interpretations of Boccaccio's text in the latter sense see: *Le menagier de Paris* [1393], vol. 1 (Paris, 1847), pp. 125–8 [repr. (Geneva, 1982)]. Baldassare Castiglione, *Book of the Courtier*, English version (London, 1561), p. 66 [repr. (New York, 1967); first published (Venice, 1528)].

14. On Juana see: Ferdinand of Aragon [Letter to De Puebla, January 1508], in: *SP Spain*, vol. 1, no. 577, pp. 452–4. On Maximilian see: Hans Herzheimer, 'Neue Zeitung' zum Tode Kaiser Maximilians I. [Ms. Vienna, Bibliothek und Kunstblättersammlung des Österreichischen Museums für Angewandte Kunst], ed. Hanna Dornik-Eger, *Albrecht Dürer und die Druckgraphik für Kaiser Maximilian I.* (Vienna, 1971), pp. 35–6.

15. Müller, *ReichsTagsTheatrum* (note 5), pp. 576–612.

16. Maximilian's parents were notorious for adhering to incompatible educational principles. See: Joseph Grünpeck, 'Historia Friderici IV. et Maximiliani I.', cap. 17, 21–4, ed. Joseph Chmel, in: *Der österreichische Geschichtsforscher* 1 (1838), pp. 79, 81–3. Eleanor of Portugal [Letter to Duchess Eleanor of Tirol, 20 June 1466], ed. Katherine Walsh, 'Deutschsprachige Korrespondenz der Kaiserin Leonora von Portugal', in: *Kaiser Friedrich III. (1440–1493) in seiner Zeit*, ed. Paul-Joachim Heinig (Cologne, Weimar and Vienna, 1993), no. IV, p. 441.

17. Leon Battista Alberti, *I libri della famiglia*, book I, ed. Renée Neu Watkins, *The Family in Renaissance Florence* (Columbia, S.C., 1969) pp. 36–40.

18. Augustine, *De vera religione*, cap. I/26, ed. Jacques-Paul Migne, *Patrologiae cursus completus*. Series Latina, vol. 34, col. 145. Isidore of Seville, *Etymologiarum sive originum libri XX*, cap. XI/2, ed. William M. Lindsay (Oxford, 1911).

19. Ed. Rolf Sprandel, in: Sprandel, *Altersschicksal und Altersmoral* (Stuttgart, 1981), pp. 164–86.

20. William Shakespeare, *As You Like it*, II. vii.

21. For details see: Harald Kleinschmidt, *Understanding the Middle Ages* (Woodbridge, 2000), pp. 293–6.

22. Paraphrase of the treaty on the marriage between Arthur and Catherine, 6 June 1500, in: *SP Spain*, vol. 1, no. 255, pp. 220–2. For a description of the pageants on the occasion of Catherine's arrival in England see: 'Here begynneth the note and trewth of the moost goodly behavior in the receyt of the Ladie Kateryne . . . yowen in marriage goinet to Prince Arthur, son and heir unto our noble Soferynge of Englond King Henry the VIIth, in the XVII yeare of his reign' [1501], ed. Francis Grose and F.G.Th. Astle, in: *The Antiquarian Repertory* II, 1 (1808), pp. 249–331. See also: John Leland, ed., 'A Narrative of the Jousts, Banquets and Disguisings Used at the Intertaynement of Katherine Wife to Prince Arthur, Eldest Sonne to King Henry VIIth, 8 November 1501',

in: Leland, *De rebus Britannicis collectanea*, vol. 5 (London, 1774), pp. 356–73 [repr. (Farnborough, 1970)].

23. Henry, Prince of Wales [Memorandum, 27 June 1505], in: *SP Spain*, vol. 1, no. 435, pp. 358–9.

24. De Puebla [Letter to Ferdinand of Aragon, 15 April 1507], Catherine of Aragon [Letter to her father, 5 October 1507], in: *SP Spain*, vol. 1, nos 511, 541, pp. 408–10, 426–8.

25. Gerard de Pleine [Letter to Margaret, 30 June 1514], in: *LP*, vol. 1, no. 3041, pp. 1306–7.

26. On Henry VIII and the imperial succession see: Robert Wingfield [Letter to Wolsey, 10 January 1516 (reports Maximilian's view that the imperial crown should be offered to Henry)]; Pace [Letter to Wolsey, 12 May 1516 (Maximilian willing to adopt Henry as his son)]; Robert Wingfield [Letter to Henry VIII, 17 May 1516 (Maximilian offered to adopt Henry as his son and to designate him as his successor in the empire but wants subsidies)]; Henry VIII [Letter to Wolsey, 27 July 1516 (believes that Maximilian will resign the imperial crown)]; treaty between Maximilian and Henry VIII, art. 5, October 1516 (Henry pledges to accept the imperial crown), in: *LP*, vol. 2, nos 1398, 1878, 1902, 2218, 2463, pp. 386–7, 539–40, 549–50, 675–6, 767–8.

27. Prudencio Sandoval, *Historia de la vida y hechos del Emperador Carlos V* (Antwerp, 1681), vol. 1, p. 196 [new edn (Madrid, 1955)].

28. For Henry VII's embassy see: Henry VII [Instruction to Francis Marsin, James Braybrooke and John Stile to investigate the Old Queen of Naples and her daughter for the marriage project between himself and the younger Queen of Naples, June 1505], in: *Materials for a History of the Reign of Henry VII*, ed. William Campbell, vol. 2 (London, 1877), pp. 223–39 [repr. (Nendeln, 1965)].

29. Maximilian's instruction is recorded in the earliest version of Mennel's calendar of Habsburg saints. See: Jakob Mennel, 'After-Kalender' [1513/14], ed. Wolfgang Irtenkauf, *Der Habsburger-Kalender* (Göppingen, 1979), p. 21. Also in: Maximilian, Instruction to Mennel, *c.* 1515, Ms Vienna, Österreichische Nationalbibliothek, Cod. 2834, fol. 1r-v. In the introductions to the manuscript and the printed versions of his chronicle, Mennel referred explicitly to the fact that he had been commissioned by Maximilian to write the work. See: Ms Vienna, Österreichische Nationalbibliothek, Cod. 3072*, fol. 1r–2v. Jakob Mennel, 'Fürstlich Chronickh kayser maximilians geburt spiegel', 5 vols in 6 parts. Ms Vienna, Österreichische Nationalbibliothek Cod. 3072x, fol. A IIr–v. Printed in: *Jahrbuch der Kunsthistorischen Sammlungen des Allerhöchsten Kaiserhauses* 3 (1885), Reg. 2977, pp. XCI–XCII. Joseph Chmel, *Die Handschriften der K.k.Hofbibliothek Wien*, vol. 1 (Vienna, 1840), p. 1.

30. Mennel, 'Chronickh' (note 29), vol. 2, Ms Vienna, Österreichische Nationalbibliothek Cod. 3073.

31. Aeneas Sylvius Piccolomini [Pope Pius II], *De Bohemorum origine ac gestis historia*, in: Piccolomini, *Opera quae extant omnia* (Basle, 1551), p. 84.

32. Georg Kugler, 'Eine Denkschrift Dr. Jakob Mennels, verfaßt im Auftrage Maximilians I. für seinen Enkel Karl', Ph.D. Diss. (University of Vienna, 1960), fol. 74.

33. Fredegar, *Chronicarum quae dicuntur Fredegarii scholastici libri IV*, cap. II/4–9, cap. III/2,3,5,9, ed. Bruno Krusch, *Fredegarii et aliorvm Chronica. Vitae Sanctorvm, MGH, SS rer. Merov.*, vol. 2 (Hanover, 1888), pp. 45–7, 93–5. Similarly: *Historia Daretis Frigii de origine Francorum, ibid.*, p. 199. See also: *The Anglo-Saxon Chronicle. A Collaborative Edition*, vol. 3: MS A, *s.a.* 855, ed. Janet M. Bately (Cambridge, 1986), p. 46.

34. Jakob Mennel, 'Kaiser Maximilians besonder Buch genannt der Zaiger', Ms Vienna, Österreichische Nationalbibliothek Cod. 7892.

35. Kugler, 'Eine Denkschrift' (note 32), fols 67–8, 71–2.

36. The Mennel broadsheet has the title 'De Diui Maximiliani Romanorum Cesaris Christiana vita. Et felicissimo eius obitu.' Print, *c.* 1519 (Vienna, Graphische Sammlung Albertina). An inscription on the side of the picture showing Mennel before Maximilian reads: 'Cesari antiquissime et nobilissime Genealogie eius per Manlium libri leguntur' [his most ancient and noblest genealogies are read to the emperor by Mennel]. Reprinted in: *Maximilian I. Katalog zur Ausstellung Innsbruck 1969* (Innsbruck, 1969), no. 261, pp. 66–7.

37. Kugler, 'Eine Denkschrift' (note 32), fol. 74. For a more detailed discussion of medieval traditions in Charles's world picture, see below, Chapter II.

38. Vienna, Österreichisches Staatsarchiv, Haus-, Hof- und Staatsarchiv, Kasten blau 56, fol. 5v. ed. Kugler (note 32), fol. 70.

39. Kugler, 'Eine Denkschrift' (note 32), fol. 73.

40. Jakob Mennel, *Kayser all und Babst all* (s.l., 1515).

Two

1. Maximilian [Letter to Charles, September 1513], in: Andreas Walther, *Die Anfänge Karls V* (Leipzig, 1911), p. 218. Archduchess Margaret [Instruction to her ambassador in England, 1514], in: *LP*, vol. 1, no. 3210, pp. 1360–1.

2. For a verbal description see: William Camden, *The Historie of the Most Renowned and Victorious Princesse Elizabeth, Late Queen of England* (London, 1688), fol. A [IIIv]–B [Ir] [first published (London, 1615)].

3. Henry VIII [Letter to Pope Leo X, 12 August 1514], in: *LP*, vol. 1, no. 3139, p. 1341. *Négociations diplomatiques entre la France et l'Autriche durant les trente premières années du XVIe siècle*, ed. André Joseph Ghislain Le Glay, vol. 2 (Paris, 1845), no. 29, p. 96.

4. André Joseph Ghislain Le Glay, ed., *Correspondence de l'empereur Maximilien et de Marguerite d'Autriche, sa fille*, vol. 1 (Paris, 1837), p. 394. For a record

Notes

of Maximilian's own tournament skills see: *Freydal des Kaisers Maximilian I., Turniere und Mummereien*, ed. Quirin von Leitner, 3 vols (Vienna, 1880–2).

5. Memorandum by Manrique de Lara for Cardinal Jimenez de Cisneros, 8 March 1516, ed. Salvador de Madariaga, *Charles Quint* (Paris, 1969), pp. 305–17. Also in: Kohler, ed., *Quellen*, p. 34. The treaty of Noyon (13 August 1516), in which the return of Navarre to French control was pledged, is in: Jean Dumont, *Corps diplomatique universel*, vol. 4, pt 1 (The Hague, 1726), no. 106, pp. 224–8, 240.

6. Remy du Puys, *La tryumphante entrée de Charles Prince des Espagnes en Bruges. 1515*, reprint, ed. Sidney Anglo (New York and Amsterdam 1973).

7. William of Croy [Letter to Wolsey, 6 August 1517], in: *LP*, vol. 2, no. 3562, p. 113.

8. Lara's memorandum (note 5), in: Kohler, ed., *Quellen*, p. 35.

9. Charles V [Letter to Archduchess Margaret, 5 March 1519], in: *RTA*, vol. 1, pp. 352–5. Also in: Kohler, ed., *Quellen*, pp. 41–4.

10. Verbatim report of Charles's address to the States General of the Netherlands, 25 October 1555, ed. William Stirling, *The Cloister Life of the Emperor Charles the Fifth* (London, 1853), pp. 7–9. Also in: Kohler, ed., *Quellen*, pp. 466–8.

11. Baldassare Castiglione, *Book of the Courtier* (London, 1561) [repr. (New York, 1967); first published (Venice, 1528)].

12. Niccolò Machiavelli, *Il principe*, cap. 21, in: Machiavelli, *Opere*, ed. Mario Bonfantini (Milan and Naples, 1963), pp. 71–4.

13. Jean Bodin, *Les six livres de la République*, cap. 8, vol. 1 (Paris, 1576), pp. 179–80 [repr., ed. Christiane Frémont, Marie-Dominique Couzinet and Alain Rochais (Paris, 1986)].

14. Andreas Knichen, *De iure territorii* (Frankfurt, 1600), cap. I, no. 33, p. 59.

15. Engelbert of Admont, 'De ortu et fine Romani imperii', cap. 2, ed. Melchior Goldast of Haiminsfeld, *Politica imperialia* (Frankfurt, 1614), p. 755. John Quidort of Paris, *De potestati regia et papali*, cap. 1, ed. Fritz Bleienstein (Stuttgart, 1969), pp. 75–8.

16. Justus Lipsius, *Two Bookes of Constancie* [tr. John Stradling (London 1584)], ed. R. Kirk and C. M. Hall (New Brunswick, 1939), pp. 95–6. Lipsius, *Sixe Bookes of Politickes or Civil Doctrine* [1589], ed. William Jones (London, 1594), p. 128 [repr. (Amsterdam and New York, 1970)]. William of Orange, *Apologie ofte verantwoordinghe des derluchtigen ende hoogeborenen Vorsts end Heeren, Heeren Wilhelms van Gods ghenade prince van Orangien* (Leiden, 1581), ed. Hans Wansink (Leiden, 1969) [first published English version (London, 1581)].

17. Mercurino Arborio di Gattinara [Memorandum to the Royal Council of Castile, July 1526], ed. Carlo Bornate, 'Historia vite et gestorum per dominum magnum Cancellarium, con note, aggiunte et documenti', in: *Miscellanea di storia Italiana* 48 (1915), pp. 492–3.

18. Lazarus Spengler, 'Bedenken' [*c.* 1529], ed. Wolfgang Steglich, *RTA*, vol. 8, pp. 502–3.

19. Augustine, *De civitate Dei*, cap. XIX/14, ed. Bernard Kalb and Alphons Dombart (Turnhout, 1955), pp. 680–2 (Corpus Christianorum. Series Latina, 48 B).

20. Leon Battista Alberti, *De re aedificatoria* [editio princeps (Paris, 1512)], cap. V/17, ed. Max Theuer (Darmstadt, 1991), p. 272 [first edn (Vienna and Leipzig, 1912)].

21. Ulrich von Hutten [Letter to Willibald Pirckheimer, 25 October 1518], in: Hutten, *Schriften*, vol. 1, ed. Eduard Böcking (Leipzig, 1859), pp. 201–3.

22. Anthony Fitzherbert, *Loffice et auctoryte des Justyces de peas* (1538), fols XCVIr–XVCIIIr.

23. For miles discs as schematic route maps of the late sixteenth century using the model of the planetary spheres while recording the distances between cities, see the Nuremberg cases printed by Georg Kreydlein, *c.* 1575 (Nuremberg, Germanisches Nationalmuseum, HB 23191, Kapsel 1288), and by Johann Schirmer in 1612 (*ibid.*, HB 4242, Kapsel 1377, the Augsburg miles discs printed by Hans Rogel, *c.* 1565 (Augsburg: Staats- und Stadtbibliothek, Graph 29/140a) and by Kaspar Augustin in 1629 (*ibid.*, Graph 29/140a), the Erfurt miles disc of the late sixteenth century (*ibid.*, HB 21662, Kapsel 1377), and the London miles disc of *c.* 1600 (Short Title Catalogue Br 10021.7; Society of Antiquaries of London). The Ogilby map is in: John Ogilby, *Britannia* (London, 1675), frontispiece.

24. Erhard Etzlaub, *Das ist der Rom Weg von meylen zu meylen mit puncten verzeychnet.* Printed broadsheet (Nuremberg, *c.* 1502).

25. John Bucius, *Evropa prima pars terrae in forma virginis.* Single sheet (Paris, 1537).

26. Sebastian Münster, *Cosmographia*, vol. 1 (Basle, 1628), p. 54.

27. The original appeared at Magdeburg in 1585.

28. On the methodology of eighteenth-century statistics see: Gottfried Achenwall, *Vorbereitung zur Staatswissenschaft der heutigen fürnehmsten Europäischen Reiche und Staaten* (Göttingen, 1748). Anton Friedrich Büsching, *Vorbereitung zur gründlichen und nützlichen Kenntnis der geographischen Beschaffenheit und Staatsverfassungen* (Hamburg and Vienna, 1758) [fourth edn (*ibid.*, 1768)].

29. Domenico di Bandino, 'Fons memorabilium rerum', part III, Ms. Florence, Biblioteca Medicea Laurenziana, Ms. Gadd reliq. 126. *Libro del Conoscimiento de todos los reynos y tierras y senorios que son por el mundo y de las senales y armas que han cada tierra y senorio por sy de los reyes señores que los proueen escrito por un franciscano español á mediados del siglo XIV*, ed. Marcos Jiménez de la Espada (Madrid, 1877) [repr. (Barcelona, 1980)].

30. For references to a larger island in the vicinity of a number of smaller islands see: the Cantino map of 1501 or 1502 and Francesco Roselli in his world map of 1508 [ed. in: Peter Whitfield, *The Image of the World* (London, 1994) [repr. (London, 1997)], pp. 44–7, 50–1]. In verbal references the plural is used in the edicts in the name of Alexander VI, whereas Columbus himself and the Catholic kings preferred the singular. The plural form *'terrae firmae'* in the papal edicts renders the assumption unlikely that the phrase was meant to denote continents of the tri-continental *ecumene*. However, in his 'Testament and Codicil of 19 May 1506', Columbus referred to himself as representative of 'the already discovered and newly to be discovered islands and the firm land of India' [ed. John Boyd Thacher, *Christopher Columbus. His Life, His Work, His Remains*, 3 vols, 3 (New York, 1904), pp. 658–60] and thus associated the singular form of the phrase with a part of the tri-continental *ecumene*. Elsewhere, Columbus used the singular *'Tierra firma'* for lands off the Asian coast, as in his *Lettera rarissima* of 1503, that he had been willing to approach a *'Tierra firma'* from 'Janahica' (Jamaica) ['Relación de Cuarto Viaje' = 'Lettera rarissima', 7 July 1503, in: *Relazioni e lettere sul secondo, terzo e quarto viaggio*, ed. Paolo Emilio Taviani, Consuelo Varela, Juan Gil and Marina Conti, vol. 1 (Rome, 1992), p. 131]. The charters of the Catholic kings for Columbus and other seafarers have the singular throughout but connect it with the classification of the seaways under consideration as 'el Mar oceano que es nuestro' [instruction for Columbus, 28 May 1493, ed. Martín Fernández de Navarrete, *Colección de los viages y descubrimientos que hicieron por mar los españoles desde fines del siglo XV*, vol. 2, second edn (Madrid, 1859), pp. 69–70; instruction for the fourth voyage to Columbus where he is styled 'nuestro Almirante de las islas e tierra firme que son en el mar oceano a la parte de las Indias', ed. Navarrete, *Colección*, vol. 1, second edn, p. 427; instruction by Isabel of Castile to Nicolas de Ovando, 16 September 1501, ed. in: *Colección de documentos inéditos . . . en América y Oceania*, vol. 31 (Madrid, 1879), p. 13]. Likewise the Tordesillas treaty of 1494 stipulated in Art. 1 that a *rraya* or maritime borderline should be drawn by which the discovered or henceforth to be discovered islands or a firm land were to be assigned to either of the signatory parties. See: *Fontes Historiae Iuris Gentium*, No. 11, ed. Wilhelm Georg Carl Grewe, vol. 2 (Berlin and New York, 1988), pp. 110–16.
31. Amerigo Vespucci, *Mundus novus*, facsimile, ed. Emil Sarnow and Kurt Trübenbach (Strasbourg, 1903).
32. See: Martin Waldseemüller, *Cosmographiae Introductio* (Strasbourg, 1507) [ed. Franz Ritter von Wieser (Strasbourg, 1907)].
33. The section on fol. A IIv with the passage in which the name 'Americi terram siue Americam' appears is in: Franz Wawrick, 'Das Amerika-Bild in Österreich', in: *Die Neue Welt. Österreich und die Erforschung Amerikas*, ed. Franz Wawrick, Elisabeth Zeilinger, Jan Mokre and Helga Hühnel (Vienna,

1992), p. 24. Cf.: Martin Waldseemüller, 'In Claudii Ptolemei Supplementum', in: Claudius Ptolemaus, *Geographia* (Strasbourg, 1513), pl. 2. Alexander von Humboldt was already aware of the fact that the earliest references to the name America concerned the *terra* in the southern part of the ocean only. For the beginning of the discussion on the naming of America see: Friedrich Heinrich Alexander von Humboldt, *Examen critique de l'histoire de la géographie du nouveau continent*, vol. 5 (Paris, 1839), pp. 180–225. Humboldt, 'Ueber die ältesten Karten des Neuen Continents und den Namen Amerika', in: Friedrich Wilhelm Ghillany, *Geschichte des Seefahrers Ritter Martin Behaim* (Nuremberg, 1853), p. 8.

34. Johann Adolph Muehlich and Johann Grüninger, *Der welt kugel* (Strasbourg, 1509), fol. C IIv. Johann Schöner applied the phrase 'AMERICA VEL BRASILIA SIVE PAPAGALLI TERRA' to the north-eastern part of the *terra* which, by that time, was larger than that of Muehlich/Grüninger of 1509. Printed in Franz Ritter von Wieser, *Magalhâes-Strasse und Austral-Continent auf den Globen des Johannes Schöner* (Innsbruck, 1881).

35. Christoph Egenolf, *Chronica. Beschreibung vng gemeyne anzeyge Vonn aller Welt herkommen* (Frankfurt, 1535), fols CIIIv–CIIIr, CVIr. Likewise: Sebastian Franck, *Chronica. Zeitbuch vnnd Geschichtslibell* (Ulm, 1536), fol. CCXv.

36. See: Peter Whitfield, *New Found Lands. Maps in the History of Explorations* (London, 1998), p. 68.

37. Florence, Biblioteca Nazionale, Magl. VIII, 81, fol. 60v, 57r. Printed in: Franz Ritter von Wieser, 'Die Karte des Bartolomeo Colombo über die vierte Reise des Admirals', *Mitteilungen des Instituts für Österreichische Geschichtsforschung, Ergänzungsband* 4 (1893), after p. 498. The best edn is: *Cristoforo Colombo e l'apertura degli spazi*, ed. Guglielmo Cavallo (Rome, 1992), vol. 2, p. 669.

38. See: Raleigh Ashlin Skelton, *Decorated Printed Maps of the Fifteenth to Eighteenth Centuries* (London, 1952).

39. John III, archbishop of Sultanyeh, 'Libellus de notitia orbis [Ms. Cod. Lat. University Library Leipzig, 1404]', ed. Anton Kern, 'Der "Libellus de Notitia orbis" Iohannes' III. (de Galonifontibus?) O.P. Erzbischofs von Sultanyeh', *Archivum Fratrum Praedicatorum* 8 (1938), p. 120.

40. Nicolae Iorga, *Notes et extraits pour servir à l'histoire des Croisades au XVe siècle*, vol. 1 (Paris, 1899).

41. For a description of the conquest of Malacca see: François de Sa de Menesses, *The Conquest of Malacca*, ed. Edgar C. Knowlton (Kuala Lumpur, 1970).

42. Printed in: Christopher Columbus, *Relazioni e lettere sul secondo, terzo e quarto viaggio*, ed. Paolo Emilio Taviani, Consuelo Varela, Juan Gil and Marina Conti, vol. 2 (Rome, 1992), p. 339.

43. See on the continuity of the theory of a vast 'fourth' or 'southern' continent into and beyond the sixteenth century: *America. Das frühe Bild der Neuen*

Welt, ed. Hans Wolff (Munich, 1992), p. 57 (prints a map of the Pacific by Guillaume Broucon, Huntington Library, 1543), *ibid.*, p. 138 (prints a map of the Pacific by Battista Agnese, Munich, Bayerische Staatsbibliothek. *c.* 1535–42, showing Magellan's route). *Portugaliae monumenta cartographica*, ed. Armando Cortesão and Avelino Teixeira da Mota, vol. 5 (Lisboa, 1960), p. 529 (prints a map of the world from the atlas by António Sanches, The Hague, Koninklijke Bibliotheek, 1641).

44. Peter Martyr d'Anghiera, 'De orbo novo decades', cap. I/1 [1493], in: Anghiera, *La scoperta del Nuovo Mondo negli scritti di Pietro Martire d'Anghiera*, ed. Ernesto Luneardi, Elisa Magioncalda and Rosanna Mazzacane (Rome, 1988), p. 218.

45. See: Antonio Pigafetta, *Magellan's Voyage. A Narrative of the First Circumnavigation* (New Haven and London, 1969).

46. For a survey of the cartography of the Pacific see: Lawrence C. Wroth, 'The Early Cartography of the Pacific', in: *Papers of the Bibliographical Society of America* 38 (1944), pp. 87–268.

47. For examples, see the world map first printed by Willem Blaeu in 1630, ed. John Goss, *Blaeu's The Grand Atlas of the Seventeenth-Century World* (London, 1990), pp. 24–5. Lucien Louis Joseph Gallois, *De Orontio Finaeo* (Paris, 1890).

48. See: *Focus Behaim Globus*, 2 vols (Nuremberg, 1992).

49. Waldseemüller's printed gores of 1507; see: *Die älteste Karte mit dem Namen Amerika aus dem Jahre 1507 und die Carta marina aus dem Jahre 1516 des M. Waldseemüller (Ilacomilus)*, ed. Joseph Fischer and Franz Ritter von Wieser (Innsbruck and London, 1903).

50. Giovanni Contarini in his world map of 1506 [ed. Whitfield, *Image* (note 30), pp. 46–7.

51. Printed in: Whitfield, *Image* (note 30), pp. 52–3.

52. For the Schöner globe see: Wieser, *Magalhâes-Strasse* (note 34), pp. 9–19.

53. For Apian's globe see: Whitfield (note 30), pp. 56–7.

54. For two-dimensional depictions of the globe see: Peter Apian, *Cosmographicus liber* (Landshut, 1524). Muehlich/Grüninger, *Welt kugel* (note 34). Johannes de Sacrobosco, *Opusculum* (Vienna, 1518). Johann Schöner, *Luculentissima quaedam terrae totius descriptio* (Nuremberg, 1515).

55. Marco Polo, *Das Buch der Wunder*, cap. III/1 [*Le Livre des Merveilles du Monde*, Paris, Bibliothèque nationale de France, Ms. Fr. 2810, fols 71–2], ed. Marie-Hélène Tesnière, François Avril and Marie-Thérèse Gousset (Munich, 1999), pp. 148–52.

56. For Columbus's belief that he reached the proximity of Zipangu see the entry for 23 October 1492 in his *Diario de a bordo*, ed. Luis Arranz (Madrid, 1985), p. 106 (where he identifies Cuba with Zipangu). Cf. the entry for 24 December 1492, *ibid.*, p. 166 (where Columbus reports on a gold island seemingly known

by the local population under the name Cibao). The same name also appears in the form Civao on a map autograph of Columbus preserved in the archives of the duke of Alba in Madrid (printed in Cavallo, ed., *Apertura* (note 37), vol. 2, p. 618).

57. For reproductions of maps relevant to the early European cartography of Japan, see: Paul [Pál] Graf Teleki, *Atlas zur Geschichte der Kartographie der Japanischen Inseln* (Budapest, 1909) [repr. (Nendeln, 1966)].

58. Gerhard Mercator, *Atlas minor* (Amsterdam, 1569).

59. Simon Grynaeus, *Novus Orbis ac insularum veteribus incognitarum*, vol. I (Basle, 1532), s.p.

60. For a recent study of the motto see: Hans-Joachim König, 'PLUS ULTRA. Ein Weltreichs- und Eroberungsprogramm? Amerika und Europa in politischen Vorstellungen im Spanien Karls V', in: *Karl V*, ed. Alfred Kohler *et al.* (Vienna, 2002), pp. 197–222.

61. On the making of the *Requerimiento* see: Bartolomé de Las Casas, *Historia de las Indias*, lib. III, cap. 57, ed. Agustín Millares Carlo, vol. 2 (Madrid, 1957), p. 58, attested to Rubios's authorship.

62. For a description of the enforcement of the *Requerimiento* see: Antonio de Herrera Tordesillas, *Historia general de las hechos de los Castellanos en las Islas y Tierra Firme del Mar Oceano* [first published 1601], ed. J. Natalacio González, vol. 2 (Asunción, Buenos Aires, 1944), Dec. I, lib. VII, cap. 4, vol. 3 (Madrid, 1934), pp. 170–2.

63. Diego Velázquez [Instruction to Hernán Cortés, 23 October 1518], ed. Beatríz Artega Garaz, Guadalupe Pérez San Vicente, *Cedulario Cortesiano* (Mexico, 1949), pp. 9–33. Also edited by José Luis Martinez, *Documentos Cortesianos*, vol. 1 (Mexico, 1990), pp. 45–57.

64. Hernán Cortés, 'Primera Carta' [10 July 1519], in: *Cartas y documentos*, ed. Mario Hernández Sanchez-Barba (Mexico, 1963), pp. 7, 27–8.

65. Hernán Cortés, 'Segunda Carta' [30 October 1520], in: Cortés, *Cartas* (note 64), p. 33. Gonzalo Fernández de Oviedo y Valdés, *Sumario del Natural Historia de las Indias*, ed. José Miranda (Mexico, 1950), pp. 79, 272–5, repeated these claims, probably on the basis of Cortes's *cartas* and stated that Charles had gained an 'imperio occidental de las Indias, isles y tierra-firme del mar Oceano'. He added that the islands that Columbus had first visited were identical with the 'Islas Hespéridas', named after Hespero, the alleged twelfth original king of Spain, believed to have flourished 1658 BC.: Oviedo y Valdés, *ibid.*, p. 297.

66. Cortés, 'Segunda Carta' (note 64), pp. 58–60, 68–9. Versions of Moctezuma's speech are also contained in: Gonzalo Fernández de Oviedo y Valdés, *Historia general y natural de las Indias, Islas y Tierra-Firme del Mar Oceano* [1535], ed. José Amador de los Rios, vol. 1 (Madrid, 1851), pp. 278–87, 531–5. Juan Ginés de Sepúlveda, *De rebus Hispanorum gestis ad novum orbem*

Mexicumque, lib. V, cap. 21, in: Sepúlveda, *Opera cum edita tum inedita* (Madrid, 1780), pp. 134–6.

67. Bartolus of Sassoferato, *In secvndvm Digesti noui partem commentaria*, ad dig. XLIX/15,22, in: Bartolus, *Opera*, vol. 6 (Venice, 1570–1), pp. 227–8. For a case of the reception of Bartolus's theory in the late fifteenth century see: Juan de Torquemada, 'Opusculum ad honorem Romani imperii et dominorum Romanorum' [1467/68], ed. Hubert Jedin, 'Juan de Torquemada und das Imperium Romanum', in: *Archivum Fratrum Praedicatorum* 12 (1942), pp. 275–6.

68. Charles V, instruction to Hernán Cortés, 26 June 1523, in: Cortés, *Cartas* (note 64), pp. 585–92.

69. *Translatio Sancti Liborii*, cap. 5, ed. Georg Heinrich Pertz, *MGH SS*, vol. 4, p. 151.

70. Maximilian developed his crusading plans most famously in his memorandum of 1517 under the title 'Kayser Maximilian Anslag wider die Türcken', Ms. Österreichisches Staatsarchiv, Haus-, Hof- und Staatsarchiv, Maximiliana, Fz 30b (1517) 2, fols 131r–40v. See for edited parts of the memorandum: Georg Wagner, 'Der letzte Türkenkreuzzugsplan Kaiser Maximilians I. aus dem Jahre 1517', in: *Mitteilungen des Instituts für Österreichische Geschichtsforschung* 77 (1969), pp. 320–47. Also in: *Quellen zur Geschichte Maximilians I. und seiner Zeit*, ed. Hermann Wiesflecker and Inge Wiesflecker-Friedhuber (Darmstadt, 1996), pp. 268–79.

71. On the sculptures see: José García Icazbalceta, ed., *Colección de documentos para la historia de México*, 2nd edn, vol. 2 (Mexico, 1971), pp. 365, 407–10, 426, 432–3. Richard Karl Nebel, *Altmexikanische Religion und christliche Heilsbotschaft* (Immensee, 1983), pp. 116–17. Cortés described buildings found on the *Tierra Firme* as done in the Muslim style, thereby categorising Native Americans as if they were Muslims. See: Cortés, *Primera Carta*, in: Cortés, *Cartas* (note 64), pp. 7, 11–2, 24.

72. Bernal Díaz del Castillo, *Historia verdadera de la conquista de la nueva España*, cap. 20, ed. Joaquím Ramirez Cabañas, vol. 1 (Mexico, 1960), p. 31. See also: Juan de Torquemada, *Ia – IIIa parte de los veynte y un libros rituals y Monarquía Indiana con el origin y guerras de los Indias Occidentales de sus poblaçones descubrimiento, conquista, conversion y otras cosas marvillosas de la esma tierra*, lib. I, cap. 4, vol. 1 (Sevilla, 1615), pp. 387–91. Ginés de Sepúlveda, *Rebus* (note 65), lib. III, cap. 17, p. 74–5.

73. Alfonso V, king of Portugal, issued a decree on 22 October 1443 regarding crusades and the fifth of all profits from the campaigns. For the claims by the Castilian Crown that Cortés himself recognised, see: Cortés 'Primera Carta' (note 64), p. 27. Díaz del Castillo, *Historia* (note 72), cap. 105, pp. 89–91, confirmed that Cortés claimed one fifth of the spoils for the Crown.

74. Matías de Paz, 'Del dominio de los Reyes de España sobre los Indios', ed. Silvio Zavala in: Juan Lopez de Palacio Rubios, *De las islas del mar Océano*, cap. IV, § 7, cap. V (Mexico and Buenos Aires, 1954), p. 215.

75. Martín Fernández Enciso, 'Memorial que dió el Bachiller Enciso de lo ejecutao por él en defensa de los Reales derechos en la materia de los indios', ed. Luís Torres de Mendoza, *Colección de documentos ineditos relativos al descubrimiento, conquista y organización de las posesiones españoles en América y Oceanía, sacerdos, en su mayor parte, del Real Archivio de Indias*, vol. 1 (Madrid, 1864), p. 443 [repr. (Vaduz, 1964)].

76. Gregory VII, Registrum, lib. VIII, ep. 6 [1075], ed. Jacques-Paul Migne, *Patrologiae cursus completus*. Series Latina, vol. 158, cols 454–5.

77. Pope Eugene IV, Bull, 8 January 1443, in: *Monumenta Henricina*, ed. António Joaquim Dias Dinis, vol. 7 (Coimbra, 1965), no. 232, pp. 344–50. See also: Pope Eugene IV, Bull, 9 January 1443, in: *ibid.*, vol. 8 (1967), no. 1, pp. 1–4.

78. Ginés de Sepúlveda's *Rebus* (note 66), lib. III, cap. XVIII, pp. 74–5.

79. Foremost among the theorists of 'natural slavery' was: John Major, *In secundum liber Sententiarum [Petri Lombardi]* (Paris, 1519), fol. CLXXXVIIr. According to Las Casas, Bishop Juan de Quevedo, a Franciscan, advised the newly elected Emperor Charles V that the Indians were 'slaves by nature'. See: Lewis Hanke, *All Mankind is One. A Study of the Disputation between Bartolomé de Las Casas and Juan Ginés de Sepúlveda in 1550 on the Intellectual and Religious Capacity of the American Indians* (DeKalb, IL, 1974), p. 11. On his deathbed Betanzos revoked his view and admitted that he had been mistaken. For an edition of the revocation text see: Bartolomé de Las Casas, *Tratado de Indias y el doctor Sepúlveda*, ed. Manuel Giménez Fernández (Caracas, 1962), pp. 184–6. For attitudes of the pope see: Clement VII, Bull Intra Arcana, 8 May 1529, partly ed. Lewis Hanke, 'Pope Paul III and the American Indians', in: *Harvard Theological Review* 30 (1937), p. 77.

80. Paul III, Bull Sublimis Deus, 1 June 1537, ed. Alberto Hera, 'El derecho delos Indios a la libertad y a la fé. La bula "Sublimis Deus"', in: *Anuario de la historia del derecho español* 36 (1956), pp. 161–2. Paul III, Bull Veritas Ipsa, 2 June 1537, ed. Josef Metzler, *America Pontifica primi saeculi evangelizationis. 1493–1592*, vol. 1 (Vatican City, 1991), pp. 364–6. Some influence came from a colleague of Las Casas, Julián Garcés, *De habilitate et capacitate gentium sive Indorum novi mundi nuncupati ad fidem Christi . . . suscipiat* (Rome, 1537).

81. The text of the revocation is in: Paul III, Edict Non indecens, 19 June 1538, in: Metzler, *America* (note 80), vol. 1, pp. 373–5.

82. As late as 1550, Juan Ginés de Sepúlveda upheld the same view that Native Americans had to the servants of the Spanish *conquistadores*. He did so in a grand debate, which was called by Charles V and began in Valladolid on 7 July 1550 between Sepúlveda and Las Casas as the contender in the presence of high-ranking representatives of the Catholic Church in Spain. The debate was called

to settle the dispute over the question of whether Native Americans ought to be converted to Christianity and, if so, by what legitimate means. The debate ended without a formal verdict. See for the records of the debate: Bartolomé de Las Casas, *Aqui se contiene vna disputa o controversia entre el bispo dom fray Bartholome de las Casas o Casaus Obispo que fue dela ciudad Real de Chtpa que es en las Indias parte de la nueva España y el doctor Ginés de Sepúlueda Coronista del Emperador nuestro señor* (Valladolid, 1552) [summary of the debate by Domingo de Soto], ed. Lewis Hanke and Manuel Giménez Fernández, *Tratados de Fray Bartolomé de Las Casas*, vol. 1 (Mexico, 1965), pp. 217–459. Also in: Las Casas, *Die Disputationen von Valladolid (1550–1551)*, ed. Mariano Delgado (Paderborn, 1994), pp. 339–436. Also printed separately s.t.: Las Casas, *Disputa o controversia de Sepúlveda contendiendo acerca a licitud de las conquistas de las Indias reproducida literalmente de la edición de Sevilla de 1552 y colejada con la de Barcelona de 1646* (Madrid, 1908)ʹ [repr. (Zug, 1985)]. A separate manuscript of Las Casas's part in the debate has been edited by Stafford C. M. Poole, *In Defense of the Indians* (DeKalb, IL, 1974).

83. The treaty of Alcacovas has been published in *Documentos referentes a las relaciones con Portugal durante el reinado de los Reyes Católicos*, ed. Antonio de la Torre y del Cerro and Luis Suarez Fernandez, vol. 1 (Valladolid, 1958–63), pp. 245–84. Also in: *European Treaties Bearing on the History of the United States and Its Dependencies to 1648*, no. 3, ed. Frances Gardiner Davenport (Washington, 1971), pp. 33–48. Also in: *Descobrimentos portugueses*, ed. João Martins da Silva Marques, vol. 3, no. 142 (Lisbon, 1971), pp. 181–209.

84. See for papal crusading bulls in favour of the kings of Portugal: Benedict XII, Gaudemus et exultamus, 30 April 1341, in: *Monumenta Henricina* (note 77), vol. 1, no. 84 (1960), pp. 178–86 [concedes the crusading tithe for military actions against 'infidels' in Africa]. Martin V, Rex Regum, 4 April 1418, *ibid.*, vol. 2, no. 143 (1967), pp. 282–5. Eugene IV, Rex Regum, 8 January 1443, *ibid.*, vol. 7, no. 232 (1965), pp. 344–50 [authorises a crusade]. Nicholas V, Dum diversis, 10 June 1452, *ibid.*, vol. 11, no. 146 (1970), pp. 197–202 [authorises a crusade]. Nicholas V, Romanus Pontifex, 8 January 1455, *ibid.*, vol. 12, no. 36 (1971), pp. 71–9 [authorises a crusade]. Calixtus III, Ad summj pontificatus apicem, 15 May 1455, *ibid.*, vol. 12, no. 64 (1972), pp. 123–9 [authorises a crusade]. Calixtus III, Etsi cuncti, 15 February 1456, *ibid.*, vol. 12, no. 116 (1972), pp. 225–9 [authorises a crusade]. Calixtus III, Inter cetera, 13 March 1456, *ibid.*, vol. 13, no. 137 (1972), pp. 286–8 [inserts the Romanus pontifex of Nicholas V and confirms the authorisation of a crusade].

85. Sixtus IV, Romanus pontifex, 28 January 1481, Archivio Vaticano, Reg. Lat. 805, fol. 253r–v. [obliges the Portuguese clergy to make missionary efforts among the Muslims in Africa]. Sixtus IV, Aeterni Regis, 21 June 1481, ed. in: *Alguns documentos do Archivo Nacional da Torre do Tombo* (Lisbon, 1892),

pp. 46–53 [stipulates a crusade to be conducted by the Portuguese king]. Sixtus IV, 11 September 1481, in: *Monumenta missionaria africana. Africa Ocidental*, ed. António Brásio, vol. 1 (Lisbon, 1952), p. 7 [promises indulgences for Christians to choose to live in the newly built and to be built fortress El Mina under the control of the Portuguese king]. Sixtus IV, Rationi congruit, 12 September 1484, ed. Odoricus Raynald, *Compendium annalium ecclesiasticorum*, vol. 12 (Prague, 1727), pp. 97–100 [obliges the Portuguese king to conduct a crusade]. Innocent VIII, 18 February 1486, edited in *Alguns documentos* (as above), p. 57 [renews bulls of Sixtus IV].

86. On the crusading bulls for Spain see: José Goñi Gaztambide, *Historia de la Bula de la Cruzada en España* (Vitoria, 1958).

87. Tommaso de Vio, Cardinal Cajetan, *Sancti Thomae Aquinatis doctoris angelica opera omnia cum commentariis Thomas de Vio Caetani*, vol. 9 (Rome, 1897), p. 94.

88. Desiderius Erasmus [Preface to his edition of works by Suetonius, 1517], in: Erasmus, *Opus Epistolarum*, vol. 2, ed. Percy Stafford Allen (Oxford, 1910), pp. 579–86. Erasmus [Letter to Alfonso Valdés, secretary to Charles V, 2 March 1529], in: Erasmus, *Opus Epistolarum*, vol. 8, ed. Percy Stafford Allen and Helen Mary Allen (Oxford, 1934), pp. 89–96.

89. Charter of 17 April 1492, ed. Navarrete, *Colección* (note 30), vol. 2, no. V, second edn (Madrid, 1859), pp. 11–13. Further instructions by the Spanish rulers for Columbus and other expedition leaders contained the name in its singular form (charter of 30 April 1492, ed. Navarrete, *Colección*, vol. 2, no. VIII, second edn, pp. 19–20) but connected it with the qualification of the waterway under consideration as 'el Mar oceano que es nuestro' and referred to Columbus as 'nuestro Almirante de la islas e tierra firme que se han descubierto ó han de descubrir en el Mar Oceano à la parte de las Indias' (Charter of 28 May 1493, ed. Navarrete, *Colección*, vol. 2, no. XLI, 2nd edn, p. 75); instruction for the fourth voyage to Columbus as 'nuestro Almirante de las islas e tierra firme que son en el mar oceano a la parte de las Indias' (ed. Navarrete, *Colección*, vol. 1, 2nd edn, 1858, p. 427). Instruction by Isabel of Castile to Nicolas de Ovando of 16 September 1501 ('Islas e Tierra firme del Mar Oceano'), ed. in: *Colección* (note 30), vol. 31 (Madrid, 1879), p. 13. The Catholic kings, Letter to Columbus, 5 September 1493, ed. Navarrete, *Colección* (note 30), vol. 2, no. LXXI, 2nd edn, p. 124.

90. Alexander VI, Inter cetera, 3 May 1493, ed. Metzler, *America* (note 80), vol. 1, p. 73. Note the plural of the formula for the 'islands and firm lands' in this privilege.

91. The Spanish version of the treaty has been edited with translations into English and German by Grewe, *Fontes* (note 30), vol. 2, pp. 110–16. The ratification charter is available in: *Colección de documentos* (note 75), vol. 30, p. 258. Another edition of the treaty together with the ratification charters of the kings

of Portugal and Castile is in: Davenport, *Treaties* (note 83), vol. 1, pp. 86–93. On the negotiations see: *Corpus documental del tratado de Tordesillas*, ed. L. Adão da Fonseca (Lisbon, 1995).

92. The map has the title 'Carta da navigar per le isole Novamente trovate in la parte de l'India (Carta Cantino)'. 1501 or 1502. Printed in Cavallo, *Apertura* (note 37), vol. 2, between pp. 736 and 737. The map shows the demarcation line of the Tordesillas treaty. The western part of the *terra* is identified as under the control of the 'King of Castile' whereas the south-eastern part of *terra*, east of the demarcation line, bears no inscription. However, a large hypothetical island north-east of the island world visited by Columbus and, again, located east of the demarcation line is identified as 'Terra del Rey de portugall'. There is no reason to doubt the mapmaker's intention to say that this inscription also classifies the areas further south as being under the control of the Portuguese king. Consequently, the Strasbourg edition of Vespucci's report which appeared in 1505 from the workshop of Martin Hupuff shows two pictures of inhabitants of South America under the headline 'De ora antarctica per regem Portugallie pridem inuenta'.

93. Ms. Munich, Bayerische Staatsbibliothek, cim 315: 'tota terra inuenta per Cristoforo Colombo januensis de Re de Spania'; 'tota ter[r]a vocatur sancta cruces de Re de portogale'. Zuazo [Letter to Charles I, 1518], in: *Collecion de documentos ineditos relativos al descubrimiento, conquista y colonización de las posesiones españoles en América y Occeanía*, vol. 1 (Madrid, 1864), p. 296.

94. See above, note 75.

95. Juan Lopez de Palacio Rubios, *De las islas del mar Océano*, cap. IV, § 7, cap. V, praefatio, ed. Silvio Zavala (Mexico and Buenos Aires, 1954), pp. 100–5, 128 [written before 1516; first edition s.t.: *Del dominio de los Reyes de España* (Madrid, 1933)]. Rubios 'De iustitita et iure obtentionis ac retentionis regni Navarrae', in: Rubios, *Opera varia* (Antwerp, 1616), p. 718. Rubios derived what he understood as the papal capability to 'donate' islands in the ocean from the papal claim for universal rule as it had been articulated by Pope Innocent III and used the Latin *donatio* in the Justinian sense of the transfer of power to govern a *dominium*.

96. *The Cabot Voyages and Bristol Discovery under Henry VII*, ed. James A. Williamson (Cambridge, 1962), pp. 175–7.

97. Philip II [Letter to Charles V, 14 December 1544], in: *SP Spain*, vol. 7, no. 260, pp. 495–6.

98. Mary of Hungary [Instruction, February 1554], ed. Lanz, *Staatspapiere*, p. 141.

99. In a note of 29 December 1503 to his chancellor Cyprian of Serntein: Ms. Innsbruck, Tiroler Landesarchiv, Autographen.

100. Philip Melanchthon, *Chronicorum ab orbe condito pars secunda* (Basle, 1650), p. 12.

Notes

Three

1. Maximilian I, 'Kayser Maximilian Anslag wider die Türcken', Ms. Vienna, Österreichisches Staatsarchiv, Haus-, Hof- und Staatsarchiv, Maximiliana, Fz 30b (1517) 2, fol. 131r–40v. ed. in: *Quellen zur Geschichte Maximilians I. und seiner Zeit*, ed. Hermann Wiesflecker and Inge Wiesflecker-Friedhuber (Darmstadt, 1996), pp. 268–79.

2. Hans Burgkmair did much of the work for the printed edition of Maximilian's Triumphal Procession. Moreover, one of Mennel's genealogical manuscripts, Vienna, Österreichische Nationalbibliothek, Cod. 8018, fol. CXVr, has a woodcut by Hans Burgkmair and the subscription 'Hector genuit Francionem primum'. For further contributions by Burgkmair to Maximilian's imperial propaganda see: Josef Bellot, 'Konrad Peutinger und die literarisch–künstlerischen Unternehmungen Kaiser Maximilians', in: *Philobiblon* 11 (1967), p. 179. Beate Borowka-Clausberg, *Balthasar Springer und der frühneuzeitliche Reisebericht* (Munich, 1999). Paul Geissler, 'Hans Burgkmairs Genealogie Kaiser Maximilians I.', in: *Gutenberg-Jahrbuch* (1965), p. 251. Cäcilie Quetsch, 'Die "Entdeckung der Welt" in der deutschen Graphik der beginnenden Neuzeit'. Ph.D. Diss. (University of Erlangen, 1983), vol. 1, pp. 77–8, 161–2. Hildegard Zimmermann, 'Hans Burgkmair des Älteren Holzschnittfolge zur Genealogie Kaiser Maximilians I.', in: *Jahrbuch der Königlich Preussischen Kunstsammlungen* 36 (1915), pp. 39–64.

3. Dürer and his workshop contributed much to Maximilian's imperial propaganda, mainly the *Ehrenpforte* to which Dürer himself assigned the date AD 1515. Likewise, in 1515 Albrecht Dürer thought it appropriate to illustrate a leaf in his book of hours for Maximilian, which relates to Psalm 24 ('Domini est terra et plenitudo eius orbis terrarum et universi qui habitant in eo'), with a picture of Native Americans shown in feather garments. For a facsimile edition see: Karl Giehlow, *Kaiser Maximilians I. Gebetbuch mit Zeichnungen von Albrecht Dürer*, vol. 1 (Vienna, 1907), fol. 41r [partly reprinted s.t.: *Das Gebetbuch Kaiser Maximilians. Der Münchner Teil mit den Randzeichnungen von Albrecht Dürer und Lucas Cranach d. Ä. Rekonstruierte Wiedergabe*, ed. Hinrich Sieveking (Munich, 1987)]. A note by Maximilian's secretary Marx Treitzsaurwein of 1512 (Ms. Vienna, Österreichische Nationalbibliothek, Cod. 2835, fol. 39), tells us that the book of hours was commissioned by Maximilian as a gift for the knights of the Order of St George. See: Tilmann Falk, 'Frühe Rezeption der Neuen Welt in der graphischen Kunst', in: *Humanismus und Neue Welt*, ed. Wolfgang Reinhard (Weinheim, 1987), pp. 43–4, 49, 52 (Deutsche Forschungsgemeinschaft. Kommission für Humanismusforschung, Mitteilung 15). Dürer sometimes complained about belated payments by the emperor. See his letter to Christoph Kress [30 July 1515], in: Albrecht Dürer, *Schriftlicher Nachlaß*, ed. Hans Rupprich vol. 1

(Berlin, 1956), pp. 77–8. Also in: Dürer, *Schriften und Briefe*, ed. Ernst Ullmann, 6th edn (Leipzig, 1993), p. 95.

4. For an assessment of Albrecht Altdorfer's contribution see: Franz Winzinger, 'Albrecht Altdorfer und die Miniaturen des Triumphzuges Kaiser Maximilians I.', in: *Jahrbuch der Kunsthistorischen Sammlungen in Wien* 62 (1966), pp. 158–69.

5. This goal of Maximilian's crusading plans is recorded in: Hartmann Schedel, *Buoch der Chronicken*, German version (Nuremberg, 1493), fol. CCVIIIv [repr. (Grünwald, 1975)]. Another ed. s.t.: Schedel, *Weltchronik. Kolorierte Gesamtausgabe von 1493* [facsimile ed. of Inc. 119 in the Herzogin Anna Amalia Bibliothek Weimar], ed. Stephan Füssel (Cologne, London, Madrid, New York, Paris and Tokyo, 2001).

6. Maximilian [Letters to his daughter Margaret, dated 18 January 1516, and 17 February 1518], in: *Jahrbuch der Kunstsammlungen des Allerhöchsten Kaiserhauses* 29 (1910/11), pp. 78, 79. In a letter dated 19 May 1517 Maximilian put much pressure on the historian Johannes Stabius to speed up the printing process for the Triumphal Arch. See: Eduard Chmelarz, 'Die Ehrenpforte des Kaisers Maximilian I.', in: *Jahrbuch der Kunstsammlungen des Allerhöchsten Kaiserhauses* 4 (1886), pp. 310–1.

7. *RTA*, vol. 1, p. 110.

8. Printed in: *Jahrbuch der Kunstsammlungen des Allerhöchsten Kaiserhauses* 1 (1883), p. LXXV.

9. For a discussion of proto-nationalism see: Eva Dorothea Marcu, *Sixteenth Century Nationalism* (New York, 1976). Herfried Münkler, Hans Grünberger and Kathrin Mayer, *Nationenbildung. Die Nationalisierung Europas im Diskurs humanistischer Intellektueller. Italien und Deutschland* (Berlin, 1998).

10. On early modern grammarians see: Bertil Sundby, *English Word Formation as Described by English Grammarians. 1600–1800* (Oslo, 1995). Hiroyuki Takada, *Grammatik und Sprachwirklichkeit von 1640–1700. Zur Rolle deutscher Grammatiker im schriftsprachlichen Ausgleichsprozeß* (Tübingen, 1998), pp. 1–13.

11. For dress code books see: Ferdinando Bertelli, ed., *Omnivm fere gentivm nostrae aetatis habitvs nvnqvam ante hac aetatis* (Venice, 1563) [repr. (Unterschneidheim, 1969)]. Hans Weigel, ed., *Habitvs praecipvorvm popvlorvm tam virorvm qvam foeminarvm singvlaris arte depicti. Trachtenbuch. Darin fast allerley vnd der furnehmbsten Nationen / die heutigen tags bekandt sein / Kleidungen / beyde wie es bey Manns vnd Weibspersonen gebreuchlich / mit allem vleiss abgerissen sein* (Nuremberg, 1577) [repr. (Zwickau, 1913)]. Cesare Vecellio, *De gli habiti antichi et moderni di diversi arti del mondo* (Venice, 1590) [repr. (Bologna, 1982)].

12. For the Habsburgs and the German-speaking areas: Jakob Mennel, 'Fürstlich Chronickh kayser maximilians geburt spiegel', 5 vols in 6 parts. Ms. Vienna,

Österreichische Nationalbibliothek Cod. 3072x, 3073, 3074, 3075, 3076, 3077. Johannes Naucler, *Chronica* (Cologne, 1579). For England: *Polydore Vergil, Angliae historiae libri XXVII* (Basle, 1534). Edward Hall, *Chronicle, Containing the History of England during the Reign of Henry the Fourth and the Succeeding Monarchs to the End of the Reign of Henry the Eighth* (London, 1548). Raphael Holinshed, *The First and Second Volumes of the Chronicles* (London, 1587). For Italy: Francesco Guicciardini. *La historia d'Italia* (Florence, 1561). For Spain: Alonso de Santa Cruz, *Cronica del Emperador Carlos V* (Madrid, 1920–5). Juan de Mariana, *Historia general de España* (Madrid, 1678). For France: Paulus Aemilius, *De rebus gestis Francorum libri X* (Paris, 1539–43).

13. For the later reception of these traditions see: David Hume, 'Of National Character', in: Hume, *Essays Moral, Political and Literary*, vol. 1, ed. Thomas Hill Green and Thomas Hodge Grose (London, 1882), pp. 244–58.

14. Dress codes as reflected in people's tables have been studied in: *Europäischer Völkerspiegel*, Franz Karl Stanzel, ed. (Heidelberg, 1999). The work also features facsimiles of two eighteenth-century people's tables.

15. Kohler, ed., *Quellen*, pp. 46–8.

16. Werner Goez, *Translatio imperii. Ein Beitrag zur Geschichte des Geschichtsdenkens und der politischen Theorie im Mittelalter und in der frühen Neuzeit* (Tübingen, 1958).

17. For an edition of the bill see: Bernhard Greiff, 'Was Kayser Carolus dem Vten die Römisch Küniglich Wal cost im 1520. Jar', in: *Jahresbericht des Historischen Kreis-Vereins in Schwaben und Neuburg* 34 (1868), pp. 19–44. Abridged version in: Kohler, ed., *Quellen*, pp. 63–70.

18. For the text of Francis's campaign announcement see: Kohler, ed., *Quellen*, pp. 48–52.

19. *RTA*, vol. 1, pp. 794–5.

20. Paul Kalkoff, *Die Kaiserwahl Friedrichs IV. und Karls V.* (Weimar, 1925). For a critical review see: Karl Brandi, 'Die Wahl Karls V.', in: *Nachrichten von der Gesellschaft der Wissenschaften zu Göttingen*, Philologisch–Historische Klasse (1925), pp. 109–33.

21. *Des allerdurchlauchtigsten vnd großmechtigsten fursten vnd herren, herren Karls Romischen vnd hyspanischen Konigs vnd künfftigen Kaysers Einzug yezt zu Aach am XXII, tag Octobris beschehen gantz historlich vnd kurtzweylig zu lesen*. Print (s.l., 1519). See also: *RTA*, vol. 2, pp. 65–106.

22. Martin Luther, 'An den christlichen Adel deutscher Nation' [1520], in: *D Martin Luthers Werke. Kritische Gesammtausgabe*, vol. 6 (Weimar, 1888), p. 381–469 [repr. (Weimar, 1966)].

23. See: Cornelius Graphius, *Divi Caroli Imperatoris Caesaris Opt[timi] Max[imi] desyderatissimus ex Hispania in Germaniam reditus* (Antwerp, 1520), fol. A3. Conrad Peutinger, *Celeberrimi viris D[octoris] Chonradi Peutingeri Augustani*

Ivris vtrvsqve Doctoris et oratoris disertissimi oratio pro sacrosancto Romani Imperij Ciuitate Augusta Vindelicorum (Boxlege, 1521), fols A4–B4. Alofresant of Rhodes, *Keyserliche practica und prognostication auss allen alten Weyssagungen . . . das eben . . . Carolus V der sey, so reformiren und allein das regiment von orient biss in occident [führen kann]* (s.l. [1519]), fol. B1. Georg Sauermann, *Hispaniae consolatio* (Louvain, 1520), fols BIIr–v, C [I]r. Bernhard Wurmser, 'Rede zur Wahl Karls V. am 30. September 1519', in: *Orationes procerum Europae eorumdemque ministorum ac legatorum*, ed. Johann Christian Lünig (Leipzig, 1713), pp. 207–9.

24. [Memorandum by the imperial estates on the relations with France and the Swiss Confederacy, 23 May 1521], in: *RTA*, vol. 2, pp. 387–8. Also in: Kohler, ed., *Quellen*, pp. 80–1.

25. Treaty between Charles V and Henry VIII, relating to the formalities of Charles's visit to England, 11 April 1520, in: *SP Spain*, vol. 2, no. 274, pp. 296–9.

26. Treaty between Charles V and Henry VIII, 25 August 1521, in: *SP Spain*, vol. 3, no. 355, pp. 369–71.

27. As already suggested in a letter by Ferdinand of Aragon to his daughter Catherine of England, 3 December 1509, in: *SP Spain*, vol. 2, no. 22, pp. 31–2.

28. *RTA*, vol. 3.

29. Beginning with the publication of his tract 'De captivitate Babylonica' [1520], in: *D Martin Luthers Werke. Kritische Gesammtausgabe*, vol. 6 (Weimar, 1888), pp. 497–573 [repr. (Weimar, 1966)].

30. *RTA*, vol. 2, pp. 449–661.

31. *RTA*, vol. 2, pp. 594–6. Also in: Kohler, ed., *Quellen*, pp. 74–5.

32. Jerome Aleander [Dispatch from the Worms imperial diet, 29 April 1521], in: *Die Depeschen des Nuntius Aleander vom Wormser Reichstage*, ed. Paul Kalkhoff (Leipzig, 1886), no. 22, p. 159 (Veröffentlichungen des Vereins für Reformationsgeschichte. 17). Worms edict, 8/26 May 1521, in: *RTA*, vol. 2, pp. 640–59. Also in: Kohler, ed., *Quellen*, pp. 76–9.

33. The first meeting took place in 1520. *Wie der allerdeurchleuchtigste grossmechtigte etc. künig Karl von Hispanien . . . erstlich geschifft nac Engellandt, nachmaln fürterhin auffs Niderlandt gen Flyssingen etc. mit was triumphierung und freuden yr Kay[serliche] Ma[jestät] empfangen worden.* Print (s.l.et.a.). See also: Antonio Surian and Gasparo Contarini, Venetian ambassadors to England [Report to the Senate of Venice, 31 May 1522] in: *Cal. Venice*, vol. 2, no. 463, pp. 230–3.

34. Augustine, *Dei civitate Dei*, cap. XIX/13, ed. Bernhard Kalb and Alphonse Dombart (Turnhout, 1955), pp. 678–82 (Corpus Christianorum. Series Latina. 48 B).

35. Dante Alighieri, *De monarchia*, book I, cap. XI/2–3, in: Dante, *Opere minori*, ed. Bruni Nardi, vol. 2 (Milan and Naples, 1979), pp. 328–30.

36. Engelbert of Admont, 'De ortu et fine Romani imperii', cap. 2, ed. Melchior Goldast von Haiminsfeld, *Politica imperialia* (Frankfurt, 1614), p. 755. Enea

Silvio Piccolomini [Pope Pius II], 'De ortu et auctoritate imperii Romani' [1 March 1446], in: Piccolomini, *Der Briefwechsel*, part II: Briefe als Priester und als Bischof von Trient, ed. Rudolph Wolkau (Vienna, 1912), pp. 7–8.

37. See: Joseph Hürblin, ed., 'Der "Libellus de Caesarea monarchia" von Hermann Peter aus Andlau', in: *Zeitschrift der Savigny-Stiftung für Rechtsgeschichte*, Germanistische Abteilung 13 (1892), pp. 212–13. Antonio de Rosellis, 'Monarchia siue tractatus de potesta imperatoris et Papae', Pars I, cap. 32 and 56, ed. Melchior Goldast of Haiminsfeld, *Monarchia Sancti Romani Imperii*, vol. I (Hanover, 1611), pp. 268, 282–4 [repr. (Graz, 1960)].

38. Miguel de Ulcurrum, *Catholicum opus imperiale regiminis mundi* (Saragossa, 1525), fols XXV, XXVIII, XXXI, XXXIII, XXXVIII. Excerpts printed in: *Tractatus universi iuris*, vol. 1 (1584), fol. XXIIv. Luciano Pereña Vicente, 'Miguel de Ulcurrun'. El emperador organo y garantia del derecho de gentes positivo', *Revista Española de Derecho Internacional* 6 (1953), pp. 320–1. See also: Jacob de Antonisz, *De praecellentia potestais Imperatoriae* (Antwerp [1503]), fols C2, D5, E6.

39. Gattinara explicitly quoted Augustine in a memorandum addressed to Charles in or after 1519. See: Mercurino Arborio di Gattinara, 'Mémoire du chancellier de Gattinara sur les droits de Charles-Quint au duché de Bourgogne', ed. Carlo Bornate, in: *Bulletin de la Commission Royale d'Histoire de Belgique* 76 (1907), p. 395. Gattinara's ownership of a copy of Dante's *Monarchia* is reported in a letter that he wrote to Erasmus of Rotterdam on 12 March 1527, in which he asked Erasmus to edit Dante's work. See: Erasmus, *Opus Epistolarum*, vol. 6, ed. Percy Stafford Allen and Helen Mary Allen (Oxford, 1926), pp. 470–1.

40. Mercurino Arborio di Gattinara, 'Consigli del Gran Cancelliere all' Imperatore' [12 July 1519], ed. Carlo Bornate, 'Historia vitae et gestorum per dominum magnum Cancellarium, con note, aggiunte et documenti', in: *Miscellanea di storia Italiana* 48 (1915), pp. 406–8.

41. Bartolus of Sassoferato, *In secvndvm Digesti noui partem commentaria*, ad dig. XLIX/15, 22, in: Bartolus, *Opera*, vol. 6 (Venice, 1570–71), pp. 227–8.

42. See above, chapter II, note 64.

43. See: Lazarus Spengler, 'Bedenken' [*c.* 1529], ed. Wolfgang Steglich, *RTA*, vol. 8, pp. 502–3.

44. See: Andreas Walther, 'Kanzleiordnungen Maximilians, Karls I. und Ferdinands I.', in: *Archiv für Urkundenforschung* 2 (1909), pp. 379–83.

45. [Charles V reflects on the current state of political affairs, late in 1524 or early in 1525], ed. Karl Brandi, 'Eigenhändige Aufzeichnungen Karls V. aus dem Anfang des Jahres 1525', in: *Nachrichten von der Gesellschaft der Wissenschaften zu Göttingen*, Philol.-Hist. Kl. (1933), p. 259. Also in: Kohler, ed., *Quellen*, pp. 107–8.

46. On the term 'amnesty' see Jörg Fisch, *Krieg und Frieden im Friedensvertrag* (Stuttgart, 1979).

47. Desiderius Erasmus, 'Querela pacis', in: Erasmus, *Opera omnia*, vol. 4 (Leiden, 1723), col. 641c [repr. (Hildesheim, 1962)].

48. Gattinara, 'Memoriale del gran Cancelliere all Imperatore', ed. Bornate, 'Historia' (note 40), p. 429.

49. Desiderius Erasmus, 'Institutio principis Christiani', in: Erasmus, *Opera omnia*, ed. Otto Herding, vol. 4, 1 (Amsterdam, 1974), p. 187.

50. Thomas Rymer, *Foedera, conventions, litterae et cujusque generic acta publica inter reges Angliae et alios quosvius imperatores, reges, pontifices, principes vel communitates*, vol. 13 (London, 1714), pp. 624–49. Jean Dumont, *Corps diplomatique universel*, vol. 4, pt 1 (The Hague, 1726), no. 125, pp. 269–75.

51. For the accessions see: *SP Spain*, vol. 2, no. 264, pp. 290–3.

52. Treaty between the pope, Emperor Maximilian I, Francis I, Charles I and Henry VIII, 2 October 1518, in: Dumont (note 50), no. 124, p. 267.

53. *Ibid.*, p. 268.

54. See: Ludwig Freiherr von Pastor, *Geschichte der Päpste*, vol. 4, part 2, 13th edn (Freiburg, 1957), pp. 687–8.

55. *LP*, vol. 2, nos 1288–9. *Cal Venice*, vol. 2, p. 448.

56. For the pope's military career see: Leone di Paride de' Grassi, *Il diario*, vol. 1, ed. M. Armellini (Rome, 1884), p. 95.

57. For early medieval promises see: *The Laws of the Kings of England*, ed. Agnes Jane Robertson (Cambridge, 1925), pp. 42–3. Percy Ernst Schramm, *Kaiser, Könige und Päpste*, vol. 2 (Stuttgart, 1969), pp. 190–1, 243. Felix Liebermann, 'Zum angelsächsischen Krönungseid', in: *Archiv für das Studium der neueren Sprachen und Literaturen* 109 (1902), pp. 375–6.

58. Charles V, *Die verschrybung vnd verwilligung des aller durchleuchtigsten/großmechtigsten herrn, Herren Karls Römischer vnd Hispanischer Kunig etc. Gegen dem heiligen Reich das gar leblich zu hören yst.* Print (s.l., 3 July 1519). Ed. in: *RTA*, vol. 1, pp. 865–76. Also in: Kohler, ed., *Quellen*, pp. 53–8.

59. Hernán Cortés, 'Primera Carta' [10 July 1519], in: *Cartas y documentos*, ed. Mario Hernández Sanchez-Barba (Mexico City, 1963), p. 20.

60. This was the radical interpretation of the imperial constitution by the seventeenth-century jurist Bogislaw of Chemnitz [Hippolytus a Lapide], *Dissertatio de ratione status imperii nostro Romano-Germanico* (Freistadt, 1647), pp. 25, 40, 50.

Four

1. Francesco Guicciardini, *Storia d'Italia*, in: Guicciardini, *Opere*, ed. Vittorio de Caprariis (Milan and Naples, 1961), p. 374.

2. Alberico Gentili, *De jure belli libri tres*, vol. 2 (Hanau, 1612), p. 65 [first published (Hanau, 1598); parts of the edn of 1612 have been republished in:

Notes

Moorhead Wright, ed., *Theory and Practice of the Balance of Power 1486–1914* (London and Totowa, NJ, 1975), pp. 13–14].

3. Mercurino Arborio di Gattinara [Memorandum on the war with France, 30 July 1521], in: Lanz, ed., *Staatspapiere*, pp. 1–9. Also in: Kohler, ed., *Quellen*, p. 84.

4. *Ibid.*, pp. 85–6.

5. For a study of legalist approaches to international politics at Spanish courts see: Viktor Frankl, 'Hernán Cortés y la tradición de las Siete Partidas', in: *Revista de historia de América 54/55* (1962), pp. 9–74. See also above, Chapter II.

6. Charles V [Reflections on the current state of affairs, winter 1524/25], ed. Karl Brandi, 'Eigenhändige Aufzeichnungen Karls V. aus dem Jahre 1525. Der Kaiser und sein Kanzler', in: *Nachrichten von der Gesellschaft der Wissenschaften zu Göttingen*, Philologisch–Historische Klasse (1933), p. 224. Also in: Kohler, ed., *Quellen*, p. 107.

7. Charles V [Letter to Ferdinand I, 27 July 1526], in: *Die Korrespondenz Ferdinands I. Familienkorrespondenz*, vol. 1, ed. Wilhelm Bauer (Vienna, 1912), p. 408 (Veröffentlichungen der Kommission für Neuere Geschichte Österreichs, 11). Also in: Kohler, ed., *Quellen*, p. 118.

8. Charles V [Address to his advisers, 16 September 1528], in: Brandi, 'Aufzeichnungen' (note 6), p. 231. Also in: Kohler, ed., *Quellen*, p. 138.

9. Alonso de Santa Cruz, *Cronica del Emperador Carlos V* (Madrid, 1920–5).

10. In his secret instruction of September 1528 to Philibert of Chalon, prince of Orange, Charles noted down in his own hand what he expected the prince to do while commanding the imperial troops stationed in the Italian peninsula. He instructed the prince to act in conformity with his intention of gaining and aggrandising his honour and to prepare for war to accomplish these goals. There is no reference to the imperial coronation issue in this text. See: Weiss, ed., *Papiers*, vol. 1, pp. 427–32.

11. The Archbishop of Armagh, John Bourchier, Lord of Berners, and Anthony Spinelli [Letter to Henry VIII, 15 December 1518], in: *LP*, vol. 2, no. 4658, pp. 1424–5.

12. *LP*, vol. 3, pp. 339, 385, 403, 429.

13. *Ibid.*, pp. 440, 443.

14. Mercurio Arborio di Gattinara [Memorandum to Charles V on the question of whether a truce should be concluded with France or the current war should be continued], 30 July 1521, in: Lanz, ed., *Staatspapiere*, pp. 1–9. Also in: Kohler, ed., *Quellen*, pp. 81–9.

15. The report on the conference has been edited by Weiss, ed., *Papiers*, vol. 1, pp. 125–241.

16. Kohler, ed., *Quellen*, p. 95.

17. Margaret [Letter to Jean de Berghes, 14/15 November 1521], partly ed. in: Karl Brandi, *Kaiser Karl V*, vol. 2 (Munich, 1941), p. 123.

18. Wolsey [Letter to Henry, 14 August 1521], in: *LP*, vol. 3, pp. 1480, 1493.

19. Treaty between Charles V and Henry VIII, 25 August 1521, in: *SP Spain*, vol. 3, no. 355, pp. 369–71.

20. Treaty between Charles and Henry VIII, 2 July 1522, in: *SP Spain*, vol. 2, no. 442, pp. 449–51.

21. Bernardino de Mesa [Letter to Charles V, 5 March 1522], Ms Vienna, Haus-, Hof- und Staatsarchiv, England, fasc. 2, partly ed. by Garrett Mattingly, 'An Early Non-Aggression Pact', in: *Journal of Modern History* 10 (1938), p. 27, fn 68.

22. Adrian VI [Letters to Charles V, 2 July 1522 and 1 January 1523], in: *SP Spain*, vol. 2, nos 518, 532, pp. 520–1, 531–2. Adrian VI [Letter to Catherine of Aragon, 23 February 1523], in: *Correspondence de Charles-Quint et d'Adrien VI*, ed. Louis Prosper Gachard (Brussels, 1859), appendix no. 22, pp. 272–4.

23. Charles V [Letter to Luis Fernandez de Cordova, duke of Sessa, his ambassador to the Holy See, 15 April 1523], in: *SP Spain*, vol. 2, no. 542, pp. 541–5.

24. Charles V [Letter to Gerard de Plaine, Seigneur de la Roche, his ambassador to the Holy See, 14 May 1524], in: *SP Spain*, vol. 2, no. 650, pp. 629–38.

25. Martin Luther, 'Wider die räuberischen und mörderischen Rotten der Bauern' [1525], in: *D Martin Luthers Werke. Kritische Gesammtausgabe*, vol. 18 (Weimar, 1908), pp. 357–61 [repr. (Weimar, 1964)].

26. The abbot of Nagera [Letter to Charles V, 24 February 1525], in: *SP Spain*, vol. 2, no. 722, pp. 708–9. *LP*, vol. 4, nos 1124, 1164, pp. 494, 513.

27. John Sampson, English ambassador to Spain [Letter to Wolsey, 15 March 1525], in *LP*, vol. 4, no. 1189, pp. 520–1. Gasparo Contarini [Letter to the duke of Venice, 12 March 1525], in: Contarini, *Regesten und Briefe 1483–1542*, ed. Franz Dittrich (Braunsberg, 1881), p. 21.

28. Charles V [Letter to Louise of Savoy, 25 March 1525], in: Weiss, ed., *Papiers*, vol. 1, p. 263. Also in: *LP*, vol. 4, no. 1208, pp. 527–8.

29. *Die Schlacht vor Pauia. Mit dem Kayser Carl den funfften des namens. Und Kunig Francisco vonn Franckreich, geschehen auff den XXIIII tag des Hornungs [February 1525]* (s.l., 1525).

30. Francis I [Letter to Charles V, March 1525], in: *LP*, vol. 4, no. 1229, p. 537. For further records concerning the battle of Pavia see: Antonio Bonardi, *L'assedio e la battaglia di Pavia. Diario inedito* (Pavia, 1895).

31. *Captivité du roi François I*, ed. Aime Champollion-Figeac (Paris, 1847), no. 134, pp. 300–3.

32. Manuel de Foronda y Aguilera, *Estancias y viajes de Carlos V* (Madrid, 1895), p. 260.

33. Charles reported triumphantly on the marriage deal to Augustin Grimaldi on 26 January 1526, in: *Recueil des letters de l'empereur Charles-Quint qui sont conservées dans les archives du palais de Monaco*, ed. Léon Honoré Labande (Monaco, 1910), no. 8, pp. 16–17. Gattinara recorded his scepticism in:

Mercurino Arborio di Gattinara, 'Historia vitae', ed. Carlo Bornate, 'Historia vitae et gestorum per dominum magnum Cancellarium, con note, aggiunte et documenti', in: *Miscellanea di storia Italiana* 48 (1915), p. 317.

34. Charles V [Letter to Henry VIII, 7 June 1525], in: *SP Spain*, vol. 3, no. 106, pp. 186–7.

35. [Report on the relations between Henry VIII and Charles V, 11 June 1525], in: *LP*, vol. 4, no. 1409, pp. 627–8.

36. Charles V [Letter to Henry VIII, 11 August 1525], in: *LP*, vol. 4, no. 1559, pp. 701–2.

37. *Articuli tractatus a Cæsare non observati* [undated], in: *LP*, vol. 4, no. 1629, p. 730.

38. The treaty of Moore [30 August 1525] has been published in: Thomas Rymer, *Foedera, conventions, litterae et cujusque generic acta publica inter reges Angliae et alios quosvius imperatores, reges, pontifices, principes vel communitates*, vol. 14 (London, 1714), p. 77. Henry VIII [Letter to his ambassadors at the Spanish courts, 21 September 1525], in: *LP*, vol. 4, no. 1655, pp. 740–3.

39. Luis Fernandez de Cordova, duke of Sessa, Charles's ambassador to the Holy See [Letter to Charles V, 13 November 1525], in: *SP Spain*, vol. 3, no. 260, pp. 458–9.

40. Pope Clement VII [Letter of dispensation, 13 November 1525], in: *SP Spain*, vol. 3, no. 263, pp. 462–3.

41. For editions of key sources on the Sack of Rome see: Marcelo Alberini, *Il sacco di Roma. L'edizione di Domenico Orano del 'I ricordi'* (Rome, 1997). Alessandro Corvisieri, ed., *Documenti inediti sul sacco di Roma* (Rome, 1873). *Descriptio urbis. The Roman Census of 1527*, ed. Egmont Lee (Rome, 1985). Carlo Milanesi, *Il sacco di Roma* (Florence, 1867). Hans Schulz, *Sacco di Roma* (Halle, 1893), pp. 176–8. See also the autobiography of one of the participating lansquenets: Sebastian Schertlin von Burtenbach, *Leben und Taten des weiland wohledlen Ritters Sebastian Schertlin von Burtenbach* ed. Engelbert Hegaur (Munich, 1910), pp. 12–16.

42. Iñigo de Mendoza, imperial ambassador to England [Letter to Charles V, 13 July 1527], in: *SP Spain*, vol. 3, no. 113, pp. 271–8.

43. Gattinara, 'Historia' (note 33), p. 361. Weiss, ed., *Papiers*, vol. 1, no. 58, pp. 311–12.

44. Charles V [Letter to Henry VIII, 27 January 1528], in: *LP*, vol. 4, no. 3844, pp 1713–16.

45. Treaty of Cambrai [5 August 1529], in: Jean Dumont, *Corps diplomatique universel*, vol. 4, pt 2 (The Hague, 1726), no. 2, pp. 7–17.

46. Quoted in: Alfred Kohler, *Karl V. 1500–1558* (Munich, 1999), p. 201.

47. Martin Luther, 'Heerpredigt wider den Türken' [28 October 1528], in: *D Martin Luthers Werke. Kritische Gesammtausgabe*, vol. 30 (Weimar, 1909), pp. 160–97 [repr. (Weimar, 1964)].

48. See: Juan Ginés de Sepúlveda, *Ad Carolum V Imperatorem invictissimum ut facta cum omnibus Christianis pace bellum susciperet in Turcos . . . cohortatio* (Bologna, 1529) [new ed. in: Sepúlveda, *Opera*, vol. 4 (Madrid, 1780), pp. 358–74]. For Charles's correspondence with Ferdinand see: Kohler, ed., *Quellen*, pp. 146–56.
49. Dante Alighieri, *De Monarchia*, lib. I/xi, 2–3, in: Dante, *Opere minori*, ed. Bruno Nardi (Milan and Naples, 1979), pp. 328–30.
50. Aristotle, *Nicomachean Ethics*, 1129a–b.
51. See above, note 1.
52. Niccolò Machiavelli, *Il principe*, cap. 21, Machiavelli, *Opere*, ed. Mario Bonfantini (Milan and Naples, 1963), pp. 71–4.
53. Among them the drawing by Hans Holbein the Younger of a lansquenet battle of 1530, now held by the Öffentliche Kunstsammlung in Basle. For an account see: Geoffrey Trease, *Die Condottieri* (Munich, 1974), p. 239. The equilibrium bearing is depicted in detail in a miniature contained in Ms Vienna, Österreichische Nationalbibliothek, Cod. 10824, fol. 115.
54. Willibald Pirckheimer, *Bellum Suitense sive Helveticum* (Zurich, 1737), pp. 70–1. Georg Kirchmair, *Denkwürdigkeiten seiner Zeit. 1519–1553*, vol. 1 (Vienna, 1855), p. 438. Maximilian I, Weisskunig, cap. 174 (Vienna, 1775), pp. 277–8 [repr., ed. Christa-Maria Dreissiger (Leipzig and Weinheim, 1985); also published (Stuttgart, 1956)].
55. Hans Bustetter, *Ernstlicher Bericht, wie sich ain Frumme Oberkayt vor, in und nach den gefärlichsten Kriegßnöten mit klugem vortayl zu ungezweyfeltem Sig, loblichen uben und halten sol* (Augsburg, 1532), fols VIv–VIIr [repr. in: Flugschriften-Sammlung Gustav Freytag, Microfiche edn, no. X/1423; newly edited by Ignaz Peters (Bonn, 1887), p. 9]. Jacques Chantereau, 'Le miroir des armes militaires et instruction des gens de piece', Ms. Paris, Bibliothèque nationale de France, fonds franç. 650, fols 12–41 [the work was dedicated to King Francis I]. Jean Surquet, *Histoire des guerres et troubles de Flandres*, ed. Jean Joseph Suret (Brussels, 1865), p. 558. Paolo Giovio, *Eine warhafftige Beschreybung aller nammhafftigen Geschichten*, vol. 1 (Basle, 1560), p. 152.
56. Charles V [Address to his advisers, 16 September 1528] (note 8), pp. 136–8. For a contemporary print of the address see: *Ain ernstliche red Kayserlicher Majestet Caroli des fünfften, die er zu den Hispaniern gethon hat, von seinem Abschied auss Hispania, und war er im, in Welchen und Teutschen Landen, zu endern und zu thun hatt fürgenommen* (s.l.et a. [Basle, 1528]).
57. Charles V [Letter to Ferdinand I, 11 January 1530], in: *Die Korrespondenz Ferdinands I. Familienkorrespondenz*, vol. 2, ed. Wilhelm Bauer and Robert Lacroix (Vienna, 1937–8), pp. 554–63 (Veröffentlichungen der Kommission für Neuere Geschichte Österreichs, 30). Also in: Kohler, ed., *Quellen*, pp. 146–56.
58. Ferdinand I [Letter to Charles V, 28 January 1530], in: Bauer, ed., *Korrespondenz*, vol. 2 (note 57), pp. 577–91. Margaret [Letter to Charles V,

18 March 1530], ed. Alessandro Bardi, 'Carlo V e l'assedio di Firenze', in: *Archivio Storico Italiano* 11 (1893), p. 35.

59. For Gattinara's memorandum see: Andreas Walther, 'Kanzleiordnungen Maximilians, Karls I. und Ferdinands I.', in: *Archiv für Urkundenforschung* 2 (1909), pp. 379–83.

60. The formula was first used in 806. Its vernacular Middle High German rendering as 'mêrer des rîches', augmenter of the empire, first appeared in an enfeoffment letter in 1301.

Five

1. Charles V [Reflections on the current state of affairs, winter 1524/25], ed. Karl Brandi, 'Eigenhändige Aufzeichnungen Karls V. aus dem Jahre 1525', in: *Nachrichten von der Gesellschaft der Wissenschaften zu Göttingen*, Philologisch–Historische Klasse (1933), p. 222. Also in: Kohler, ed., *Quellen*, p. 105.

2. See: Klaus Schreiner and Gerd Schwerhoff, eds, *Verletzte Ehre. Ehrkonflikte in Gesellschaften des Mittelalters und der frühen Neuzeit* (Cologne, Weimar and Vienna, 1995).

3. Charles V Reflections (note 1), in: Brandi, 'Aufzeichnungen', p. 224. Also in: Kohler, ed., *Quellen*, p. 107.

4. Charles V [Address to his advisers, 16 September 1528], ed. Brandi, 'Aufzeichnungen' (note I), p. 232. Also in: Kohler, ed., *Quellen*, p. 137.

5. Charles V [Secret instructions to his son Philip, 6 May 1543], ed. Karl Brandi, 'Die Testamente und politischen Instruktionen Karls V., insbesondere diejenigen der Jahre 1543/44', in: *Nachrichten von der Gesellschaft der Wissenschaften zu Göttingen*, Philologisch–Historische Klasse (1935), p. 69. Also in: Kohler, ed., *Quellen*, p. 291.

6. Saragossa treaty [22 April 1529], Art. 2, in: *European Treaties Bearing on the History of the United States and Its Dependencies to 1648*, no. 3, ed. Frances Gardiner Davenport, vol. 1 (Washington, 1971), pp. 171–84; also in: *Fontes Historiae Iuris Gentium*, edited by Wilhelm Georg Carl Grewe, vol. 2 (Berlin and New York, 1988), pp. 117–34, pp. 120–2.

7. See: Alfred Kohler, *Karl V. 1500–1558* (Munich, 1999), p. 234.

8. Charles V [Instructions to Adrian of Croy, Count of Roeulx, for his mission to the imperial estates, 19 April 1535], in: Weiss, ed., *Papiers*, vol. 2, pp. 340–1. Also in: Kohler, ed., *Quellen*, p. 200.

9. [Opinion by Charles's advisers, October 1536], in: Lanz, ed., *Correspondenz*, vol. 2, p. 263. Kohler, ed., *Quellen*, p. 221.

10. *Ibid.*, in: Lanz, ed., *Correspondenz*, vol. 2, pp. 266–7. Also in: Kohler, ed., *Quellen*, pp. 226–7.

11. For the coronation see the report by Margaret's court historian Henricus Cornelius Agrippa, *De duplici coronatione Caesaris apud Bononiam historiola*

(Cologne, 1535). At fols H[VII]r–I[II]v, Agrippa gave a verbal account of the procession following the coronation. For additional records see: *Gaetano Giordani, Della venuta e dimora in Bologna del sommo pontifico Clemente VII per la coronazione di Carlo V imperatore celebrate l'anno 1530* (Bologna, 1842). For Gattinara's comment see: Mercurino Arborio di Gattinara, 'Historia vitae', ed. Carlo Bornate, 'Historia vitae et gestorum per dominum magnum Cancellarium, con note, aggiunte et documenti', in: *Miscellanea di storia Italiana* 48 (1915), p. 348. For records on Charles's stay at Bologna see: *Giuseppe Romano, ed., Cronaca del soggiorno di Carlo V in Italia dal 26 giuglio 1529 al 25 aprile 1530* (Milan, 1892).

12. Günther Gassmann, ed., *Das Augsburger Bekenntnis*, revidierter Text, 6th edn (Göttingen, 1988).

13. Charles V [Letter to Pope Clement VII, 14 July 1530], ed. Gotthold Heine, *Briefe an Kaiser Karl, geschrieben von seinem Beichtvater* (Berlin, 1848), pp. 288–9. Also in: Kohler, ed., *Quellen*, pp. 168–9.

14. Charles V [Memorandum on the competences of his brother Ferdinand as Roman king, 12 February 1531], in: Lanz, ed., *Staatspapiere*, pp. 59–62. Also in: Kohler, ed., *Quellen*, pp. 181–3. For documents relevant to Ferdinand's election see: Melchior Goldast of Haiminsfeld, *Politische Reichshändel*, pt 1 (Frankfurt, 1614). *Senckenbergische Sammlung von ungedruckten und raren Schriften zu Erläuterung derer Rechte und Geschichten von Teutschland*, ed. Heinrich Christian von Senckenberg, vol. 4 (Frankfurt, 1751), pp. 135–48, 165–89.

15. Charles V [Letter to Ferdinand I, 12 May 1533], in: Lanz, ed., *Correspondenz*, vol. 2, p. 63. Also in: Kohler, ed., *Quellen*, p. 191.

16. Francis I [Letter to the imperial estates, 1/25 February 1535], in: *Corpus Reformatorum*, ed. Carl Gottlieb Bretschneider, vol. 2 (Halle, 1835), pp. 830–1. Also in: Kohler, ed., *Quellen*, pp. 196–7.

17. Charles V, Instructions (note 8), 350–1. Also in: Kohler, ed., *Quellen*, pp. 200–1.

18. Muley Hassan, *Lettere inedite a Ferrante Gonzaga, vicere di sicilia (1537–1547)*, ed. Federico Odorici and Michele Amari (Modena, 1865).

19. Charles V [Letter to Ferdinand I, 23 June 1538], ed. Peter Rassow, *Die Kaiser-Idee Karls V., dargestellt an der Politik der Jahre 1528–1540* (Berlin, 1932), pp. 438–9 (Historische Studien. 217). Kohler, ed., *Quellen*, p. 234.

20. Eustace de Chapuys, imperial ambassador in England [Letter to Charles V, 10 January 1531], in: *LP*, vol. 5, no. 40, pp. 16–18.

21. [Undated memorandum discussing the divorce issue, *c.* 1531], in: *LP*, vol. 5, no. 468, p. 222.

22. Eustace de Chapuys [Letter to Charles V, 10 September 1533], in: *LP*, vol. 6, no. 1112, p. 465.

23. [Dispatch recording a meeting of the State Council at Toledo, 22 March 1534], in: *LP*, vol. 7, no. 353, p. 147.

24. Charles V [Instructions to Count Henry of Nassau, his ambassador in France, 12 August 1534], in: Weiss, ed., *Papiers*, vol. 2, p. 186. Also in: *LP*, vol. 7, no. 1060, pp. 413–14.

25. Henry's support for a crusade was communicated by Eustace de Chapuys [Letter to Charles V, 13 January 1531], in: *LP*, vol. 5, no. 45, pp. 19–21. For the new marriage plans see: *Correspondence politique de MM. de Castillon et de Marillac. Ambassadeurs de France en Angleterre. 1537–42*, ed. Jean Kaulek (Paris, 1885), no. 18, pp. 13–15.

26. Charles V, Instructions (note 5), in: Brandi, 'Testamente', pp. 57–8. Also in: Kohler, ed., *Quellen*, p. 285.

27. Quoted from: Karl Brandi, *Kaiser Karl V*, vol. 1, 3rd edn (Munich, 1941), p. 437.

28. Decree by the Speyer imperial diet, 10 June 1544, in: *Neue und vollständige Sammlung der Reichs-Abschiede, welche von den Zeiten Kayser Conrads des II. bis jetzo auf den Teutschen Reichs-Tägen abgefasset worden*, vol. 2 (Frankfurt, 1747), pp. 496–7 [repr. (Osnabruck, 1967)]. Also in: Kohler, ed., *Quellen*, p. 302.

29. Bernardino Navagero [Report on the imperial war against France, July 1546], in: *Relazioni di ambasciatori veneti al Senato*, vol. 2: Germania ed. Eugenio Albèri (Florence, 1841), pp. 484–92 [repr., ed. Luigi Tirpo (Turin, 1970)]. Also in: Kohler, ed., *Quellen*, pp. 328–34.

30. Henry, Dauphin of France [Protestation against the treaty of Crépy, 12 December 1544], in: Jean Dumont, *Corps diplomatique universel*, vol. 4, pt 2 (The Hague, 1726), pp. 288–9. Also in: Kohler, ed., *Quellen*, pp. 317–19.

31. *Ursprung unnd ursach diser Auffrur Teütscher Nation* [1546], in: Kohler, ed., *Quellen*, p. 339.

32. Charles V, *Commentaires de Charles-Quint [à son fils Philippe, Prince d'Espagne]*, ed. Kervyn de Lettenhove (Brussels, 1862), pp. 12–17, 24–41. Charles V [Address to the States General of the Netherlands, Brussels, 25 October 1555], ed. William Stirling, *The Cloister Life of the Emperor Charles the Fifth* (London, 1853), p. 7. Also in: Kohler, ed., *Quellen*, p. 466.

33. Sebastian Fischer, *Chronik besonders von Ulmischen Sachen* [Munich, Bayerische Staatsbibliothek, Cgm 3091, fol. 262], ed. Karl Gustav Veesenmeyer (Ulm, 1896), p. 138 (Ulm und Oberschwaben. 5–8).

34. See: René Macé, *Voyage de Charles-Quint par la France. Poème historique*, ed. Gaston Raynaud (Paris, 1879).

35. See: Gabriele von Trauchberg, *Häuser und Gärten Augsburger Patrizier* (Munich and Berlin, 2001), pp. 34–5.

36. The figures are given in the report by Bernardino Navagero to the Senate of the Republic of Venice (note 29), in: Albèri, *Relazioni*, pp. 485–7. Also in: Kohler, ed., *Quellen*, pp. 329–30. Brandi, *Karl* (note 27), vol. 1, p. 42, calculated

higher numbers and believed that Charles had 7,000 cavalry and about 24,000 infantry.

37. See: Wilhelm Beck, ed., *Die aeltesten Artikelsbriefe für das deutsche Fußvolk* (Munich, 1908).

38. Charles V [Letter to Mary of Hungary, 9 June 1546], in: Lanz, ed., *Correspondenz*, vol. 2, pp. 490–1. Also in: Kohler, ed., *Quellen*, p. 327.

39. Emperor Maxmilian I, 'Ordnung des gemeinen Pfennigs', ed. Hanns Hubert Hofmann, *Quellen zum Verfassungsorganismus des Heiligen Römischen Reiches Deutscher Nation. 1495–1815* (Darmstadt, 1976), pp. 15–18.

40. For a discussion of the evidence see: Clemens Bauer, 'Die wirtschaftlichen Machtgrundlagen Karls V', in: Bauer, *Gesammelte Aufsätze zur Wirtschafts- und Sozialgeschichte* (Freiburg, 1965), pp. 346–55. Ramón Carande, 'Das westindische Gold und die Kreditpolitik Karls V.', in: *Gesammelte Aufsätze zur Kulturgeschichte Spaniens* 10 (1955), pp. 1–22. Carande, *Carlos V y sus banqueros*, 3 vols (Madrid, 1943–67). Earl J. Hamilton, *American Treasure and the Price Revolution in Spain. 1501–1650* (Cambridge, MA, 1934).

41. Weiss, ed., *Papiers*, vol. 3, pp. 267–8.

42. Soardino, Mantuan ambassador in France [Report to the marquis of Mantua, 19 June 1520] in: *Cal. Venice*, vol.2, no. 90, pp. 71–2. The most famous of the visits occurred at the Field of the Cloth of Gold outside Guines in northern France, where Charles met with Francis and Henry in June 1520. For a description see: Sidney Anglo, 'Le Camp du Drap d'Or et les entrevues d'Henri VIII et de Charles Quint', in: *Fêtes et cérémonies au temps de Charles Quint*, ed. Jean Jacquot (Paris, 1960), pp. 116–25. Anglo, 'The Hampton Court Painting of the Field of the Cloth of Gold [June 1520] Considered as an Historical Document', in: *Antiquaries Journal* 46 (1966), pp. 287–307.

43. Charles V, Instructions (note 5), in: Brandi, 'Testamente', pp. 81–95. Also in: Kohler, ed., *Quellen*, pp. 293–300.

44. Charles V, Memorandum (note 14), in: Lanz, ed., *Staatspapiere*, pp. 59–62. Also in: Kohler, ed., *Quellen*, pp. 181–3.

45. Antonio Vázquez de Espinosa, *Compendium and Description of the West Indies*, ed. Charles Upton Clark, vol. 1 (Washington, 1942), p. 39.

46. *Ordenanzas reales para la cosa de contratación y para otras cosas de las Indias y de la navigación* (Valladolid, 1643), fol. Ir.

47. Francisco de Vitoria, *De Indis sive de iure belli Hispanorum in barbaros relectio posterior*, Sectio II, tit. I, ed. Ernest Nys (Washington, 1917), p. 234 [repr. (New York, 1964); (Buffalo, 1995)].

48. See: Kohler, *Karl* (note 7), pp. 231–2.

49. See: Bartolomé de Las Casas [In Defence of the Indians], Ms. Paris, Bibliothèque Nationale de France, Nouveaux Fonds Latin, no. 12926, ed. Stafford Poole, *In Defence of the Indians* (DeKalb, 1974), pp. 54–70, 262–6,

Notes

326–9. Las Casas, *Aqui se contiene vna disputa o controuersia entre el Obispo dom fray Bartholome de las Casas o Casaus obispo que fue dela cuidad Real de Chiapa que es enlas Indias parte dela nueua Espana y el dictor Gines de Sepulueda Coronista del Emperador nuestro senor sobre que el doctor contendia que las conquistas delas Indias contra los Indios eran lícitas y el obispo por el contrario defendio y affirmo euer si do y ser impossibile no serlo tiranicas injustas y iniquas* (Seville, 1552). New edn in: Las Casas, *Tratados*, ed. Lewis Hanke and Manuel Giménez Fernández, vol. 1 (Mexico City, 1965), pp. 217–459. German ed. in: Las Casas, *Werkauswahl*, ed. Mariano Delgado, vol. 1 (Paderborn, 1994), pp. 347–436.

50. For Sepúlveda's historiographical work see: Juan Ginés de Sepúlveda, *De rebus gestis Caroli Quinti imperatoris et Regis Hispaniae*, 2 vols (Madrid, 1780) (Sepúlveda, *Opera*, vol. 1–2).

Six

1. Charles V [Instruction to his son Philip, 25 October 1555], in: Bruno Stübel, ed., 'Die Instruktion Karls V. für Philipp II. vom 25 Oktober 1555', in: *Archiv für österreichische Geschichte* 93 (1905), p. 190. Also in: Kohler, ed., *Quellen*, p. 471.
2. State Council [Statement concerning policies towards the Ottoman Turkish Empire, November 1526], in: *Corpus documental de Carlos V*, ed. Manuel Fernández Alvarez, vol. 1 (Salamanca, 1973), p. 118. Also in: Kohler, ed., *Quellen*, p. 122.
3. Charles V [Address to the Augsburg imperial diet, delivered by Frederick Count Palatine, 20 June 1530], in: Karl Eduard Förstemann, ed., *Urkundenbuch zu der Geschichte des Reichstages zu Augsburg im Jahre 1530*, vol. 1 (Halle, 1833), p. 304 [repr. (Osnabrück, 1966)]. Also in: Kohler, ed., *Quellen*, p. 160. Charles V [Letter to Juan Antonio Muxetula, 23 September 1530], in: Eduard Wilhelm Mayer, 'Forschungen zur Politik Karls V. während des Augsburger Reichstages von 1530', in: *Archiv für Reformationsgeschichte* 13 (1916), pp. 68–71. Also in: Kohler, ed., *Quellen*, pp. 172–5.
4. Martin Luther, 'Heerpredigt wider den Türken' [28 October 1528], in: *D Martin Luthers Werke. Kritische Gesammtausgabe*, vol. 30 (Weimar, 1909), pp. 160–97 [repr. (Weimar, 1964)].
5. Charles was advised to conduct a war against Turkish allies in Asia and Africa by Baptista Pizacharus, *Ad Carolem V Caesarem augustissimum pro Francisco Sfortia Insubrum duce oratio* (Rome, *c.* 1529), fol. C 1. For sources on Charles's concerns about the security of the Mediterranean sea routes see: Karl Brandi, *Kaiser Karl V*, vol. 2 (Munich, 1941), p. 247.
6. Muley Hassan, *Lettere inedite a Ferrante Gonzaga, vicere di sicilia (1537–1547)*, ed. Federico Odorici and Michele Amari (Modena, 1865).

259

Notes

7. For Tavera's protest see: Fritz Walser, ed., 'Denkschrift Juan Taveras zum geplanten Zuge gegen Tunis und nach Italien, Madrid, Jan. 1535', in: *Nachrichten von der Gesellschaft der Wissenschaften zu Göttingen*, Philologisch–Historische Klasse (1932), pp. 167–72.

8. For reports on military aspects of the campaign see: Luis de Avila y Zuñiga, 'Lo de la Goletta y Tunez año de 1535', in: *Colección de documentos ineditos*, vol. 1 (Madrid, 1842), p. 159. Guillaume de Montoiche, 'Voyage et expedition de Charles-Quint au Pays de Tunis, de 1535', in: *Collection des voyages des souverains des Pays-Bas*, ed. Louis Prosper Gachard, vol. 3 (Brusselx, 1875), pp. 317–403. C[hristoph] S[cheurl von Defersdorf], *Römischer Kayserlicher Maiestat Christenliche Kriegs Rüsstung wider die Vnglaubigen / anzůg in Hispanien vnd Sardinien / Ankunfft in Africa / vnd eroberung des Ports zů Thunis / im Monat Junio / Anno 1535* (s.l., 1535). *La conquête de Tunis en 1535, racontée par deux écrivains franç-comtois*, ed. Auguste Castan (Besançon, 1891). *Tunesi. Spedizione di Carlo V imperatore*, ed. Damiano Muoni (Milan, 1876).

9. Caravaggio's sketch for the Messina triumphal arch is extant in Berlin, Kupferstichkabinett, K.d.Z.26541.79 D 34. Reprinted in: Roy Strong, *Art and Power: Renaissance Festivals* (Woodbridge, 1984), pp. 148–9.

10. Giorgio Vasari, *Le vite de' piu eccellenti pittori, scultori ed architettori*, ed. Gaetano Milanesi, vol. 5 (Florence, 1906), pp. 151–2. See also: Strong, *Art* (note 9), p. 149.

11. See: *Triumphierlich einreiten Röm[isch] Keyserlicher Maiestat zu Messina den 21. Octobris und zu Neapolis den 25. Novembris Anno 1535* (s.l., 1535). Marco Guazzo, *Historia di tutte le cose degni d memoria del anno 1524 sino a questo presenta* (Venice, 1540), fols 139v–40v. 'Embellissement des voyage et conqueste de la cité de Thunes en Affrique, faicte par l'Impérialle Majesté figure à Gédéon', in: *Documents inédits relatifs à la conquête de Tunis par l'empereur Charles-Quint*, ed. Emile Léonard Jean Baptiste Gachard (Brussels, 1844), p. 49.

12. See the anonymous sketch of the Rome triumphal arch in: Strong, *Feste* (note 9), p. 150.

13. For contemporary prints reporting on the Tunis expedition see: *Newe zeytung / von der Römischen Kay[serlichen] May[estät] zug/vnd erorberung des Künigsreyches Thunesse* (s.l., 1535). *Verteuscht Schreiben von Kayserlicher Majestat wunderbarlicher Eroberung der Statt Tunis in Africa doselbst den XXIII Julij 1535* (Nuremberg, 1535). *La felice vitoria de Tunis i Goletta fatta de la Cesarea Maiesta de Carlo V. imperatore* ([Milan], 1535).

14. For the tapestries, completed in 1554/55, see: *Der Kriegszug Kaiser Karls V. gegen Tunis. Kartons und Tapisserien*, ed. Wilfried Seipel (Vienna, 2000). For an edition of materials relevant to the making of the Tunis tapestries see: *Jules*

Houdoy, *Tapisseries représentantes la conqueste du royaulme de Thunes* (Lille, 1873).

15. Charles V [Letter to his sister Mary of Hungary, 26 July 1535], in: Lanz, ed., *Correspondenz*, vol. 2, pp. 193–5. Also in: Kohler, ed., *Quellen*, pp. 203–5.

16. Sebastian Fischer, *Chronik besonders von Ulmischen Sachen* [Munich, Bayerische Staatsbibliothek, Cgm 3091, fol. 262v], ed. Karl Gustav Veesenmeyer (Ulm, 1896), p. 138 (Ulm und Oberschwaben. 5–8).

17. Museum Nordico, Linz, Inv-No. 11009.

18. Gregory I, *Moralia in Job*, cap. XI/ 10, 14, *S. Gregorii Magni Moralia in Iob*, ed. Marcel Andriaen (Turnhout, 1979), p. 249.

19. The PLVS VLTRA emblem appeared in prints of imperial edicts and decisions of imperial diets, most prominently in the prints published in the aftermath of the Augsburg imperial diet of 1548. For the prints see: Historisches Archiv der Stadt Köln, Bestand 50, No. 109, e.g., fols 46r, 81r, 133v, 134r, 158v, 192r, 194r.

20. Charles reported on his address in a letter to Jean Hannart, sieur de Likerke, dated 17/18 April 1536, in: Lanz, ed., *Correspondenz*, vol. 2, pp. 223–9. Also in: Kohler, ed., *Quellen*, pp. 211–18.

21. The German version has been edited in: Peter Rassow, *Die Kaiser-Idee Karls V. Dargestellt an der Politik der Jahre 1528–1540* (Berlin, 1932), pp. 265–8 (Historische Studien. 217) [repr. (Vaduz, 1965)]. Also in: Kohler, ed., *Quellen*, pp. 218–21.

22. Reported by: Nicolo Tiepolo *et al.* [Letter to the doge of Venice, 4 June 1538], in: *Dispacci di Germania. Venetianische Depeschen vom Kaiserhof*, ed. Gustav Turba, vol. 1 (Vienna, 1889), no. 25, pp. 99–105.

23. Nicolo Tiepolo *et al.* [Letter to the doge of Venice, 24 May 1538], in *ibid.*, no. 19, pp. 67–76.

24. Mary of Hungary [Letter to Charles V, August 1541], in: Lanz, ed., *Staatspapiere*, pp. 263–8.

25. Tiepolo, Letter (note 23).

26. On the Algiers campaign see: *Documents musulmans sur le siège d'Alger en 1541*, ed. René Basset (Oran, 1890). Jean Vandenesse, 'Journal 1514–1551', in: Louis Prosper Gachard, ed., *Collection des voyages des souverains des Pays-Bas*, vol. 2 (Brussels, 1874), pp. 612–17. See also: Gachard, ed., *Collection des voyages des souverains des Pays-Bas*, vol. 3 (Brussels, 1875), pp. 403–48.

27. Nicolas Perrenot de Granvelle [Memorandum for Charles V, 28 November 1541], ed. Walter Friedensburg, 'Aktenstücke zur Politik Kaiser Karls V. im Herbst 1541', in: *Archiv für Reformationsgeschichte* 29 (1932), pp. 46–64. Also in: Kohler, ed., *Quellen*, pp. 268–74.

28. See: Kohler, ed., *Quellen*, pp. 274–5, fn 1.

29. *Negociations de la France dans le Levant*, ed. Ernest Charrière, vol. 1 (Paris, 1848), pp. 116–29. It needs to be taken into consideration that the Viennese

court took a less fundamentalist stance than Charles, sent diplomatic emissaries to Istanbul from 1530 and began to establish regular diplomatic relations with the sultan in 1554. See: Benedikt Kuripešič, *Itinerarium der Gesandtschaft König Ferdinands I. von Ungarn nach Konstantinopel 1530*, ed. Srecko M. Džaja and Jozo Džambo (Bochum, 1983) (Materialia Turcica. Beiheft 6) [repr. of the original edn (Augsburg, 1531)]. Ogier Ghiselin de Busbecq, *The Turkish Letters of Ogier Ghiselin der Busbecq, Imperial Ambassador at Constantinople. 1554–1562* (Oxford, 1968).

30. See: *Correspondence politique de MM. De Castillon et de Marillac, ambassadeurs de France en Angleterre. 1537–42*, ed. Jean Kaulek (Paris, 1885), no. 279, p. 249.

31. See: Alfred Kohler, *Karl V. 1500–1558* (Munich, 1999), pp. 256–8.

32. Granvelle, Memorandum (note 27), in: Friedensburg, 'Aktenstücke', pp. 50–1. Also in: Kohler, ed., *Quellen*, pp. 269–70.

33. State Council [Statement on the policy towards Lutheranism after the submission of the Confessio Augustana, June 1530], in: Leopold von Ranke, *Deutsche Geschichte im Zeitalter der Reformation*, vol. 6, ed. Paul Joachimsen (Munich, 1926), p. 115. Also in: Kohler, ed., *Quellen*, pp. 164–5.

34. Garcia de Loaysa [Letters to Charles V, 25 August 1530, 1 October 1530], in: *Briefe an Kaiser Karl, geschrieben von seinem Beichtvater*, ed. Gotthold Heine (Berlin, 1848), pp. 33, 41–2.

35. *RTA*, vol. 7.

36. Charles V [Memorandum addressed to the Augsburg imperial diet, 8 September 1530], ed. Rassow, *Kaiser-Idee* (note 21), p. 402.

37. Günther Gassmann, ed., *Das Augsburger Bekenntnis*, revidierter Text, 6th edn (Göttingen, 1988).

38. Herbert Immenkötter, ed., *Die Confutatio Augustana vom 3. August 1530* (Munster, 1979) (Corpus catholicorum. 33).

39. Huldreich Zwingli, *Von götlicher vnd menschlicher grechtigheit* (Zurich, 1523). Zwingli, *Ad Carolem Rom[anum] imperatorem* (Zurich, 1530). Also in: Zwingli, *Sämtliche Werke*, vol. 2, ed. Emil Egli and Georg Finsler (Leipzig, 1908), pp. 458–525 (Corpus Reformatorum. 89.) Zwingli, *Schriften*, vol. 1, ed. Thomas Brumschweiler, Samuel Lutz et al. (Zurich, 1995), pp. 155–213. Heinrich Bullinger, *De testamento seu foedere Dei unico et aeterno* (Zurich, 1534). Tr. in: Charles S. McCoy, J. Wayne Baker, *Fountainhead of Federalism. Heinrich Bullinger and the Covenantal Tradition* (Louisville, KY, 1991). Pope Leo X [Letter to Henry VIII, 11 October 1521], in: Jean Dumont, *Corps diplomatique universel*, vol. 4, pt 1 (The Hague, 1726), no. 158, pp. 355–7.

40. See: Friedrich Hortleder, *Der Rom[ischen] Keys[erlichen] u[nd] Koniglichen Maiesteten, auch des Heil[igen] Rom[ischen] Reichs geistl[icher] und weltl[icher] Stende, Churfursten, Fursten etc. Handlungen und Anschreiben,*

Sendbrieff, Klag und Supplikationsschreiben von den Ursachen des Teutschen Krieges Keyser Carls des Funften wider die Schmalkaldischen Bundesobersten Chur- und Fursten, Sachsen und Hessen und Mitverwandten anno 1546 und 47, vol. 1 (Frankfurt, 1617), pp. 104–5.

41. Matthias Held [Report to Charles V, autumn 1537], ed. Ludwig Cardauns, in: *Quellen und Forschungen aus italienischen Archiven und Bibliotheken* 12 (1909), p. 354.

42. For a report about the disputation see Charles's letter to his brother Ferdinand, dated 22 January 1541, in: Ignaz von Döllinger, ed., *Dokumente zur Geschichte Karls V., Philipps II. und ihrer Zeit aus spanischen Archiven* (Regensburg, 1862), pp. 32–6.

43. See: Reginald Pole, 'Apologia Reginaldi Poli ad Carolum V. Caesarem' [February 1539], in: Pole, *Epistolarum Reginaldi Poli S.R.E. Cardinalis et aliarum ad ipsum*, pt 1, ed. Johann Georg Schelhorn (Bressanone, 1744), pp. 66–170 [repr. (Farnborough, 1967)]. Pole sought to retain the unity of Catholicism as a means to mobilise resistance against the Ottoman Turkish Empire. See: Reginald Pole, *The Seditious and Blasphemous Oration of Cardinal Pole* (London, 1560), fols Aiiv–Aiiir.

44. Jean Calvin, *Institutio Christianiae religionis*, cap. II [Strasbourg, 1539], ed. Henri Châtelain and Jacques Pannier (Paris, 1911), vol. 1 (Bibliothèque des Hautes Etudes. 176 and 177).

45. See: Peter Abelard, *Liber dictus scito te ipsum*, cap. III, ed. Jacques-Paul Migne, *Patrologiae cursus completus*. Series Latina, vol. 178, col. 636. New edition s.t.: *Ethical Writings. Know Yourself* (Indianapolis, 1995).

46. Thomas Aquinas, *Summa theologiae*, secunda secundae, qu 132, ar 1, in *S. Thomae Opera omnia*, ed. Roberto Busa, SJ, vol. 2 (Stuttgart, 1980), p. 688.

47. On Anabaptism see: Heinold Fast, ed., *Der linke Flügel der Reformation. Glaubenszeugnisse der Täufer, Spiritualisten, Schwärmer und Antitrinitarier* (Bremen, 1962), pp. 219–46 (Klassiker des Protestantismus. 4).

48. Martin Luther, 'Von weltlicher Obrigkeit, wie man ihr Gehorsam schuldig sei' [March 1523], in: *D Martin Luthers Werke. Kritische Gesammtausgabe*, vol. 11 (Weimar, 1900), pp. 229–81 [repr. (Weimar, 1966)].

49. Martin Luther, 'Ein Sendbrief von dem harten Buchlein wider die Bauern' [1525], in: *D Martin Luthers Werke. Kritische Gesammtausgabe*, vol. 18 (Weimar, 1908), pp. 384–401 [repr. (Weimar, 1964)].

50. For example, see: Charles V [Letter to Jean Hannart, sieur de Likerke, 14 December 1535], ed. Rassow, *Kaiser-Idee* (note 21), pp. 416–17. Also in: Kohler, ed., *Quellen*, pp. 208–10.

51. Charles V [Address to his advisers, 16 September 1528], ed. Karl Brandi, 'Eigenhändige Aufzeichnungen Karls V. aus dem Jahre 1525', in: *Nachrichten vn der Gesellschaft der Wissenschaften zu Göttingen*, Philologisch–Historische Klasse (1933), pp. 230–2. Also in: Kohler, ed., *Quellen*, pp. 136–8.

Notes

52. Charles V, *Romisch–Kayserlicher Majestät Ordnung und Reformation guter Policey im Heiligen Romisch Reich* ([Augsburg], 19 November 1530). New edn (Mainz, 1548; 1551; 1577). For a comprehensive list of editions see: Karl Härter and Michael Stolleis, eds, *Repertorium der Policeyordnungen der Frühen Neuzeit*, vol. 1 (Frankfurt, 1996), pp. 61–106 (Ius commune. Beihefte 84).

53. *Die peinliche Gerichtsordnung Kaiser Karls V. von 1532 (Carolina)* (Stuttgart, 1962).

54. Charles V [Secret instructions to his son Philip, 6 May 1543], ed. Karl Brandi, 'Die Testamente und politischen Instruktionen Karls V., insbesondere diejenigen der Jahre 1543/44', in: *Nachrichten von der Gesellschaft der Wissenschaften zu Göttingen*, Philologisch–Historische Klasse (1935), pp. 68–9. Also in: Kohler, ed., *Quellen*, pp. 290–1.

55. On meals see: Alfred de Ridder, 'Les reglements de la cour de Charles-Quint', in: *Messager des sciences historiques ou archives des arts et de la bibliographie de Belgique* (1893), pp. 392–418.

56. Paul Herre, *Barbara Blomberg, die Geliebte Kaiser Karls V. und Mutter Don Juans de Austria* (Leipzig, 1909), pp. 15–16, 134 [Melchior de Camargo, Letter to Philip II, 1569].

57. *Ursprung unnd ursach diser Auffrur Teütscher Nation* [1546], in: Kohler, ed., *Quellen*, p. 340.

58. Paolo Giovio, 'De bello Germanico', in: Burkhard Gotthelf Strube, ed., *Collectanea manuscriptorum ex codicibus*, vol. 2, pt 1 (Jena, 1713), pp. 85–92.

59. Luis Avila y Zuñiga, *Geschichte des Schmalkaldischen Krieges* (Berlin, 1853), p. 144. Also in: Kohler, ed., *Quellen*, p. 362.

60. [Anonymous legal opinion on the question of how Elector John Frederick of Saxony should be punished, after 24 April 1547], ed. Walter Friedensburg, 'Ein Aktenstück zur Frage der Betrafung des gefangenen Kurfürsten Johann Friedrich von Sachsen', in: *Archiv für Reformationsgeschichte 5* (1908), pp. 214–15. Also in: Kohler, ed., *Quellen*, pp. 373–5.

61. *Abschied der Rom[isch] Keys[erlichen] Maiest[at] vnd gemeyner Stend/vff den Reichstag zu Augspurg vffgericht/Anno Domini M.D.XLVIII* (Mainz, 1548), Historisches Archiv der Stadt Köln, Bestand 50, no. 105, fols 91r–133v.

62. Charles V and the imperial estates [Burgundian Treaty, 26 June 1548], in: *Urkunden und Aktenstücke des Reichsarchivs Wien zur reichsrechtlichen Stellung des Burgundischen Kreises*, vol. 1, ed. Robert von Lacroix and Lothar Gross (Vienna, 1944), pp. 439–47. Also in: Kohler, ed., *Quellen*, pp. 392–9.

63. The numbers are from: Walter Breywisch, 'Quedlinburgs Säkularisation und seine ersten Jahre unter der preußischen Herrschaft. 1802–1806', in: *Sachsen und Anhalt 4* (1928), p. 212.

64. For the sources see: Hermann Lorenz, *Werdegang von Stift und Stadt Quedlinburg* (Quedlinburg, 1922), pp. 195–6.
65. *Ibid.*, p. 201.
66. *Ibid.*, p. 208.
67. *Ibid.*, p. 210.
68. *Ibid.*, p. 247.
69. *Ibid.*, pp. 282–3.
70. *Ibid.*, p. 269.
71. On Charles's visit to Ghent in 1540, the entry, the execution of the leaders of the uprising, the eventual submission of the burghers and the new constitution, known as the Caroline Concession, see: *Relations des troubles de Gand sous Charles-Quint*, ed. Louis Prosper Gachard (Brussels, 1846), pp. 62–6, 87–90, 98–134, 368–70. *Discourse des troubles advenuz en la ville de Gand*, ed. Cornelius Hoynck van Papendrecht (The Hague, 1743), pp. 487–517. *Coutume de la ville de Gand*, ed. Louis de Hondt and Adolphe du Bois, vol. 2 (Brussels, 1887), pp. 140–83.
72. Diploma in the name of Charles V, 4 November 1520, Ms. Nuremberg, Staatsarchiv, Rep. 1a, no. 612.
73. Staatsarchiv Nürnberg, Rep. 67, no. 1, fols 132–81.
74. Christoph Scheurl of Defersdorf, 'Epistel über die Verfassung der Reichsstadt Nürnberg', 15 December 1516, in: *Die Chroniken der fränkischen Städte. Nürnberg*, vol. 5 (Leipzig, 1874), pp. 781–2 (Die Chroniken der deutschen Städte. 11).
75. See: Eberhard Naujoks, ed., *Kaiser Karl V. und die Zunftverfassung. Ausgewählte Aktenstücke zu den Verfassungsänderungen in den oberdeutschen Reichsstädten (1547–1556)* (Stuttgart, 1985), pp. 72–7, 86–91 (Veröffentlichungen der Kommission für geschichtliche Landeskunde in Baden-Württemberg. Reihe A, vol. 36).
76. See the description and edition of sources by: Philipp Ernst Spiess, *Geschichte des kaiserlichen neunjährigen Bundes vom Jahr 1535 bis 44 als eine neue Erscheinung in der Teutschen Reichsgeschichte, aus den Originalakten dargestellt* (Erlangen, 1788), esp. pp. 97–142.
77. [Report on Charles's entry into Augsburg, 15 June 1530], in: Förstemann, *Urkundenbuch* (note 3), pp. 257–62. Kohler, ed., *Quellen*, pp. 157–60. For the publication of a series of prints (from the Herzog-Anton-Ulrich-Museum at Brunswick) showing Charles's entry into Augsburg see: Max Geisberg and Walter L. Strauss, eds, *The German Single-leaf Woodcut. 1500–1550*, vol. 4 (New York, 1974), pp. 327–37.
78. Mandate in the name of Charles V, 3 February 1528, Ms. Frankfurt, Institut für Stadtgeschichte, Reichtsgasakten 43, fol. 45. The mandate was issued at the time of the Anglo-French war against the emperor and sought to prevent the entry of the emperor's subjects into the service of Francis I and Henry VIII. See:

Reichsgeschichtliche Quellen. 1500–1555, ed. Harry Gerber (Frankfurt, 1936) (Mitteilungen aus dem Frankfurter Stadtarchiv. 2).

79. Oath of allegiance to Charles V, 1543. Ms Ulm, Stadtarchiv, Bestand A 1, fol. 3r.

80. The Secret Council of Ulm [Letter to the XIII Directors of Strasbourg, 19 December 1546], in: *Politische Correspondenz der Stadt Strassburg im Zeitalter der Reformation*, ed. Otto Winckelmann, vol. 4, pt 1, eds J. Bernays and Harry Gerber (Heidelberg, 1931), no. 491, pp. 524–5.

81. The XIII Directors of Strasbourg [Letter to the Secret Council of Ulm, 25 December 1546], in: Winckelmann, *Correspondenz* (note 80), no. 497, pp. 532–3. Mayor and Council of Ulm [Letters to the Council of Strasbourg, 28 December 1546 and January 1547], in: Winckelmann, *Correspondenz* (note 80), nos 503 and 507, pp. 541–3, 546–9.

82. See: Paul Hector Mair, 'Chronica, angefangen nach Christi, unnsers lieben herrn und haylandts geburt, als man zelt M.D.XLVII', in: *Die Chroniken der schwäbischen Städte. Augsburg*, vol. 7 (Leipzig, 1917), pp. 23–4 (Die Chroniken der deutschen Städte. 32).

83. *Ibid.*, pp. 25–57.

84. Georg Sigismund Seld, Kurze anzaig Welchermassen, auch auß was ursachen, die Rö[misch] Kay[serliche] May[estät] Verenderung Regiments der Statt Ulm . . . furgenommen. Ms. 19 August 1548, Stadtarchiv Ulm, A3409. Fischer, *Chronik* (note 16), pp. 139–44. See also: Wolfgang Glockengiesser, Von alten geschichten so zu Vlm vnnd anderen Orhten firgangen. Ms. Ulm, Stadtarchiv, Bestand G 3, fols 20v–22v. Glockengiesser was one of the guild masters who had lost their office in consequence of the imperial intervention in Ulm. Nikolaus Mameranus, *Caroli V Rom[ani] Imp[eratoris] Aug[usti] iter ex inferiore Germania ab anno 1545 usque in cometia apud Augustam Rhetian indicta anni 1547* (Augsburg, 1548), fol. B [XXX]r.

85. Fischer, *Chronik* (note 16), fol. 267, p. 141.

86. The 'Neue Schwörbrief' (new charter concerning oaths of allegiance), dated 22 August 1558, in: *Juristisches Magazin für die deutschen Reichsstädte*, ed. Tobias Ludwig Ulrich Jäger, vol. 2 (Ulm, 1791), pp. 329–43. The new date for the oaths was to fall on a day in August, whereas according to the old *Schwörbrief* of 1397 the annual swearing day had been 23 April.

87. See: *Beschlüsse des Rates der Stadt Köln. 1320–1550*, 5 June 1548, ed. Manfred Groten, vol. 3 (Düsseldorf, 1988), p. 595 (Publikationen der Gesellschaft für Rheinische Geschichtskunde. 65,3).

88. Groten, ed., *Beschlüsse* (note 87), 27 August 1548, pp. 616–17.

89. Groten, ed., *Beschlüsse* (note 87), 7 September 1548, p. 621; 12 September 1548, p. 622.

90. Groten, ed., *Beschlüsse* (note 87), 6 April 1549, pp. 671–2.

Seven

1. During and after the war against the Schmalkaldic League, Charles could no longer conceal the seriousness of his illnesses before diplomats present in his entourage. Hence, the emperor's frailty featured frequently in diplomatic reports. For example, see: Alois Mocenigo [Report about Charles V, written in 1548], no. 3, in: *Relationen venetianischer Botschafter über Deutschland und Österreich im 16. Jahrhundert*, ed. Joseph Fiedler (Vienna, 1870), pp. 14–15.

2. For a report on Philip's journey see: Juan Cristobal de Calvate de Estrella, *El Felicissimo viaie del muy alto y muy poderoso Principe Don Phelippe, Hijo del Emperador Don Carlos Quinto Maximo, desde España a sus tierras dela baxa Alemaña* (Antwerp, 1552), fols 170v–71r, 225v–51v.

3. Francis van de Velde, *Arcus triumphales quinque a S.P.Q. Gand Philippo Austriae et Caroli imp[eratoris] Principis Flandiarum filio et haeredi et futuro principi Flandiarum exstituti fuere* (Ghent, 1549).

4. Charles V [Comments on complaints by the imperial estates, June 1552], in: *Briefe und Akten zur Geschichte des sechzehnten Jahrhunderts*, vol. 3, ed. August von Druffel (Munich, 1875), pp. 444–7. Also in Kohler, ed., *Quellen*, pp. 418–22. Charles V [Letter to his sister Mary of Hungary, 16 July 1552], in: Lanz, ed., *Correspondenz*, vol. 3, pp. 377–8. Also in: Kohler, ed., *Quellen*, pp. 422–3.

5. Treaty of Chambord, ed. Druffel, *Briefe* (note 4), pp. 340–50.

6. Charles, Comments (note 4), Druffel, p. 446. Also in: Kohler, ed., *Quellen*, p 421. [Manifesto of the War Princes, 1552], ed. Friedrich Hortleder, *Der Rom[ischen] Keys[erlichen] u[nd] Koniglichen Maiesteten, auch des Heil[igen] Rom[ischen] Reichs geistl[icher] und weltl[icher] Stende, Churfursten, Fursten etc. Handlungen und Anschreiben, Sendbrieff, Klag und Supplikationsschreiben von den Ursachen des Teutschen Krieges Keyser Carls des Funften wider die Schmalkaldischen Bundesobersten Chur- und Fursten, Sachsen und Hessen und Mitverwandten anno 1546 und 47*, vol. 1 (Frankfurt, 1617), pp. 117–18, 1295.

7. For the treaty of Passau, signed by Charles V on 15 August 1552, see: Druffel, *Briefe* (note 4), vol. 3, pp. 444–569.

8. Quoted from: Alfred Kohler, *Karl V. 1500–1558* (Munich, 1999), p. 340.

9. Charles V [Letter to Ferdinand, 9 December 1553], in: Druffel, *Briefe* (note 4), vol. 4, ed. Karl Brandi (Munich, 1896), p. 331. Ferdinand [Letter to Charles V, 29 December 1553], in: Lanz, ed., *Correspondenz*, vol. 3, p. 596.

10. Mary, Queen of England [Letter to Charles V, 7 August 1553], in: *SP Spain*, vol. 11, p. 153.

11. Simon Renard [Letter to Charles V, 8 December 1553], in: *SP Spain*, vol. 11, pp. 414–19.

12. Charles V [Letter to Ferdinand, 8/10 June 1554], in: Lanz, ed. *Correspondenz*, vol. 3, pp. 623–4. Also in: Kohler, ed., *Quellen*, p. 455. Using failing health as

a pretext was not a far-fetched argument, as reports on Charles's weakening health were circulating at the courts. For an example see: Andrew Dudley and Richard Morysine [Letter to the Council of England, 25 January 1553], in: *Calendar of State Papers, Foreign Series, of the Reign of Edward VI. 1547–1553*, ed. William B. Turnbull (London, 1861), no. 611, pp. 239–40.

13. Treaty of Munster, 24 October 1648, Art. VII, in: *Kaiser und Reich*, ed. Arno Buschmann (Munich, 1984), pp. 336–8.

14. *Der Augsburger Religionsfriede vom 25. September 1555*, ed. Karl Brandi, 2nd edn (Göttingen, 1927). Also in: Buschmann, ed., *Kaiser* (note 13), pp. 224–9, 273.

15. Charles V [Letter to Ferdinand, 15 August 1555], in: Lanz, ed., *Correspondenz*, vol. 3, pp. 673–5. Also in: Kohler, ed., *Quellen*, pp. 464–5.

16. Charles V [Letter to Ferdinand I, 15 August 1555], in: Lanz, ed., *Correspondenz*, vol. 3, p. 673. Also in: Kohler, ed., *Quellen*, p. 464.

17. Charles V [Address to the States General of the Netherlands, Brussels, 25 October 1555], ed. William Stirling, *The Cloister Life of the Emperor Charles the Fifth* (London, 1853), pp. 7–8. Also in: Kohler, ed., *Quellen*, p. 467.

18. Stirling, *Cloister Life* (note 17), p. 9. Also in: Kohler, ed., *Quellen*, p. 468.

19. Charles V [Instruction for the abdication mission to Ferdinand I, 3 August 1556], ed. Gustav Turba, 'Beiträge zur Geschichte der Habsburger', pt III, in: *Archiv für österreichische Geschichte* 90 (1901), pp. 314–16. Also in: Kohler, ed., *Quellen*, pp. 480–2. For a report on the procedure of Charles's abdication as emperor see: Edward Carne [Letter to Queen Mary, 26 March 1558], in: *Calendar of State Papers, Foreign Series, of the Reign of Mary. 1553–1558*, ed. William B. Turnbull (London, 1861), no. 747, p. 367.

20. [List of jewels, garments and furniture found at Yuste upon the death of Charles V, 1558], ed. Stirling, *Cloister Life* (note 17), pp. 322–8. Also in: Kohler, ed., *Quellen*, pp. 483, 485. For sources relevant to Charles's retirement at Yuste see: *Retraite et mort de Charles-Quint au Monastère de Yuste. Lettres inédites publiées d'après les originaux conservés dans les Archives royales de Simancas*, ed. Louis Prosper Gachard, 3 vols (Brussels, 1854–5).

21. Quoted from: Kohler, *Karl* (note 8), p. 362.

22. *La magnifique pompe funèbre faite en la ville de Bruxelles le 29 déc. 1558 aux obsèques de l'empereur Charles* (Antwerp, 1559).

23. Cuthbert's Letter on the Death of Bede, in: Bede, *Historia ecclesiastica gentis Anglorum*, eds Bertram Colgrave and Roger Aubrey Baskervill Mynors (Oxford, 1969), pp. 579–87 [repr. (Oxford, 2003)]. *Vita Eigilis*, cap. 25, ed. Georg Waitz, MGH, *SS* 15, pp. 231–3.

24. Orderic Vitalis, *Ecclesiastical History*, cap. VII/14, vol. 4, ed. Marjorie Chibnall (Oxford, 1973), p. 78.

25. For an edition of some relevant high and late medieval texts see: Rolf Sprandel, *Altersschicksal und Altersmoral. Die Geschichte der Einstellungen zum Altern nach der Pariser Bibelexegese* (Stuttgart, 1981), esp. pp. 164–86.

26. See: Josef Karl Mayr, 'Die letzte Abdankung Karls V. (16. Jänner 1556)', in: *Nachrichten von der Gesellschaft der Wissenschaften zu Göttingen*, Philologisch–Historische Klasse (1931), pp. 143–58.

27. Leon Battista Alberti, *I Libri della famiglia*, book I, ed. Renée Neu Watkins, *The Family in Renaissance Florence* (Columbia, S.C., 1969), pp. 36–40. Also in: Klaus Arnold, *Kind und Gesellschaft in Mittelalter und Renaissance* (Paderborn, 1980), p. 147.

28. Charles, Address (note 17), in: Stirling, *Cloister Life*, p. 7. Also in: Kohler, ed., *Quellen*, p. 468.

29. Charles V, *Commentaires de Charles-Quint [à son fils Philippe, Prince d'Espagne]*, ed. Kervyn de Lettenhove (Brussels, 1862).

30. Charles, Address (note 17).

31. Charles V, *Commentaires* (note 29), pp. 7–55.

32. *Ibid.*, pp. 7–10.

33. *Ibid.*, pp. 27, 33, 41.

34. *Ibid.*, pp. 46–54.

35. See: Laurent Vital, 'Rélation du premier voyage de Charles-Quint en Espagne', in: *Collection des voyages des souverains des Pays-Bas*, ed. Louis Prosper Gachard, vol. 3 (Brussels, 1875), pp. 583–8.

36. Luis de Avila y Zuñiga, *Comentario de la guera de Alemaña* (Berlin, 1854), p. 134. Also in: Kohler, ed., *Quellen*, p. 360.

37. List (note 20), p. 483.

38. Charles V [Instruction to his son Philip, 25 October 1555], in: Bruno Stübel, ed., 'Die Instruktion Karls V. für Philipp II. vom 25 Oktober 1555', in: *Archiv für österreichische Geschichte* 93 (1905), pp. 223, 232. Also in: Kohler, ed., *Quellen*, pp. 474, 476–7.

39. Charles V, Address (note 17).

40. Jean-Jacques Rousseau, 'Extrait d'un projet de paix perpétuelle de M. Abbé de Saint-Pierre' [1756], in: Rousseau, *The Political Writings*, ed. Charles Edwyn Vaughan, vol. 1 (Cambridge, 1915), pp. 370–1 [repr. (Oxford, 1962)].

Selected Further Reading

Angermeier, Heinz: *Die Reichsreform. 1410–1555* (Munich, 1984)

Black, Jeremy M., ed.: *The Origin of War in Early Modern Europe* (Edinburgh, 1987)

Bosbach, Franz: *Monarchia universalis. Ein politischer Leitbegriff der Frühen Neuzeit* (Göttingen, 1988) (Schriftenreihe der Historischen Kommission bei der Bayerischen Akademie der Wissenschaften. 32)

Brandi, Karl: *Kaiser Karl V. Werden und Schicksal einer Persönlichkeit und eines Weltreiches*, vol. 1, 3rd edn (Munich, 1941) [first published (Munich, 1937)]; vol. 2 (Munich, 1941) [English version of vol. 1 (London, 1939)]

Brummett, Palmira: *Ottoman Seapower and Levantine Diplomacy in the Age of Discovery* (Albany, NY, 1994)

Cardauns, Ludwig: *Von Nizza bis Crépy. Europäische Politik in den Jahren 1534 bis 1544* (Rome, 1923) (Bibliothek des Preußischen Historischen Instituts in Rom. 15)

Chaunu, Pierre: *Charles Quint* (Paris, 2000)

Fernández Alvarez, Manuel: *Politica mundial de Carlos V y de Felipe II* (Madrid, 1966)

Fernández-Santamaria, J.A.: *The State, War and Peace. Spanish Political Thought in the Renaissance. 1516–1559* (Cambridge, 1977)

Gan Giménez, Pedro: *El consejo real de Carlos V* (Granada, 1988)

García Simon, Agustín: *El ocaso del Emperador. Carlos V en Yuste* (Madrid, 1995)

Groß, Lothar, ed.: *Die Reichsregistraturbücher Karls V. 1519–1556* (Vienna and Leipzig, 1930)

Hartung, Fritz: *Karl V. und die deutschen Reichsstände. 1546–1555* (Halle, 1910)

Headly, John M.: *The Emperor and His Chancellor. A Study of the Imperial Chancellery under Gattinara* (Cambridge, 1983)

Hinrichs, Carl: *Luther und Müntzer. Ihre Auseinandersetzung über Obrigkeit und Widerstandsrecht* (Berlin, 1952)

Höffner, Joseph: *Kolonialismus und Evangelium. Spanische Kolonialethik im Goldenen Zeitalter*, 3rd edn (Trier, 1972) [first published under the title *Christentum und Menschenwürde* (Trier, 1947)]

Immenkötter, Herbert, ed.: *Die fromme Revolte* (Sankt Ottilien, 1982)

Iserloh, Erwin, ed.: *Confessio Augustana. Der Augsburger Reichstag 1530 und die Einheit der Kirche*, 2nd edn (Munster, 1980) (Reformationsgeschichtlich Studien und Texte. 118)

Knecht, Robert J.: *Francis I* (Cambridge, 1982)

Kohler, Alfred: *Karl V. 1500–1558. Eine Biographie* (Munich, 1999) [3rd edn (Munich, 2001)]

——, and Friedrich Edelmayer, eds: *Hispania–Austria. Die Katholischen Könige, Maxmilian I. und die Anfänge der Casa de Austria in Spanien. Akten des Historischen Gespräches – Innsbruck, Juli 1992* (Munich and Vienna, 1993)

——, Barbara Haider and Christine Ottner, eds.: *Karl V. 1500–1558. Neue Perspektiven seiner Herrschaft in Europa und Übersee* (Vienna, 2002) (Österreichische Akademie der Wissenschaften, Philosophisch–Historische Klasse, Historische Kommission. Zentraleuropa-Studien. 6)

Langenn, Albert Friedrich von: *Biographie Moritz' von Sachsen*, 2 vols (Leipzig, 1841)

Lapeyre, Henri: *Charles-Quint* (Paris, 1971)

Leva, Giuseppe de: *Storia documentata di Carlo V in correlazione all' Italia*, 2 vols (Venice, 1864)

Ludolphy, Ingeborg: *Friedrich der Weise* (Göttingen, 1984)

Lutz, Heinrich: *Christianitas afflicta. Europa, das Reich und die päpstliche Politik im Niedergang der Hegemonie Kaiser Karls V. (1552–1556)* (Göttingen, 1964)

——, ed.: *Das römisch-deutsche Reich im politischen System Karls V.* (Munich and Vienna, 1982) (Schriftenreihe des Historischen Kollegs. Kolloquien. 1)

——, and Alfred Kohler, eds: *Aus der Arbeit an den Reichstagen unter Karl V.* (Vienna, 1986)

Macdonald, Stewart: *Charles V. Ruler, Dynast and Defender of the Faith. 1500–1558* (London, 1992)

Majoros, Ference: *Karl V.* (Graz, 2000)

Martín Rubio, Maria del Carmen: *Carlos V, Emperador de las Islas y Tierra Firme del Mar Océano* (Madrid, 1987)

Maurenbrechter, Wilhelm: *Karl V. und die deutschen Protestanten. 1545–1555. Nebst einem Anhang von Aktenstücken aus dem spanischen Staatsarchiv von Simancas* (Düsseldorf, 1865)

Menéndez Pidal, Ramón: *Idea imperial de Carlos V*, 6th edn (Madrid, 1971) [first published (Madrid, 1940)]

Parker, Geoffrey: *Philip II*, 3rd edn (Chicago and La Salle, 1995) [first published (London, 1995)]

——: *The Grand Strategy of Philip II* (New Haven and London, 1998)

Pietschmann, Horst: *Staat und staatliche Entwicklung am Beginn der spanischen Kolonisation Amerikas* (Munster, 1980)

Rabe, Horst, ed.: *Karl V. Politik und politisches System. Berichte und Studien aus der Arbeit an der Politischen Korrespondenz als Kaiser* (Constance, 1996)

271

Rady, Martyn: *Emperor Charles V* (London and New York, 1988)

Rapp-Buri, Anna, and Monica Stucky-Schürer: *Burgundische Tapisserien* (Munich, 2001)

Rassow, Peter: *Die Kaiser-Idee Karls V., dargestellt an der Politik der Jahre 1528–1540* (Berlin, 1932) (Historische Studien. 217) [repr. (Vaduz, 1965)]

Ritter, Gerhard: *Luther*, 6th edn (Munich, 1959) [first published (Munich, 1925)]

Sallmann, Jean-Michel: *Carlo V* (Milan, 2000)

Scarisbrick, John Joseph: *Henry VIII* (London, 1976) [first published (London, 1968)]

Schäfer, Ernst: *El Consejo Real y Supremo de las Indias*, 2 vols (Seville, 1935–47)

Seibt, Ferdinand: *Karl V. Der Kaiser und die Reformation* (Berlin, 1998) [first published (Berlin, 1990)]

Seipel, Wilfried, ed.: *Kunst um 1492. Hispania–Austria. Die Katholischen Könige, Maximilian I. und die Anfänge der Casa de Austria in Spanien* (Milan, 1992) [Spanish and Italian version (Milan, 1992)]

——, ed.: *Kaiser Karl V. (1500–1559). Macht und Ohnmacht Europas* (Vienna, 2000)

Soly, Hugo, ed.: *Charles V (1500–1558)* (Amsterdam, 1999)

Sutter-Fichtner, Paula: *Ferdinand of Austria. The Politics of Dynasticism in the Age of Reformation* (Boulder, CO, and New York, 1982)

Tracy, James D.: *Emperor Charles V. Impresario of War* (Cambridge, 2002)

Walser, Fritz, and Rainer Wohlfail: *Die spanischen Zentralbehörden und der Staatsrat Karls V. Grundlagen und Aufbau bis zum Tode Gattinaras* (Göttingen, 1959) (Abhandlungen der Akademie der Wissenschaften zu Göttingen, Philologisch–Historische Klasse. III.F., vol. 43.)

Walther, Andreas: *Die Anfänge Karls V.* (Leipzig, 1911)

——: *Die burgundischen Zentralbehörden unter Maximilian I. und Karl V.* (Leipzig, 1909)

Wernham, Richard B.: *Before the Armada. The Emergence of the English Nation. 1485–1588* (London, 1966)

Wiesflecker, Hermann: *Kaiser Maximilian I. Das Reich, Österreich und Europa an der Wende zur Neuzeit*, 5 vols (Munich, 1971–86)

Yates, Frances Amelia: *Astraea. The Imperial Theme in the Sixteenth Century* (London and Boston, 1975)

Index

(The dates given for church and secular rulers refer to periods of incumbency of office)

Index

284

285

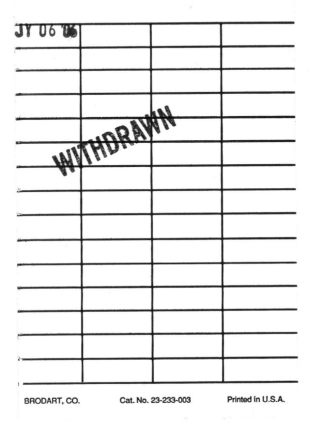
Please remember that this is a library book,
and that it belongs only temporarily to each
person who uses it. Be considerate. Do
not write in this, or any, library book.